T0328433

Heidegger on Ontotheology
Technology and the Politics of Education

Heidegger is now widely recognized as one of the most influential philosophers of the twentieth century, yet much of his later philosophy remains shrouded in confusion and controversy. Restoring Heidegger's understanding of metaphysics as "ontotheology" to its rightful place at the center of his later thought, this book explains the depth and significance of his controversial critique of technology, his appalling misadventure with Nazism, his prescient critique of the university, and his important philosophical suggestions for the future of higher education. It will be required reading for those seeking to understand the relationship between Heidegger's philosophy and National Socialism as well as the continuing relevance of his work.

Iain D. Thomson is assistant professor of philosophy at the University of New Mexico, where he received the Gunter Starkey Award for Teaching Excellence. His articles on Heidegger have been published in *Inquiry, Journal of the History of Philosophy,* the *International Journal of Philosophical Studies,* and the *Journal of the British Society for Phenomenology.*

Heidegger on Ontotheology

Technology and the Politics of Education

IAIN D. THOMSON

University of New Mexico

CAMBRIDGE UNIVERSITY PRESS
Cambridge, New York, Melbourne, Madrid, Cape Town, Singapore,
São Paulo, Delhi, Dubai, Tokyo, Mexico City

Cambridge University Press
The Edinburgh Building, Cambridge CB2 8RU, UK

Published in the United States of America by Cambridge University Press, New York

www.cambridge.org
Information on this title: www.cambridge.org/9780521616591

© Iain D. Thomson 2005

This publication is in copyright. Subject to statutory exception
and to the provisions of relevant collective licensing agreements,
no reproduction of any part may take place without the written
permission of Cambridge University Press.

First published 2005

A catalogue record for this publication is available from the British Library

Library of Congress Cataloging in Publication Data
Thomson, Iain D. (Iain Donald), 1968–
Heidegger on ontotheology : technology and the politics of education /
Iain D. Thomson.
p.   cm.
Includes bibliographical references (p.).
isbn 0-521-85115-7 (hardback) – isbn 0-521-61659-x (pbk.)
1. Heidegger, Martin, 1889–1976. 2. Metaphysics – History – 20th century.
3. Technology – Philosophy – History – 20th century.
4. Education – Philosophy – History – 20th century. I. Title.
b3279.h49t48   2005
193–dc22   2004026256

isbn 978-0-521-85115-2 Hardback
isbn 978-0-521-61659-1 Paperback

Cambridge University Press has no responsibility for the persistence or
accuracy of URLs for external or third-party internet websites referred to in
this publication, and does not guarantee that any content on such websites is,
or will remain, accurate or appropriate. Information regarding prices, travel
timetables, and other factual information given in this work is correct at
the time of first printing but Cambridge University Press does not guarantee
the accuracy of such information thereafter.

For my mother, father, and (in memoriam) Gutcher,
Poets of public policy, healers of human being, teachers.

Time will bring to light whatever is hidden; it will conceal and cover up what is now shining with the greatest splendor.

Horace, *Epistles*

An unlimited text is one that every time gives rise to a new reading while partly escaping it.

What still remains to be read is its one chance of survival.

Edmond Jabès, *The Little Book of
Unsuspected Subversion*

Contents

Acknowledgments   *page* ix

A Note on the Notes   xiii

Abbreviations Used for Works by Heidegger   xv

Introduction: Heidegger on Ontotheology   1

1   Ontotheology? Understanding Heidegger's
    Deconstruction of Metaphysics   7
     1. *Introduction: Ontotheology?*   7
     2. *Metaphysics as Ontotheology*   11
     3. *Deconstructing Metaphysical Foundationalism*   17
     4. *"One of the Deepest Problems"*   23
     5. *Conclusions: Back to the Beginning*   39

2   Understanding Ontotheology as the Basis for Heidegger's
    Critique of Technology   44
     6. *Introduction: From Ontotheology to Technology*   44
     7. *What's Wrong with Technological Essentialism?*   47
     8. *Recognizing Nietzsche's Ontotheology as the Essence of Technology*   52
     9. *Addressing Feenberg's Objections to Heidegger's Critique of*
       Technology   58
     10. *Conclusions: Vindicating Heidegger's Critique* 76

3   Heidegger and the Politics of the University   78
     11. *Heidegger and National Socialism*   78
     12. *Heidegger's Earliest Views on University Education (1911)*   87
     13. *To Educate the Nation (1918 to 1924)*   92
     14. *Restoring Philosophy to Her Throne as the Queen of the Sciences*
       (1927 to 1934)   104

15. *Lessons Learned (after 1934)*   114
16. *Conclusions: Pöggeler and Derrida on the Confucian Question*   129

4   Heidegger's Mature Vision of Ontological Education, or How We Become What We Are   141
17. *Introduction: Deconstructing Education*   141
18. *Heidegger's Ontohistorical Critique of the Technologization of Education*   144
19. *Heidegger's Return to Plato's Cave: Ontological Education as the Essence of Paideia*   155
20. *Conclusions: Envisioning a Community of Learners*   170

References   183
Index   195

Acknowledgments

Heidegger on Ontotheology: Technology and the Politics of Education brings together and develops much of the thinking I have been doing on Heidegger over the past five years, and I owe considerable debts to the individuals and communities who, by supporting and guiding my work during this time, helped to improve it in innumerable ways. I would like to acknowledge them here, thanking them for their insight and critique without claiming to have resolved all the differences between our views. I hope these differences will prove to be productive, but where they turn out merely to reflect the limits of my views, the responsibility, of course, is entirely my own.

Many of the hermeneutic theses at the heart of *Heidegger on Ontotheology* were tested and refined at annual meetings of the International Society for Phenomenological Studies, and my work benefited immensely from these small but intense gatherings of continental philosophers in serene Asilomar, California. For helpful criticisms and suggestions on these memorable occasions, I would like to thank Steve Affeldt, Ed Boedecker, Taylor Carman, Dave Cerbone, Drew Cross, Steve Crowell, Béatrice Han, Alastair Hannay, John Haugeland, Randall Havas, Piotr Hoffman, Stephan Käufer, Sean Kelly, Cristina Lafont, Jeff Malpas, Wayne Martin, Alexander Nehamas, Mark Okrent, John Richardson, Joe Rouse, Ted Schatzki, Hans Sluga, Julian Young, and – for extremely incisive and valuable critiques of the whole book – Bill Blattner, Bert Dreyfus, Charlie Guignon, and Mark Wrathall.

I also owe thanks to the other philosophical communities before whom I presented my work on Heidegger, including the American Philosophical

Association, the Parliament of Philosophers, the Society for Philosophy
and Technology, and the University of Tokyo Center for Philosophy in
the 21st Century, and so to such inimitable philosophical interlocutors
as Anne Margaret Baxley, Keith Brown, Joseph Cohen, Adrian Cussins,
Michael Eldred, Andy Feenberg, Matt George, Peter Gordon, Kevin
Hill, David Hoy, John Hughes, Yumiko Iida, Hide Ishiguro, Shunsuke
Kadowaki, Ted Kisiel, Ed Lee, Kenn Maly, Junichi Murata, Michael
Peters, Robert Pippin, Bill Richardson, Chris Rickey, Richard Rorty, Raj
Sampath, Charles Spinosa, Tracy Strong, David Stump, Mungo Thomson,
Gianni Vattimo, Samuel Weber, Gideon Yaffe, and Holger Zaborowski.
Here Jerry Doppelt deserves special mention for wise counsel and stead-
fast support.

Heidegger on Ontotheology incorporates significantly revised and extended versions of materials first published elsewhere, and I thank
those who originally published my work and allowed me to make use
of it here: For "Ontotheology? Understanding Heidegger's *Destruktion*
of Metaphysics," *International Journal of Philosophical Studies* 8: 297–327,
Dermot Moran, editor; © 2000 Taylor & Francis. For "What's Wrong
with Being a Technological Essentialist? A Response to Feenberg," *Inquiry* 43: 429–44, Alastair Hannay, editor; © 2000 Taylor & Francis. For
"Heidegger and the Politics of the University," *Journal of the History of
Philosophy* 41: 515–42, Gerald A. Press, editor; © 2003 Johns Hopkins University Press. For "Heidegger on Ontological Education, or: How We Become What We Are," *Inquiry* 44: 243–68, Alastair Hannay, editor; © 2001
Taylor & Francis.

Thanks, too, to my editors and referees at Cambridge University Press
for their wonderful enthusiasm for and care of my book. The Phi Beta
Kappa Society and the University of New Mexico were generous with
research support, as were my philosophical colleagues at UNM with
their ideas and encouragement; thanks especially to Kelly Becker, Andy
Burgess, John Bussanich, Reed Dasenbrock, Manfred Frings, Russell
Goodman, Barbara Hannan, Brent Kalar, Joachim Oberst, Paul Schmidt,
Ted Sturm, John Taber, and the students in my Heidegger seminars, with
whom, happily, I continue to learn.

Of course, I might never have developed my own interpretation of
Heidegger if I did not have great teachers who disagreed profoundly
with one another, among whom I gratefully acknowledge Taylor Carman,
Jacques Derrida, Fred Olafson, and Richard Wolin. Here, however, my
deepest thanks go to Bert Dreyfus, not only for introducing me to

Heidegger in the 1980s and encouraging my work ever since with thoughtful critiques but also for helping to inspire this work by exemplifying the virtues of the Heideggerian teacher. Finally, I would like to recognize the loving support of my wonderful wife and family, without whom this book could never have been completed.

Given all the help I have received, I feel a bit less embarrassed by my more than occasional use of the royal hermeneutic "we."

A Note on the Notes

Some of us are footnote people, but many are not. For those who find that copious footnotes disrupt the flow of the text, my (perhaps obvious) suggestion is: Do not feel compelled to read every note as you go. If you want the reference or have an unanswered question, then you should read the surrounding notes; with any luck your question will be answered there (and if it is not, then you will see that in fact I do not have *enough* notes). Otherwise, I would invite you to read through the notes at your leisure; some supplemental and specialized argument is done in the notes, and a number of *Holzwege* are preserved there as well. (The received view that by *Holzweg* Heidegger means "dead-end" is mistaken. In the prefatory epigraph to the collection of essays he titled *Holzwege*, Heidegger explains these as forest paths made by backwoods loggers and known to backcountry hikers, thus implying that a *Holzweg* is a path leading to a place in the forest from which trees have been removed – that is, a *clearing*.)

Abbreviations Used for Works by Heidegger

(*Translations frequently modified*)

A   *Antwort: Martin Heidegger im Gespräch.* Günther Neske and
Emil Kettering, eds. Pfullingen: Neske, 1988.

Auf   *Aufenthalte.* Frankfurt: V. Klostermann, 1989.

B&T   *Being and Time.* J. Macquarrie and E. Robinson, trans.
New York: Harper & Row, 1962.

CP   *Contributions to Philosophy (from Enowning).* P. Emad and
K. Maly, trans. Bloomington: Indiana University Press, 1999.

DBW   "Die Bedrohung der Wissenschaft." In Dietrich Papenfuss
and Otto Pöggeler, eds., *Zur philosophischen Aktualität
Heideggers.* Frankfurt am Main: Vittorio Klostermann, 1989.

DDP   "Documents from the Denazification Proceedings
Concerning Martin Heidegger." M. Brainard and F.-A.
Dorner, trans. *Graduate Faculty Philosophy Journal* 14–15
(1991): 528–56.

DT   *Discourse on Thinking.* J. Anderson and E. Freund, trans. New
York: Harper & Row, 1966.

EHF   *The Essence of Human Freedom: An Introduction to Philosophy.*
T. Sadler, trans. London and New York: Continuum, 2002.

EP   *The End of Philosophy.* J. Stambaugh, trans. New York: Harper
& Row, 1973.

ET   *The Essence of Truth.* T. Sadler, trans. London and New York:
Continuum, 2002.

FCM   *The Fundamental Concepts of Metaphysics: World, Finitude,
Solitude.* W. McNeill and N. Walker, trans. Bloomington:
Indiana University Press, 1995.

FD   *Die Frage nach dem Ding.* Tübingen: Max Niemeyer, 1953.

G   *Gelassenheit.* Pfulligen: Neske, 1959.
GA3   *Gesamtausgabe,* Vol. 3: *Kant und das Problem der Metaphysik.*
            Friedrich-Wilhelm von Herrmann, ed. Frankfurt:
            V. Klostermann, 1991.
GA5   *Gesamtausgabe,* Vol. 5: *Holzwege.* Friedrich-Wilhelm von
            Herrmann, ed. Frankfurt: V. Klostermann, 1977.
GA7   *Gesamtausgabe,* Vol. 7: *Vorträge und Aufsätze.*
            Friedrich-Wilhelm von Herrmann, ed. Frankfurt:
            V. Klostermann, 2000
GA9   *Gesamtausgabe,* Vol. 9: *Wegmarken.* Friedrich-Wilhelm von
            Herrmann, ed. Frankfurt: V. Klostermann, 1976.
GA10   *Gesamtausgabe,* Vol. 10. *Der Satz vom Grund.* Petra Jaeger, ed.
            Frankfurt: V. Klostermann: 1997.
GA12   *Gesamtausgabe,* Vol. 12: *Unterwegs zur Sprache.*
            Friedrich-Wilhelm von Herrmann, ed. Frankfurt:
            V. Klostermann, 1985.
GA13   *Gesamtausgabe,* Vol. 13. *Aus der Erfahrung des Denkens.*
            Hermann Heidegger, ed. Frankfurt: V. Klostermann:
            1983.
GA15   *Gesamtausgabe,* Vol. 15: *Seminare.* Curd Ochwadt, ed.
            Frankfurt: V. Klostermann, 1986.
GA16   *Gesamtausgabe,* Vol. 16: *Reden und andere Zeugnisse eines
            Lebensweges, 1910–1976.* Hermann Heidegger, ed.
            Frankfurt: V. Klostermann, 2000.
GA19   *Gesamtausgabe,* Vol. 19: *Platon: Sophistes.* Ingeborg Schüßler,
            ed. Frankfurt: V. Klostermann, 1992.
GA20   *Gesamtausgabe,* Vol. 20: *Prolegomena zur Geschichte des
            Zeitbegriffs.* Petra Jaeger, ed. Frankfurt: V. Klostermann,1979.
GA26   *Gesamtausgabe,* Vol. 26: *Metaphysische Anfangsgründe der Logik
            im Ausgang von Leibniz.* Frankfurt: V. Klostermann, 1978.
GA27   *Gesamtausgabe,* Vol. 27: *Einleitung in die Philosophie.* Ina
            Saame-Speidel, ed. Frankfurt: V. Klostermann, 1996.
GA29–30   *Gesamtausgabe,* Vol. 29–30: *Die Grundbegriffe der Metaphysik:
            Welt, Endlichkeit, Einsamkeit.* Frankfurt: V. Klostermann,
            1983.
GA31   *Gesamtausgabe,* Vol. 31. *Vom Wesen der menschlichen Freiheit.*
            Second edition. Frankfurt: V. Klostermann, 1994.
GA34   *Gesamtausgabe,* Vol. 34. *Vom Wesen der Wahrheit: Zu Platons
            Höhlengleichnis und Theätet.* Hermann Mörchen, ed.
            Frankfurt: V. Klostermann, 1988.

GA39   *Gesamtausgabe*, Vol. 39. *Hölderlins Hymnen "Germanien" und "Der Rhein."* Susanne Ziegler, ed. Frankfurt: V. Klostermann, 1980.

GA40   *Gesamtausgabe*, Vol. 40. *Einführung in die Metaphysik.* Petra Jaeger, ed. Frankfurt: V. Klostermann, 1983.

GA41   *Gesamtausgabe*, Vol. 41. *Die Frage nach dem Ding.* Petra Jaeger, ed. Frankfurt: V. Klostermann: 1984.

GA50   *Gesamtausgabe*, Vol. 50. *Nietzsches Metaphysik; Einleitung in die Philosophie: Denken und Dichten.* Petra Jaeger, ed. Frankfurt: V. Klostermann: 1990.

GA53   *Gesamtausgabe*, Vol. 53. *Hölderlins Hymne "Der Ister."* Walter Biemel, ed. Frankfurt: V. Klostermann, 1984.

GA54   *Gesamtausgabe*, Vol. 54: *Parmenides.* Manfred S. Frings, ed. Frankfurt: V. Klostermann, 1982.

GA56–57 *Gesamtausgabe*, Vol. 56–57: *Zur Bestimmung der Philosophie.* Bernd Heimbüchel, ed. Frankfurt: V. Klostermann, 1987.

GA59   *Gesamtausgabe*, Vol. 59: *Phänomenologie der Anschauung und des Ausdrucks.* Claudius Strube, ed. Frankfurt: V. Klostermann, 1993.

GA61   *Gesamtausgabe*, Vol. 61: *Phänomenologische Interpretaionen zu Aristoteles: Einführung in die Phänomenologische Forshung.* Walter Bröcker and Käte Bröcker-Oltmanns, eds. Frankfurt: V. Klostermann, 1985.

GA63   *Gesamtausgabe*, Vol. 63: *Ontologie (Hermeneutik der Faktizität).* Käte Bröcker-Oltmanns, ed. Frankfurt: V. Klostermann, 1988.

GA65   *Gesamtausgabe*, Vol. 65: *Beiträge zur Philosophie (Vom Ereignis).* Friedrich-Wilhelm von Herrmann, ed. Frankfurt: V. Klostermann, 1989.

GA66   *Gesamtausgabe*, Vol. 66: *Besinnung.* Friedrich-Wilhelm von Herrmann, ed. Frankfurt: V. Klostermann, 1997.

GA79   *Gesamtausgabe*, Vol. 79: *Bremer und Freiburger Vorträge.* Petra Jaeger, ed. Frankfurt: V. Klostermann, 1994.

H   *Holzwege.* Frankfurt: V. Klostermann, 1994.

HB   "Selected Letters from the Heidegger–Blochmann Correspondence." F. Edler, trans. *Graduate Faculty Philosophy Journal* 14–15 (1992): 559–77.

HBC   Heidegger, Martin, and Elizabeth Blochmann. *Martin Heidegger–Elizabeth Blochmann, Briefwechsel 1918–1969.* J. W. Storck, ed. Marbach: Deutsche Literaturarchiv, 1989.

HC   *The Heidegger Controversy: A Critical Reader.* Richard Wolin,
            ed. New York: Columbia University Press, 1991.

HCE   *Hegel's Concept of Experience.* K. R. Dove, trans. New York:
            Harper & Row, 1970.

HCT   *History of the Concept of Time.* T. Kisiel, trans. Bloomington
            and Indianapolis: Indiana University Press, 1985.

HHI   *Hölderlin's Hymn "The Ister."* W. McNeill and J. Davis, trans.
            Bloomington: Indiana University Press, 1996.

HJC   *The Heidegger–Jaspers Correspondence.* Walter Biemel and Has
            Saner, eds. G. E. Aylesworth, trans. Amherst, NY: Humanity
            Books, 2003.

I&D   *Identity and Difference.* J. Stambaugh, trans. New York:
            Harper & Row, 1969.

IM   *Introduction to Metaphysics.* G. Fried and R. Polt, trans.
            New Haven, CT: Yale University Press, 2000.

KPM   *Kant and the Problem of Metaphysics.* R. Taft, trans.
            Bloomington: Indiana University Press, 1997.

KTB   "Kant's Thesis About Being." T. E. Klein and W. E. Pohl,
            trans. (In P.)

MFL   *The Metaphysical Foundations of Logic.* M. Heim, trans.
            Bloomington: Indiana University Press, 1984.

N1   *Nietzsche: The Will to Power as Art.* David Farrell Krell, ed. and
            trans. New York: Harper & Row, 1979.

N3   *Nietzsche: The Will to Power as Knowledge and as Metaphysics.*
            David Farrell Krell, ed. J. Stambaugh, D. F. Krell, and
            F. Capuzzi, trans. New York: Harper & Row, 1987.

N4   *Nietzsche: Nihilism.* David Farrell Krell, ed. F. Capuzzi, trans.
            New York: Harper & Row, 1982.

NI   *Nietzsche,* vol. I. Pfullingen: G. Neske, 1961.

NII   *Nietzsche,* vol. II. Pfullingen: G. Neske, 1961.

OET   "On the Essence of Truth." T. Sheehan, trans. (In P.)

OHF   *Ontology – The Hermeneutics of Facticity.* J. van Buren, trans.
            Bloomington: Indiana University Press, 1999.

OWL   *On the Way to Language.* P. D. Hertz, trans. New York: Harper
            & Row, 1971.

P   *Pathmarks.* William McNeill, ed. Cambridge: Cambridge
            University Press, 1998.

PAR   *Parmenides.* A. Schuwer and R. Rojcewicz, trans.
            Bloomington: Indiana University Press, 1992.

PDT   "Plato's Doctrine of Truth." T. Sheehan, trans. (In P.)
PLT   *Poetry, Language, Thought.* A. Hofstadter, trans. New York:
           Harper & Row, 1971.
PR   *Principle of Reason.* R. Lilly, trans. Bloomington: Indiana
           University Press, 1991.
PT   "Phenomenology and Theology." J. G. Hart and J. C.
           Maraldo, trans. (In P.)
Q&A   Günther Neske and Emil Kettering, eds. Lisa Harries, trans.
           *Martin Heidegger and National Socialism: Questions and
           Answers.* New York: Paragon House, 1990.
QCT   *The Question Concerning Technology.* W. Lovitt, trans. New
           York: Harper & Row, 1977.
S   *Plato's* Sophist. R. Rojcewicz and A. Schuwer, trans.
           Bloomington: Indiana University Press, 1997.
S&Z   *Sein und Zeit.* Tübingen: M. Niemeyer, 1993.
T&B   *On Time and Being.* J. Stambaugh, trans. New York: Harper &
           Row, 1972.
TDP   *Towards the Definition of Philosophy.* T. Sadler, trans. London:
           Athlone Press, 2000.
TPOA   "Toward a Philosophical Orientation for Academics."
           J. Protevi, trans. *Graduate Faculty Philosophy Journal* 14–15
           (1991): 496–501.
TTL   "Traditional Language and Technological Language." W. T.
           Gregory, trans. *Journal of Philosophical Research* 23 (1998):
           129–45.
USTS   *Überlieferte Sprache und Technische Sprache.* Hermann
           Heidegger, ed. St. Gallen: Erker, 1989.
WCT   *What Is Called Thinking?* J. G. Gray, trans. New York: Harper
           & Row, 1968.
WHD   *Was Heißt Denken?* Tübingen: M. Niemeyer, 1984.
WIM   "What Is Metaphysics?" D. F. Krell, trans. (In P.)
WIP   *What Is Philosophy?* J. T. Wilde and W. Kluback, trans. New
           Haven, CT: College and University Press, 1958.
WIT   *What Is a Thing?* W. B. Barton and V. Deutsch, trans. South
           Bend, IN: Gateway Editions, 1967.
WT   *What Is a Thing?* W. B. Barton Jr. and V. Deutsch, trans.
           Chicago: Henry Regnery, 1969.
Z   *Zollikoner Seminare.* Medard Boss, ed. Frankfurt: V.
           Klostermann, 1987.

ZS   *Zollikon Seminars: Protocols – Conversations – Letters.* Medard
          Boss, ed. F. May and R. Askay, trans. Evanston, IL:
          Northwestern University Press, 2001.
ZSD   *Zur Sache des Denkens.* Tübingen: M. Niemeyer, 1969.

Introduction

Heidegger on Ontotheology

Martin Heidegger is now widely recognized as one of the most influential philosophers of the twentieth century. Until the late 1960s, this impact derived mainly from his early magnum opus, *Being and Time* (published in 1927). Many of the twentieth century's most significant continental thinkers – including Hannah Arendt, Rudolf Bultmann, Hans-Georg Gadamer, Jürgen Habermas, Emmanuel Levinas, Herbert Marcuse, Maurice Merleau-Ponty, Jean-Paul Sartre, and Paul Tillich – acknowledge profound conceptual debts to the insights elaborated in this text. *Being and Time* was never finished, however, and Heidegger continued to develop, refine, and in some places revolutionize his own thinking for another fifty years. This "later" Heidegger's prolific body of work decisively influenced the next generation of continental philosophers, helping to shape the concepts and concerns of major contemporary figures such as Jean Baudrillard, Maurice Blanchot, Jacques Derrida, Hubert Dreyfus, Michel Foucault, Luce Irigaray, Jacques Lacan, Richard Rorty, and Charles Taylor, to name but a few. Despite this unparalleled impact, however, important aspects of Heidegger's later philosophy remain obscured by confusion and controversy.

Heidegger on Ontotheology: Technology and the Politics of Education seeks to clarify five interrelated aspects of Heidegger's later thought, namely, his neglected understanding of metaphysics as ontotheology, his controversial critique of technology, his appalling misadventure with Nazism, his prescient critique of the university, and, finally, his important philosophical suggestions for the future of higher education. My title is "fortuitously ambiguous," as Heidegger would say – that is, "ambiguous in a positive sense" (KPM 157/GA3 231) – for, in *Heidegger on Ontotheology*, I first

1

explain Heidegger's philosophical understanding of ontotheology, then develop an interpretation of his later thought *on the basis of* this understanding of ontotheology. The subtitle, *Technology and the Politics of Education*, expresses my sense that the other important aspects of Heidegger's later thinking just mentioned are interrelated in a way we can appreciate only once we understand his views on ontotheology.

I thus begin, in Chapter 1, by arguing that Heidegger's unjustifiably neglected understanding of metaphysics as ontotheology in fact forms the crucial philosophical background for much of his later thought. Until now, Heidegger's complex understanding of ontotheology has been either ignored or misunderstood. When his view of "ontotheology" is mentioned at all, it is usually taken to be a dismissive way of characterizing any theology that treats God as the outermost anchor in the causal chain of creation. Yet, this reduction of the divine to "the God of the philosophers" is only one of the profound consequences of the ontotheological structure Heidegger discovers at the core of the entire tradition of Western metaphysics. To clarify this more complex and nuanced understanding of ontotheology, I show how Heidegger's historical deconstruction of the metaphysical tradition leads him to the view that all our great metaphysical systems make foundational claims best understood as *ontotheological.* His guiding idea is that the metaphysical tradition establishes both the fundamental and the ultimate conceptual parameters of intelligibility by ontologically grounding and theologically legitimating our changing historical sense of what is. Heidegger's notorious antipathy to metaphysics thus obscures the fact that, on his view, it is metaphysics which unifies and secures our successive historical "epochs." A series of metaphysical ontotheologies anchor our successive constellations of historical intelligibility, temporarily securing the intelligible order by grasping it from both ends of the conceptual scale simultaneously (as it were), both *ontologically* (from the inside out) and *theologically* (from the outside in). By first elucidating and then problematizing Heidegger's thesis that all the great systems of Western metaphysics share this ontotheological structure, I reconstruct the most important components of the original and persuasive history of metaphysics he provides in support of this thesis. It is precisely this historical narrative, I show, that generates the critical force of the later Heidegger's main philosophical project, namely, the attempt to find a philosophical path leading beyond our nihilistic, Nietzschean age. (Because it provides crucial philosophical background for the rest of the book, Chapter 1, of necessity, engages closely with Heidegger's technical vocabulary, and readers who find the going too slow might do well to skip ahead to Chapter 2 or 3, circling back once the stakes become clear.)

Chapter 1 thus presents Heidegger's rather dystopian critique of our own historical age, and Chapter 2 begins to respond to some of the controversy this critique has understandably provoked. Specifically, Chapter 2 seeks to demonstrate that three of the major criticisms advanced against Heidegger can be persuasively countered once we comprehend the way in which his famous critique of our "technological" understanding of being *follows from* his understanding of metaphysics as ontotheology. To make this case, I focus systematically on the three longstanding criticisms appropriated, refined, and leveled against Heidegger's view by the leading critical theorist of technology, Andrew Feenberg. I first make clear that Feenberg's formidable criticisms are addressed not to technological essentialism as such, but, rather, to three particular kinds of technological essentialism, namely, *ahistoricism, substantivism* (or fatalism), and *one-dimensionalism* (that is, the charge that Heidegger's understanding of technology is "totalizing" or indiscriminate). After explicating these three forms of technological essentialism and explaining why exactly Feenberg finds them objectionable, I ask whether any of them should in fact be ascribed to Heidegger. By showing how Heidegger's critique of technology follows from his understanding of ontotheology, and then drawing out the implications of the heretofore unnoticed connection, I am able to respond to each of Feenberg's criticisms in turn, establishing three important conclusions: first, that Heidegger's rather limited technological essentialism is not at all ahistoricist, but the opposite, an historical conception of the essence of technology; second, that although Heidegger does indeed advocate a substantivist technological essentialism, he also suggests a plausible, indirect response to Feenberg's voluntaristic, Marcusean objection; and, third, that Heidegger's one-dimensional technological essentialism is of a nonobjectionable variety, because it does not force him to reject technological devices *in toto.* These conclusions help vindicate Heidegger's groundbreaking ontological approach to the philosophy of technology. In so doing, moreover, they reinforce my overarching thesis that Heidegger's understanding of ontotheology needs to be recognized as the crucial philosophical background of his later thought. For, I show, deprived of this philosophical background, later views such as Heidegger's critique of technology can easily appear arbitrary and indefensible, but when this background is restored, the full depth and significance of those views begins to emerge with new clarity.

After proposing an interpretation that restores Heidegger's understanding of ontotheology to its rightful place at the center of his later
philosophy (in Chapter 1), and then, on the basis of this interpretation,
vindicating his later work against some longstanding objections (in Chapter 2), I turn in Chapter 3 to confront what is surely the greatest obsta-
cle to any sympathetic reconstruction and defense of Heidegger's work,
namely, his brief but appalling alliance with National Socialism. Why
did one of the twentieth century's greatest thinkers join forces with its
most contemptible political movement? This profoundly troubling combination has spawned a secondary literature of singular immensity. Cut-
ting through this controversy, Chapter 3 advances a new understanding
of the philosophical basis of Heidegger's infamous politics by focusing
on the development of his philosophical views on university education.
Elucidating these views and situating them within their broader historical and philosophical context, I show them to be largely responsible for
his decision to become the first Nazi Rector of Freiburg University in
1933. I then ask: Did Heidegger learn from this horrific political misadventure and so transform the underlying philosophical views that helped
motivate it? Pursuing this important question, I show that Heidegger
did indeed learn several crucial philosophical lessons here, but I also
argue, against the interpretations of Otto Pöggeler and Derrida, that
the later Heidegger continued to develop and refine the basic philosophical research program that originally motivated his failed attempt
at political activism, rather than simply abandoning this philosophical
program after 1933. Instead of using this conclusion as an excuse to dismiss Heidegger's later views on education, however, I suggest that his
prescient critique of the university has only become more relevant since
he elaborated it, and that, with the important philosophical corrections
suggested for this philosophical research program by his so-called turn,
the later Heidegger's mature vision for a reontologization of education
merits the careful attention of those of us now seeking to understand
the roots and implications of our own growing crisis in higher education. In order to justify these admittedly provocative claims, I turn in
the concluding Chapter 4 to critically appropriate, develop, and defend
several aspects of the later Heidegger's radical philosophical vision for a
university of the future.

Chapter 4 begins by showing that Heidegger presciently diagnosed
our current crisis in higher education. Important contemporary theorists such as Bill Readings extend and update Heidegger's critique,
documenting the increasing instrumentalization, professionalization,

vocationalization, corporatization, and technologization of the modern university, the dissolution of its guiding and unifying ideals, and, consequently, the growing hyperspecialization and ruinous fragmentation of its departments. Unlike Heidegger, however, these critics do not recognize such disturbing trends as interlocking symptoms of an underlying ontotheology, and, as a result, they are unable to provide a positive vision for the future of higher education. In contrast, by understanding our educational crisis in terms of its deep ontohistorical roots, Heidegger is able to develop an alternative, ontological conception of education, one devised to help bring about a renaissance in higher education. To make this case, I show how Heidegger, through a creative reading of Plato's famous allegory of the cave, excavates and appropriates the original Western educational ideal of Platonic *paideia*, thereby outlining the pedagogy of an ontological education capable of directly challenging the nihilistic but increasingly widespread conception of education that follows from our technological understanding of being and its underlying Nietzschean ontotheology. Reconstructing Heidegger's mature notion of ontological education, I suggest that his view can best be understood as a species of philosophical perfectionism, one which seeks to reessentialize the currently empty ideal of educational "excellence" in order to both reconnect teaching to research and restore a meaningful sense of communal solidarity to the academic community. In developing such a view, however, I argue that we need to recognize, criticize, and steer well clear of the authoritarian and totalitarian excesses that distorted and misdirected Heidegger's own attempt to intervene politically in 1933 on the basis of his still insufficiently clarified philosophical views on university education. *Heidegger on Ontotheology: Technology and the Politics of Education* thus concludes by suggesting that, once those aspects of Heidegger's earlier view that encouraged his disastrous politics have been isolated, criticized, and rejected, the later Heidegger's mature understanding of ontological education represents an important contribution to current philosophical efforts to both diagnosis and respond to our own growing crisis in higher education.

1

Ontotheology?

Understanding Heidegger's Deconstruction of Metaphysics

§1. INTRODUCTION: ONTOTHEOLOGY?

On hearing the expression "ontotheology," many philosophers start looking for the door. Those who do not may know that it was under the title of this "distasteful neologism," for which we have Kant to thank, that the later Heidegger elaborated his seemingly ruthless critique of Western metaphysics.[1] The forcefulness of Heidegger's "deconstruction" (*Destruktion*) of the metaphysical tradition helped turn a generation of post-Heideggerian thinkers into antimetaphysicians, but Heidegger's deconstruction is actually premised on his attribution to metaphysics of an unparalleled pride of place in the historical construction and maintenance of intelligibility.[2] Heidegger's deconstruction presupposes that

---

[1] Kant observed of philosophical neologisms that: "It is not as easy to invent new words as one thinks, because they are contrary to taste, and in this way taste is a hindrance to philosophy" (*Lectures on Metaphysics*, 120). Kant coined "ontotheology" and "cosmotheology" in order to distinguish between two opposing kinds of "transcendental theology." "Ontotheology" is his name for that kind of transcendental theology exemplified by St. Anselm's famous "ontological argument" for the existence of God, which "believes it can know the existence of an [original being, *Urwesen*] through mere concepts, without the help of any experience whatsoever" (*Critique of Pure Reason/Kritik der reinen Vernunft*, A632/B660; see also P. F. Strawson, *The Bounds of Sense*, 17). Heidegger may have appropriated the term "ontotheology" from Kant, but his use of it, as we will see, is quite different.

[2] In an erudite genealogy of "destruction," Dermot Moran traces a family of similar philosophical concepts back through medieval thought to Plato's *Euthydemus* ("The Destruction of the Destruction, 176–96; cf. Jorge Borges, "Averroës' Search," *Collected Fictions*, 235–41). Moran translates Heidegger's *Destruktion* as "destruction" in order to stress its difference from Derrida's "deconstruction." My riskier rendition of *Destruktion* as "deconstruction" throughout is justified by the fact that Derrida coined the word "deconstruction" in an attempt to translate Heidegger's *Abbau* ("quarrying, dismantling,

7

metaphysics is not simply the esoteric concern of philosophers isolated in their ivory towers but that, on the contrary: "Metaphysics grounds an age" (QCT 115/GA5 75). To put the matter too quickly, but by way of anticipation, Heidegger's claim is that by giving shape to our historical understanding of "what *is*," metaphysics determines the most basic presuppositions of what *anything* is, including ourselves.[3] "Western humanity, in all its comportment toward entities, and even toward itself, is in every respect sustained and guided by metaphysics" (N4 205/NII 343).[4]

By codifying and disseminating an understanding of what entities *are*, metaphysics provides each historical "epoch" of intelligibility with its ontological bedrock. And by furnishing an account of the ultimate source from which entities issue, metaphysics supplies intelligibility with a kind of foundational justification that (for reasons we will examine shortly) Heidegger characterizes as "theological." To assert that "metaphysics grounds history," then, is to claim that metaphysics establishes both the most basic conceptual parameters and the ultimate standards of legitimacy for history's successive epochs of unified intelligibility. These epochal "constellations of intelligibility" are thus neither contingent nor free-floating but, rather, are grounded in and reflect a series of historical

---

or decomposing"), a synonym for *Destruktion* Heidegger later employed in order to emphasize that *Destruktion* is not merely a negative act, a "destruction" (*Zerstörung*), but rather "must be understood strictly as *de-struere* [the Latin "*struere*" means "to lay, pile, or build"], *ab-bauen* [literally, "un-building" or "de-construction"]" (GA15 337, 395). (See Derrida, *The Ear of the Other*, 86–7.) As I will show, Heidegger's deconstruction of Western metaphysics does not destroy or even destructure metaphysics. On the contrary, it deconstructs, decomposes, or decompiles metaphysics' sedimented historical layers, reconstructs its obscured ontotheological structure, and seeks to uncover the "decisive experiences" responsible for this common structure, with the hope that recognizing the contingency of these experiences will help us to envision a path beyond ontotheology. I am, however, in complete agreement with Moran's concluding claim that: "The concept of destruction as used by Heidegger is ... bound to a certain view of history ... that has not been clarified" (192). Indeed, that is one of the gaps in the literature I attempt to fill here in Chapter 1.

3 As Dreyfus succinctly explains: "The practices containing an understanding of what it is to be a human being, those containing an interpretation of what it is to be a thing, and those defining society fit together. Social practices thus transmit not only an implicit understanding of what it is to be a human being, an animal, an object, but, finally, what it is for anything to be at all" ("Heidegger on the Connection between Nihilism, Art, Technology, and Politics," 295).

4 Understanding Heidegger's critique of ontotheology thus helps us see that his allegedly Occicentric views, rather than indefensibly privileging "the West," in fact result from his refusal immediately to generalize the results of his close reading of Western metaphysics to traditions not rooted in our ontotheological tradition. The colonizing spread of our Western "technological" ontotheology seems to be increasingly neutralizing such distinctions, however, and not for the better.

transformations in our metaphysical understanding of what entities *are*.[5] Straightforwardly enough, Heidegger calls such an understanding of what it means for something to be an *understanding of being*, and his famous *history of being* is simply a shorthand for designating the historical series of these epoch-grounding understandings of being.

In what follows, I shall give a more carefully nuanced exposition of Heidegger's account of the way in which the metaphysical tradition establishes the foundations for every epoch of intelligibility by ontologically grounding and theologically legitimating our changing historical sense of what is. First, however, in order to help motivate a journey through such hermeneutically uncharted terrain, let me briefly address one of the potentially most troubling presuppositions of the foregoing, namely, Heidegger's claim that our ontological bedrock is temporally variable. Explaining that I am using "bedrock" in the Wittgensteinian sense, as that inevitable point at which the explanatory spade turns, may not sufficiently alleviate the worry.[6] For, if our foundationalist intuitions are rigid enough, we are likely to feel a certain vertigo before the claim that ontology, our bedrock understanding of what is, changes with time. Nevertheless, the idea that even humanity's most fundamental sense of reality changes, and so needs to be understood in terms of its history, is indeed the later Heidegger's doctrine of *ontological historicity*, a controversial doctrine the truth of which Heidegger himself had yet to recognize in his early magnum opus, 1927's *Being and Time*. By 1941, however, Heidegger had come to consider *Being and Time*'s famous first call for a deconstruction of the ontological tradition *precritical*, precisely because of the philosophically "naive" assumption that this deconstruction would allow him to recover a transhistorically binding "fundamental ontology," that is, a substantive understanding of "the meaning of being in general" fundamental enough to have been operant within every different historical epoch of intelligibility (GA15 395; EP 15/NII 415), as we will see in Chapter 3.[7] Heidegger's

---

[5] I get this nicely descriptive phrase by combining those of Dreyfus (*Being-in-the-World: A Commentary on Heidegger's* Being and Time, *Division I*) and Schürmann (*Heidegger on Being and Acting: From Principles to Anarchy*). On Heidegger's account, as we will see, Western history presents us with what are basically five different ways of understanding what beings *are*, hence five overlapping epochs in this history of Being: the pre-Socratic, ancient, medieval, modern, and, now, the late modern – that is, "enframing" (*das Gestell*).

[6] *Philosophical Investigations*, ¶217, 85.

[7] I will suggest in Chapter 3 that the link between Heidegger's philosophy and his disastrous political commitments during the 1930s can best be understood in terms of his own metaphysical ambition (exhibited prominently in such texts as *Being and Time* and his Rectorial Address) to recover a fundamental ontology capable of unifying the German academy and, behind it, the German nation. If this is right, however, it means that the

recognition that there is no such substantive, transhistorically binding fundamental ontology encouraged him to radically historicize ontology, the move which, most scholars would agree, constitutes the *sine qua non* of his "later" thought.

However controversial this central doctrine of the later Heidegger may be, it now forms a taken-for-granted point of philosophical departure for virtually every major practitioner of poststructuralism, postmodernism, and deconstruction. Why is it, then, that in the growing philosophical literature contesting or critically appropriating these otherwise diverse schools of thought, we nowhere find a careful reconstruction of the idiosyncratic understanding of metaphysics on which Heideggerian historicity is based?[8] Even thinkers such as Derrida, Baudrillard, and Irigaray, who often speak not just of metaphysics but of philosophy *tout court* as "ontotheology," never adequately unpack the meaning of the term. This chapter (and, more broadly, this book) can be understood in part as a response to this rather glaring exegetical lacuna. But beyond clarifying an unspoken presupposition of much recent continental philosophy, and so laying some necessary groundwork for those who would understand that work on its own terms (whether to criticize it, build on it, or both), there is for me an even more important motivation for reconstructing Heidegger's deconstruction of the history of Western metaphysics, and that is this: Heidegger's conception of the foundational role played historically by the metaphysical tradition provides much of the philosophical background for his mature critical philosophy, a background without

---

later Heidegger's rejection of fundamental ontology is also a renunciation of the major philosophical motive behind his politics. This suggests, in turn, that the influential Habermasian view, which would dismiss the later Heidegger's philosophy as politically tainted, rests on a basic misunderstanding of the connection between Heidegger's philosophy and politics.

[8] For a Hegelian criticism of "historicity" and the "left Heideggerian" who espouses such a doctrine, see Robert Pippin, "Heideggerian Postmodernism and Metaphysical Politics," 17–37. My own complaint would be somewhat different: Too many post-Heideggerian "continental" philosophers (both at home and abroad) fail to appreciate the precise scope of Heidegger's critique of metaphysics as "ontotheology" and so simply disparage all manner of philosophical doctrine as "metaphysical." One result of such unfortunate overgeneralizations is that a number of self-undermining positions have been advanced, falsely, under the patrimony of Heidegger's deconstruction of metaphysics. It should become clear from what follows that, although Heidegger ascribed great importance to the experience of that which seems forever to exceed the final grasp of discursive knowledge, his deconstruction of metaphysics does not require philosophers to abandon all propositional language and silently "eff" the ineffable. Nor did Heidegger think we should dissolve all positive political programs, coherent identities, and substantive commitments into the flux of efficient flexibility. Indeed, as we will see, such ersatz radicalism merely reproduces the underlying nihilism it has not first adequately understood.

which his later views can easily appear arbitrary and indefensible. I thus take it that Heidegger's understanding of metaphysics as ontotheology is sufficiently important and complex to merit careful elaboration in its own right, and this will be my primary goal here in Chapter 1.

This chapter is structured as follows. In Section 2, I unpack and explain the meaning of Heidegger's initially strange claim that metaphysics has an ontotheological structure. Section 3 then situates Heidegger's understanding of ontotheology within the broader context of his thought, outlining the significance of his deconstruction of metaphysical foundationalism for his critique of nihilism. In Section 4, I reconstruct the most important components of the original account of the history of metaphysics that Heidegger gives in support of his claim that metaphysics is ontotheology, investigating one of the deepest problems in this account. The concluding Section 5 shows that Heidegger's deconstruction of metaphysics has a positive dimension whereby it helps motivate the elaboration of nonmetaphysical ways of understanding ourselves and our relationships with our worlds.

§2. METAPHYSICS AS ONTOTHEOLOGY

Every question specifies [*grenzt*] as a question the breadth and nature of the answer it is looking for. At the same time, it circumscribes [*umgrenzt*] the range of possibilities for answering it. In order for us to ponder the question of metaphysics adequately, it is necessary in the first place to consider it as a question, rather than considering the procession of answers descending from it in the history of metaphysics.

(N4 206/NII 344)

From the late 1920s through the mid-1940s, Heidegger worked to distill the structural commonalities of the metaphysical tradition down to a formal framework into which he could fit every "fundamental metaphysical position" in the history of the Western tradition (N3 179/NII 25). In so doing, he continued to refine the understanding of metaphysics he first set forth in 1929 (in texts such as "What Is Metaphysics?" and *Kant and the Problem of Metaphysics*) until, in 1940, he presents what he calls: "The concept of the essence of metaphysics," which states that: "Metaphysics is the truth of the totality of entities as such" (N3 187/NII 257). What does this "concept of the essence of metaphysics" tell us? Let us take the advice Heidegger gives in the epigraph to this section and consider the way in which the question of metaphysics specifies and circumscribes its own possible answers.

As Heidegger understands the history of metaphysics, "Western–European thinking is guided by the question: 'What is an entity?'

['*Was ist das Seiende?*'] This is the form in which it asks about being [*Sein*]"
(KTB 340/GA9 448–9). Metaphysics asks what it means for an entity to *be*,
and understands the answer to this question as "being." For Heidegger,
however, the answer to the question of what entities *are*, which metaphysics takes as "being," really needs to be understood more precisely as
"the being of entities [*das Sein des Seienden*]." This Heideggerian locution
may sound odd initially, but really it is a fairly straightforward philosophical clarification. Asking what entities *are* (or what an entity *is*) means
asking about the *being* of those entities. As Heidegger puts it: "Whenever
it is said of entities, the little word 'is' names the *being* of [those] entities"
(PR 125/GA10 183). To establish an answer to the question "What is an
entity?" metaphysics makes a claim about what (and how) entities *are*,
and thus about the *being* of those entities.

Heidegger's startling thesis, however, is that these metaphysical postulates about the being of entities take the same form throughout the entire
history of metaphysics: "Metaphysics speaks of the totality of entities as
such, [and] thus of the *being* of entities" (N4 151/NII 205). Metaphysics'
most basic postulates – what Heidegger terms the "fundamental metaphysical positions" – endeavor to establish "a truth about the totality of
entities as such" (N3 187/NII 258/GA50 4). His analysis of this "core
content" (*Kerngehalt*) of metaphysics leads him to a surprising discovery;
each "fundamental metaphysical position" is essentially "twofold" (KTB
340/GA9 450). That is, metaphysics actually gives two subtly different but
interrelated answers to the "question of the *being* of entities." In its sim-
plest form, Heidegger's claim is that each fundamental metaphysical position has two separable components: an understanding of entities "as such"
and an understanding of the "totality" of entities. Structurally, "What *is*
an entity?" is a "twofold question," then, because in pursuing it metaphysical inquiry follows two paths at the same time, expecting of the question
"What *is* an entity?" two very different kinds of answers (KTB 11/GA9
449).[9] As Heidegger explains, "What *is* an entity?" can be heard as asking
about either *what* makes an entity an entity (as thus as inquiring into the
"essence" or "whatness" of entities as such) or about the way *that* an entity
is an entity (and so searching for the "existence" or "thatness" of entities as
a whole). Given the ambiguous form of the question, both are legitimate
and, as we will see, historically pervasive ways of understanding "the being

---

9 The metaphysical question *par excellence*, the Socratic *to dia ti*, we will see, was formulated
   "by Aristotle as the enduring question of [metaphysical] thinking" (N4 206/NII 344); see,
   for example, Aristotle, *Physics* II.I, 192b38.

of entities." Thus, on Heidegger's analysis, the *Kerngehalt* of metaphysics (its understanding of the being of entities) turns out to be conceptually "twofold," ambiguous to the core, and out of this fractured kernel grow two historically intertwined stalks.

By 1946, Heidegger unequivocally identifies these two stalks of the metaphysical question as "ontology" and "theology" respectively, and he clearly articulates what he will henceforth understand as "the fundamentally ontotheological character of metaphysics" (N4 209/NII 348).[10] In 1961, with the advantage of hindsight, Heidegger gives us perhaps his clearest account of the ontotheological structure of the metaphysical question:

> If we recollect the history of Western–European thinking once more, then we will encounter the following: The question of being, as the question of the being of entities, is double in form. On the one hand, it asks: What is an entity in general as an entity? In the history of philosophy, reflections which fall within the domain of this question acquire the title ontology. The question "What is an entity?" [or "What is that which is?"] simultaneously asks: Which entity is the highest [or supreme, *höchste*] entity, and in what sense is it? This is the question of God and of the divine. We call the domain of this question theology. This duality in the question of the being of entities can be united under the title ontotheology.
>
> (P 340/GA9 449)

Here Heidegger succinctly outlines the formal ontotheological structure of the metaphysical question. It is a question folded over on itself so as to yield two distinct types of answers, one of which is then folded back on itself once more. Let us carefully thus explicate these folds.

---

[10] For the sake of brevity I forgo a genealogical examination of the historical development of Heidegger's own understanding of ontotheology, which he clarified only slowly. Still, most noteworthy in this respect is his fascinating but deeply confused "Appendix" to 1928's *Metaphysical Foundations of Logic* (MFL 154–9/GA26 196–202). Reading this appendix in the light of Heidegger's mature understanding of ontotheology suggests that the short-lived project of "metontology" he advocates here – "a special problematic which has as its proper theme entities as a whole" (MFL 157/GA26 199) – is best understood as Heidegger's attempt to jump from the sinking ship of "fundamental ontology" to that project's ontotheological complement, a type of "fundamental theology" or "theiology" (cf. HCE 135/H 195). Here in 1928, Heidegger still regards metaphysics as a positive "task," indeed, as "the one basic problem of philosophy itself," a task he still believes he will be able to *accomplish*. Nevertheless, he comes very close to his later recognition of metaphysics as ontotheology when he writes: "In their unity, fundamental ontology and metontology constitute the concept of metaphysics" (MFL 158/GA26 202). What this shows, I take it, is that Heidegger had to recognize the fatal flaws in his own ontotheological endeavors – "fundamental ontology" and "metontology," respectively – before decisively rejecting metaphysics as ontotheology. (On "metontology," cf. Crowell's *Husserl, Heidegger, and the Space of Meaning*, 222–43.)

"What *is* an entity?" asks, on the one hand: "What is an entity as an entity?" Heidegger calls this the *ontological* question because it gives an account (*logos*) of the *on hêi on*, entities *qua* entities, or, as he more fully puts it, "entities with regard to being, that is, solely with regard to what makes an entity the entity it is: being" (MFL 10/GA26 12). Heidegger's interpretation makes obvious appeal to the fact that in the *Metaphysics* Aristotle immediately glosses "first philosophy," the study of the *on hêi on*, as *episkopei katholou peri tou ontos hêi on*, that is, "the inquiry which investigates entities insofar as they are in being [*Sein*]."[11] (Here "being" renders Aristotle's participle *to on*. Although Aristotle does not use the infinitive or abstract noun *to einai*, "being," Heidegger's point is that he might as well have; Aristotle's first philosophy investigates entities insofar as they are entities, which is precisely what Heidegger characterizes as the metaphysical question of "the being of entities.")

Heidegger's main point here is that metaphysics functions as ontology when it searches for the most general ground of entities; it looks for what component element all entities share in common. Ontologists understand the *being* of entities in terms of that entity beneath or beyond which no more basic entity can be "discovered" or "fathomed" (*ergründt*); they then generalize from their understanding of this "exemplary entity" to explain the being of all entities. This exemplary entity thus comes to play the ontological role of "giving the ground" (*ergründen*) to all other entities; that is, this basic ontological entity becomes identified as that kind of entity in whose being all other entities share and by which they are thus unified or composed (EP 20/NII 421). In Heidegger's words, metaphysics is ontology when it "thinks of entities with an eye for the ground that is common to all entities as such" (I&D 70/139). Historically, different metaphysicians determine this universal ground according to a wide variety of different "historical molds [*Prägung*]: *Phusis, Logos, Hen, Idea, Energeia,* Substantiality, Objectivity, Subjectivity, Will, Will to Power, Will to Will" (I&D 66/134), and, of course, "*Ousia*," the proto-substance, that ontological "mold" of the being of entities with which, as we will see, Heidegger thinks "metaphysics proper begins" (EP 4/NII 403).

On the other hand, "What is an entity?" (or, as the question "*Was ist das Seiende?*" is better heard in this context, "What is that which is?") also asks: "*Which* entity is the highest (or supreme) entity, and in what sense *is* it?" As my italics and Heidegger's locution ("*Welches ist und wie ist...*") suggest, this theological dimension of the metaphysical question has two aspects. "What is that which is?" asks both (1) *Which* entity is in the supreme, paradigmatic, or exemplary sense? and (2) In what sense *is* it? Heidegger calls the first question "the question of God," the second, "the question of the divine." To answer the "question of God" (of all the entities that are, which of them *is* in the supreme sense?), metaphysics needs to ask "the question of the divine" (what is the supreme *kind* of being?). Metaphysics, as theology, seeks to understand these two interconnected aspects of the being of that which is: "*Which* entity is the highest and *in what way* is it?" (P 340, my emphasis/GA9 449).[12] Taken together, Heidegger writes, this dual "question of God and of the divine" is the *theological* question, so called because it inquires into and would give an account (*logos*) of the existence of the *theion*, "the supreme cause and the highest ground of entities" (N4 209/NII 347).

Heidegger's main point here is that metaphysics thinks theologically when it "thinks of the totality of entities as such ... with regard to the supreme, all-founding entity" (I&D 70–71/139). Since the beginning of Western metaphysics, as we will see, this "highest entity" has been conceived as the ultimate ground of the being of entities (albeit, again, in a wide variety of different ways). Heidegger thus holds that metaphysics is theology whenever it determines the supreme entity as an "all-founding entity," whether as an "unmoved mover" or "self-caused cause" (that is, a "*causa sui*," which Heidegger characterizes as "the metaphysical concept of God"), or whether this "all-founding entity" is conceived with Aristotle as a "first cause" or else with Leibniz as the *ens realissimum* (the "beingest of beings" (*Seiendsten des Seienden*), as Heidegger aptly renders Leibniz's highest entity). Likewise, Kant thinks "theologically" when he postulates "the subject of subjectivity as the condition of the possibility of all objectivity," as does Hegel when he determines "the highest entity as the absolute in the sense of unconditioned subjectivity" (I&D 60/127; N4 208/NII 347),

---

[12] This suggests that the atheistic or skeptical question, "Does this supreme kind of existence in fact exist?" would originally have seemed nonsensical. (If it did not exist, then it could not have been the supreme, exemplary, or paradigmatic entity, the entity "most in being," in the first place.) The skeptical question would first arise only when a specific answer already given to the "question of God" is called into question (suggesting, in effect, that the question of God was not answered properly), or else when we come to doubt that *any* entity "is" in a highest or paradigmatic sense (suggesting, more broadly, that the question of God is nonsensical). In my view, however, the later Heidegger is not an atheist but, rather, a polytheist, for he believes that many different kinds of entities can manifest their being in an exemplary way (he calls this phenomenon "things thinging") when properly approached – with a phenomenological comportment he calls "releasement" or *Gelassenheit*. On this latter point, see my "Ontology and Ethics at the Intersection of Phenomenology and Environmental Philosophy." For a variety of interesting, if often conflicting, attempts to develop the religious significance of Heidegger's critique of metaphysics, see the essays collected in Mark A. Wrathall, ed., *Religion after Metaphysics*.

TABLE 1.1. *The Different Ontotheologies in the*
Metaphysical Tradition

Onto-	-Theology
Entities as such	Entities as a whole
Most basic entity	Highest entity
Whatness	Thatness
Koinotaton	*Katholon*
Essentia	*Existentia*
Idea as universal	*Idea* as paradigm
Deutera ousia	*Prôtê ousia*
Ultima ratio	*Causa prima*
Ens commune	*Summum ens*
Quidditas (essentiality)	*Quomodo* (modality)
Reality	The real
Subjectivity	The subject
Substantiality	Substance
The transcendental	The transcendent
Content	Form
Action	Organization
Will-to-power	Eternal return of the same

that is, as outermost conditions on the possibility of intelligibility. According to Heidegger, even Nietzsche "thinks the *existentia* of the totality of entities as such theologically as the eternal return of the same" (N4 210/NII 348), for eternal recurrence is not just the way that the totality of entities exists (in Nietzsche's speculative cosmological understanding of their existence) but also their *highest* mode of existence (as the closest the endless stream of becoming comes to *being*).

   Thus it is that when applied to the history of Western metaphysics, Heidegger's understanding of ontotheology as the substructural frame according to which every metaphysical edifice is constructed allows him to unearth the following sets of paired ontotheological distinctions (shown in Table 1.1).[13]

---

[13] This table is not meant to be exhaustive, nor does it imply that all the pairs named here *succeeded* in metaphysically grounding an historical epoch. There is, moreover, no "master pair" that can be employed to explain all the others. (The "essence/existence" distinction comes closest, but Heidegger is being anachronistic when he writes that: "The distinction between *essentia* and *existentia* underlies all metaphysics" [EP 82/NII 489].) It is tempting to say that the pairs bear a "family resemblance" to one another, but that just raises the question: A family resemblance *in virtue of what?* Heidegger insists that they are best understood as a series of different versions of the same ontotheologically structured difference, in the sense explained in the text. I must thus part company here with the

§3. DECONSTRUCTING METAPHYSICAL FOUNDATIONALISM

In Section 4, we will return to the contents of this table and one of "the deepest problems" it harbors. (The problem can be anticipated as follows: Why should we find Heidegger's understanding of ontotheology plausible, when it leads him to throw together such a startling array of pairs of "ontotheological" concepts, seemingly without any regard for the many differences between them?) First, however, let me emphasize what for our purposes is the single most important point in the foregoing explication of Heidegger's understanding of metaphysics as ontotheology. This is his claim that the primary historical role of metaphysics is the *establishment* and – in the paradoxical continuity of "an unbroken sequence of transformations" (GA15 395) – the *maintenance* of a "ground" for what is. As Heidegger writes: "Since the early days of Western thought, being has been interpreted as the ground or foundation [*Grund*] in which every entity as an entity is grounded" (I&D 32/96). (Here, within the context of Heidegger's understanding of metaphysics, we need to recall that "'being' means always and everywhere the being *of entities*" [I&D 61/129], and thus that an "understanding of being" is his shorthand for an "understanding of the being of entities.")

In Heidegger's assertion that the being of entities *grounds* entities, I believe it is crucial to recognize that "to ground" (*gründen*) is "fortuitously ambiguous" between the ontological and theological senses in which metaphysics "grounds." Ontologically, the basic entity, once generalized and so understood as the being of all entities, *grounds* in the sense of "giving the ground" (*ergründen*) to entities; ontology discovers and sets out the bedrock beneath which the metaphysician's investigations cannot "penetrate." (*Ergründen* means not just "to fathom, penetrate, or discover," but also "to get a matter upon its ground" or "through searching to establish more precisely.") Theologically, the highest (or supreme) entity, also understood as the being of entities, *grounds* in the sense of "founding" (*begründen*) entities, "establishing" the source from which all entities ultimately issue and by which they can subsequently be "justified." (*Begründen* means not only "to give reasons for" or "justify," but also to "establish"

---

kind of orthodox Heideggerianism that would dismiss "the impulse to multiply lists of terms, order them, fix them in some set structural pattern" as "academic pedantry" which, unconsciously betraying its "Christian concern with true (correct) doctrine," treats "the slippering [*sic*], resonating, evocative primal words of thinking as if they were beings to be manipulated" (Gail Stenstad, "The Turning in *Ereignis* and Transformation of Thinking," 92–3).

or "found," in the sense of "to give for the ground."[14]) As Heidegger
puts it:

> Metaphysics thinks of the being of entities both [ontologically] in [terms of] the
> ground-giving [*ergründenden*] unity of what is most general, that is, of what is
> uniformly valid everywhere, and also [theologically] in [terms of] the founding
> [*begründenden*] unity of the all, that is, of the Most High above all others. The being
> of entities is thus thought of in advance as the grounding ground [*der gründende
> Grund*].
>
> (I&D 58/125)

I interpret this strange-sounding but crucial claim to mean that within the
metaphysical tradition, the ontotheological "grounding ground" *grounds*
in *both* the ontological and theological senses. In other words, it is by simultaneously "giving the ground" ontologically and "founding" theologically
that the ontotheologically conceived being of entities accomplishes its distinctively *double* "grounding" of our changing historical sense of what is.

Heidegger's first law of phenomenology, "the law of proximity," dictates that the obvious is most likely to escape our notice (PAR 135/GA54
201). In thinking about the preceding, let us not overlook the following. When metaphysics conceives of the being of entities ontologically,
in terms of an entity in whose being all other entities share, and theologically, in terms of an all-founding entity from which (or whom) all
entities issue, what is thereby "taken for granted" is that being (understood as the being of entities) plays the role of a "ground of entities," that
is, a *foundational* role.[15] Indeed, metaphysics reinforces its foundational
claim about what and how entities *are* – its "truth concerning the totality
of entities as such" – by coming at the problem from both ends of the
conceptual scale simultaneously: Metaphysics effects *both* a bottom-up
"ground-giving or establishing" (in which its understanding of the being
of entities, reached by generalizing from its conception of the most basic
entity, grounds the intelligible order from inside out) *and* a top-down,
theological "founding or justification" (in which its understanding of the
being of entities, derived from its conception of the highest entity, secures
the intelligible order from the outside in) (I&D 61/129; I&D 39/104).
All successful, epoch-grounding metaphysical systems *combine* these two
different forms of foundationalism, thereby securing our understanding

---

[14] See Terrell et al., eds., *HarperCollins German Dictionary*, 98, 220, and G. Wahrig, ed.,
Deutsches Wörterbuch, 289, 519.

[15] As Mark Okrent explains: "Because being is understood by metaphysics as the ground of
entities, metaphysics always drives toward ultimate grounds, the ultimate principles that
account for everything else" (*Heidegger's Pragmatism: Understanding, Being, and the Critique
of Metaphysics*, 227, terminology made consistent with my own).

of the being of entities (and so grounding the intelligible order) from *both* the inside out *and* the outside in, microscopically *and* telescopically, floor to ceiling – or, as Heidegger puts it, ontologically *and* theologically, that is, *ontotheologically*.

After painstakingly reconstructing this conception of how metaphysics, as ontotheology, grounds history, however, Heidegger asks the percussive question that pulls the rug out from under the entire history of foundationalist metaphysics: What kind of a ground is this *really*? That is, if metaphysics' ontotheological postulates concerning the being of entities doubly "ground" those entities, then *what in turn grounds the being of entities?* Only two kinds of answers can halt the regress. Either there must be something beyond the being of entities in or by which the being of entities can itself be grounded, or else the being of entities must be self-grounding. As we will see, Heidegger develops a variation of the former answer himself: "Being as such" will be his problematic name for that which makes possible – but does not ontotheologically "ground" – metaphysics' various epochal postulates of the being of entities. Heidegger is clear, however, that the metaphysical tradition chooses the latter option. For metaphysics: "The being of entities reveals itself as that ground which [ontologically] gives itself the ground and [theologically] founds itself" (I&D 57/124).

We have thus seen that the peculiar "double grounding" that metaphysics attempts would ontologically anchor its understanding of the being of entities in a basic entity and theologically derive it from (and so justify it by appeal to) a supreme entity. As we will see in Section 4, however, Heidegger's deconstructive analysis of metaphysics reveals that these ontotheologically structured "fundamental metaphysical positions" constitute neither an unimpeachable ontological *Ur-grund*, an unshakable "primal foundation" for our historical understanding of being, nor merely an unstable *Ab-grund*, as if a groundless "abyss" were constantly gaping open beneath the intelligible world. Rather, these fundamental metaphysical positions provide history with what Heidegger characterizes as an *Un-grund*, "a perhaps necessary appearance of ground" for each epochal constellation of intelligibility (IM 3/GA40 5). In other words, the peculiar "double grounding" attempted by metaphysics always leaves our understanding of the being of entities epistemically "suspended" between foundation and abyss. This insight turns out to be very important, because it helps explain why the history of metaphysics looks like a *succession* of relatively durable understandings of being, rather than either a single unbroken epoch or a continuous flux. When Heidegger reminds us that "to hold back, is in Greek, *epochē*" (T&B 9/ZSD 9), his point is that each ontotheologically structured metaphysical postulate that succeeds in establishing our understanding of the being of entities effectively "holds back" the floodwaters of ontological historicity for a time – the time of an "epoch."[16] These metaphysical suspensions endure for an "epoch," doubly grounding an historical "constellation of intelligibility," only to be replaced by the next ontotheologically grounded epoch.

And so it continues, down through the "history of being" – at the fractured core of which we find a series of unified ontotheological postulates, "fundamental metaphysical positions," which each succeeded in temporarily establishing "the truth concerning the totality of entities as such" for its epoch – until, on Heidegger's reading, Nietzsche cuts the philosophical strings of the very project of metaphysical foundationalism. Nietzsche does this, I take it, both by dislodging the ontological anchoring – when, for example, in "The History of an Error" he extends the Kantian lesson that no unbroken epistemic chain can be constructed which could anchor this world in a "true world" beyond or within it – and also by persuasively criticizing, as both cognitively unsatisfying and effectively nihilistic, the appeal to a highest being – when, for instance, his "madman" brings the news that "God is dead. . . . And we have killed him" to the marketplace. It is important to notice here that Nietzsche stages his "madman" as a messenger who would have us face up to the profound significance of an "event" that has *already* occurred. For Nietzsche it is Kant who "killed God" in this sense, by demonstrating the limits of metaphysical knowledge and the fallaciousness of the

---

[16] All the different metaphysically grounded epochs in the history of being suspend historicity by "holding back" (i.e., freezing in a necessarily incomplete conceptual account) "being as such," the phenomenological "presencing" (*Anwesen*) conditioning intelligibility. Like "the same" (see later), "being as such" is one of Heidegger's names for the inexhaustible phenomenon that, by both eliciting and defying final conceptual circumscription, makes ontological historicity possible. Because metaphysics leaves "being as such" out of account when it codifies and disseminates the fundamental conceptual parameters for each constellation of intelligibility, metaphysics' purview is not total; thought is never entirely imprisoned within its epoch. Under the influence of metaphysics, however, we tend to forget this. Indeed, we will see that for Heidegger the "greatest danger" is that our Nietzschean understanding of the being of entities (as eternally recurring will-to-power) could succeed in preemptively delegitimating the very notion of "being as such," a phenomenon which appears to be "nothing" (N4 203/NII 340), merely "the last wisp of an evaporating reality" (IM 42/GA40 43), when viewed from within the perspective established by Nietzsche's metaphysics of "sovereign becoming." Heidegger characterizes this reduction of "being as such" to "nothing" as "nihilism proper" (N4 202/NII 339), because it elides the phenomenon underwriting his hope for a non-nihilistic, postepochal age – until we recognize this reduction as such, and so enter into what Heidegger calls (we will see in Section 9C) its "freeing claim."

traditional proofs for God's existence.[17] In Heidegger's terms, Nietzsche thinks Kant's "unthought" – making explicit Kant's implicit contribution to the history of metaphysics – and Heidegger, in turn, seeks to do the same for Nietzsche.

By unearthing the "unthought" ontotheological *unity* of Nietzsche's own metaphysical doctrines of will-to-power and eternal recurrence, Heidegger argues that Nietzsche's own fundamental metaphysical position inaugurates a *nihilism* (or meaninglessness) that Nietzsche, insofar as he thinks from the basis of his own unrecognized metaphysical presuppositions, is himself helpless to combat. The central idea behind Heidegger's reductive but revealing reading of Nietzsche is that, taken together, Nietzsche's doctrines of will-to-power and eternal recurrence enact the final fulfillment and collapse of metaphysics understood as the project of providing intelligibility with an ontotheological foundation. This is why Heidegger famously, and controversially, calls Nietzsche "the last metaphysician" (that is, the final ontotheologist), presenting Nietzsche's ontotheology as the "overturning" of Plato (whom, we will see, Heidegger understands as the first ontotheologist). It is crucial to grasp, however, that Nietzsche's implosion of metaphysical foundationalism does not stop the Nietzschean metaphysics of the "atomic age" from taking the groundless free fall of eternally recurring will-to-power as its own metaphysical starting point. Because Nietzsche's groundless ontotheology of eternally recurring will-to-power implodes the project of metaphysical foundationalism while, nevertheless, supplying the ontotheological understanding of the being of entities for our own historical epoch, Heidegger holds that Nietzsche inaugurates Western metaphysics' "completed or fulfilled [*vollendet*]" and "final stage; for inasmuch as through Nietzsche, metaphysics has in a certain sense divested itself of its own essential possibility, other possibilities of metaphysics can no longer

---

[17] See Nietzsche, *The Twilight of the Idols*, 50–1; *The Gay Science*, (#125), 181. For the account that follows, see Heidegger, "Nietzsche's Metaphysics" (N3 185–251/NII 257–333). Nietzsche saw Kant as a Raskolnikov figure who set out to kill (indeed, to "kill god," that is, to make reason rather than divine authority the foundation of morality), but subsequently felt he had to steal (adopting the Judeo-Christian value system) in order to rationalize this murder (and escape its guilt). For Nietzsche, Kant thereby avoided facing up to the true radicalism of his act, the fact that "the death of god" demanded a "revaluation of values," that is, a new, non-nihilistic value-system which would not devalue this world by comparing it to an "otherworldly" beyond, forever out of our cognitive reach. See Nietzsche, "On the Pale Criminal," *Thus Spoke Zarathustra*, 149–52, my "Deconstructing the Hero," and, on Nietzsche's still underappreciated debt to Kant, R. Kevin Hill, *Nietzsche's Critiques: The Kantian Foundations of His Thought.*

appear" (EP 95/GA7 81; QCT 53/GA5 209). What does Heidegger mean by this?

Before Nietzsche, the metaphysical tradition had refused to give up the foundationalist project despite the fact that its own history, as an unbroken succession of epochal overturnings – in which each metaphysically grounded epoch rose from the ashes of the metaphysics that preceded it – shows that time and again metaphysics has proven incapable of providing itself with the epistemically unimpeachable and so historically immutable ontotheological foundations it sought. Ironically, however, the epoch of the metaphysical tradition Nietzsche inaugurates now effectively deprives itself, and thus us, of any *ground* whatsoever. For Heidegger's Nietzsche, entities *are* only concatenations of forces in the service of will-to-power, a will that strives ultimately only for its own unlimited self-aggrandizing increase, thus becoming nothing but "the will to insure the overpowering of everything," that is, sheer "will to will" (EP 64/NII 468; I&D 66/134). Yet, this groundless Nietzschean ontotheology of "eternally recurring will-to-power" (or "will to will," for short) still preconceptualizes "the totality of entities as such" as concatenations of energy, forces coming together and breaking apart with no goal beyond their own self-augmenting increase, and all entities, ourselves included, are thereby conceived of ultimately only as raw materials, intrinsically meaningless *resources* (*Bestand*) on standby merely to be optimally ordered and efficiently disposed of in an endless and unending spiral of "constant overcoming." For Heidegger, then, Nietzsche's legacy is our nihilistic "cybernetic" epoch of "enframing" (*Gestell*, about which more next chapter), which can only enact its own groundless metaphysical presuppositions by increasingly quantifying the qualitative – reducing all intelligibility to that which can be stockpiled as bivalent, programmable "information" (TTL 139–42/USTS 21–28) – and by leveling down all attempts to justify human meaning to empty optimization imperatives like: "Get the most out of your potential!" Consequentialist modes of abstract resource maximization may flourish against such a background, but Heidegger points out that this "technological" understanding of the being of entities is no longer actually in the service of any person or goal. Rather, accelerated by the proliferating technologies of cyberspace, entities are increasingly stripped and divested of their meaning in order to enter into (what Baudrillard aptly describes as) "a state of pure circulation."[18]

We do not need at this point to further elaborate Heidegger's dystopian vision of late modernity, according to which we are stuck historically,

---

[18] *The Transparency of Evil: Essays on Extreme Phenomena*, 4.

playing out a kind of cybernetic endgame to the atomic age, nor do we need now to take up the controversies Heidegger's seemingly bleak philosophical portrait of our age has understandably engendered – these tasks will occupy much of Chapter 2.[19] All we need recognize for now is that the continuing failure of metaphysics to secure its own ontotheological ground prompts Heidegger to ask: *Why* is the being of entities historically "thought in advance" as a double, ontotheological *ground*? How did it happen that, as Heidegger puts it, "being is prestamped as ground" (I&D 57/124)? How was it that being got cast in such a mold? Let us be clear from the start about the aims of this question by recognizing, with Dreyfus, that "there is no sense in looking for a cause of such profound 'events' that determine what counts as being and intelligibility; one can only try to free oneself from them by recounting their history."[20]

It is in this spirit of a genealogical deconstruction of the form that metaphysical foundationalism has taken historically, a deconstruction in which we recount its history in order to call its necessity into question, as a first step toward understanding things differently, rather than as yet another metaphysically inspired attempt to secure an unbroken epistemic chain between our present understanding of being and its historical origins, that we turn now to examine Heidegger's own response to one of the deepest problems inherent in his understanding of metaphysics as ontotheology.

§4. "ONE OF THE DEEPEST PROBLEMS"

Heidegger's extremely ambitious description of the ontotheological structure of metaphysics will initially strike students of the history of philosophy as a massive oversimplification.[21] For, although Heidegger certainly acknowledges that, as this twofold metaphysical question is pursued historically, different metaphysicians formulate the ontotheological duality in different terms, he nevertheless maintains that all the major historical "fundamental metaphysical positions" remain within this same ontotheological framework. As he so provocatively puts it: "All great thinkers think the same" (N1 36/NI 46). Heidegger recognized, of course, that

---

[19] These controversies include the Sokal-led scientistic backlash. (See Alan Sokal and Jean Bricmont, *Fashionable Nonsense: Postmodern Intellectuals' Abuse of Science.*) For a reconstruction and defense of Heidegger's ontological "critique of technology," see Chapter 2 and my "From the Question Concerning Technology to the Quest for a Democratic Technology: Heidegger, Marcuse, Feenberg."

[20] *Being-in-the-World*, 127.

[21] Derrida explicitly raises this objection; see "Interpreting Signatures (*Nietzsche/Heidegger*): Two Questions," 29–42.

such a blanket statement would call forth an immediate objection. As he observes in 1955's "What Is Philosophy?":

> It will be pointed out with ease that philosophy itself and the way in which it conceives its own nature have transformed frequently in . . . two thousand years. Who would deny this? At the same time, however, we ought not overlook the fact that philosophy from Aristotle to Nietzsche, precisely on the basis of these transformations throughout its course, has remained the same. For the transformations vouch for the kinship of the same.
>
> (WIP 61/60)

Again Heidegger puts the point provocatively: All fundamental metaphysical positions think "the same" (*das Selbe*). Certainly metaphysics' self-conception has been frequently transformed throughout the long history of the metaphysical tradition, but "these transformations vouch for the kinship of the same." How are we to understand such apparently paradoxical assertions?

Like most provocations, Heidegger's are misleading *prima facie*; their point depends on our being *provoked* to think the matter through, rather than turning away from such seemingly obvious falsehoods. In fact, Heidegger is actually making three important points here. First, as we might by now expect, he is claiming that all the different metaphysical systems have the following in common: They all attempt to "lay the ground" for entities. As Heidegger had already recognized in 1929:

> An explicit ground-laying of metaphysics never happens *ex nihilo*, but rather arises from the strengths and weaknesses of a tradition which designates in advance its possible points of departure. With reference to these this tradition is self-enclosed, for every ground-laying is, in its relation to what came before, a transformation of the same task.
>
> (KPM 2/GA3 2)

Heidegger's point is that *within* the tradition of Western metaphysics (and we will ask where this tradition begins in a minute), all Western metaphysical systems attempt a "ground-laying," and, as we have seen, one which takes the form of a "double grounding" of our understanding of the being of entities in a fundamental ontotheological duality. Nevertheless, Heidegger acknowledges, each of the various "fundamental metaphysical positions" determines this unified ontotheological duality somewhat *differently*. Indeed, the different pairs of dual, ontotheological understandings of the being of entities Heidegger lists in his work, taken together, make for an initially astounding variety of concepts: whatness and thatness (EP 2/NII 401); *koinotaton* and *katholon* (GA9 450); the *idea* as universal and as paradigm (EP 13/NII 413; PDT 268/GA9 234); *protê* and *deutera ousia* (EP 6–8/NII 405–6); *quidditas* and *quomodo* (WIT 236–8/

GA41 238–40); *ultima ratio* and *causa prima* (I&D 60/127); *ens commune* and *summum ens* (WIT 118/GA41 119); essence and existence (EP 82/NII 489); content and form (PLT 27/H 12); the real and the reality of the real (WIT 212–20/GA41 214–18); subjectivity and the subject (I&D 60/127, 66/134); substantiality and substance (*ibid.*); the transcendental and the transcendent (N4 211/NII 349); organization and action (EP 66/NII 471);[22] and even, as we have seen, will-to-power and the eternal return of the same (EP 70/NII 476). At first, this may seem like an implausibly broad array of concepts, but Heidegger maintains that the inner history of metaphysics is composed of a series of such "original and therefore unique" fundamental metaphysical positions, only some of which succeeded in temporarily supplying the structural scaffolding for Western history's successive constellations of intelligibility (GA66 75). How, then, can we best make sense of his view?

There are only five basic epochs in Heidegger's mature history of being (which we could call the pre-Socratic, Platonic, medieval, modern, and late-modern ages), so many of the "unique" metaphysical positions that he lists must have been relatively *inert* ontohistorically. That is, they cannot be credited with the revolutionary inauguration of a new understanding of being, nor with providing the substructural support for an historical constellation of intelligibility, and so are not crucial to his account of the history of being. For Heidegger is not claiming that every ontotheology *succeeded* in "doubly grounding" historical intelligibility, nor that every major philosopher in the Western canon was a metaphysician. Some important thinkers, such as Kierkegaard and Hume, clearly are not "metaphysicians" in Heidegger's distinctive sense, since they do not even attempt to reconceive the being of entities, let alone successfully advance an epoch-grounding ontotheology. Although the influence of such thinkers may still, of course, be considerable, this influence will not operate directly on our ontohistorical self-understanding, and it is the fact that such thinkers do not significantly impact our historical understanding of being which makes them of little interest to the later Heidegger. Indeed, Heidegger's later focus is directed primarily toward ontohistorically revolutionary philosophers such as Plato, Descartes, and Nietzsche, and secondarily toward those philosophers who significantly refine the epoch-grounding understanding of being those metaphysicians inaugurate, such as Aristotle and Kant. Moreover, although Heidegger thinks that: "What is essential in the discovery of reality happened and happens

---

[22] With this distinction, Heidegger attributes an ontotheologically structured metaphysics to American "pragmatism."

not through science, but through primordial philosophy, as well as through great poetry and its projections" (ET 47/GA34 64) – a provocative claim to which we will return in Chapter 3 – he does not thereby deify the agency of particular metaphysicians. The great metaphysicians do not legislate their own private, creative insights but, rather, focus and disseminate the fundamental and ultimate truths of (and, subsequently, for) their respective historical ages. Because Heidegger recognizes that the tradition of Western metaphysics provides the context even for those who transform it radically, he never claims that the great metaphysicians articulate a new understanding of the being of entities *ex nihilo*. Rather, as he puts it with respect to Plato's ontohistorically revolutionary doctrine of the *ideas*: "This discovery was not some far-flung speculation on the part of Plato, but relates to what everyone sees and grasps in their comportment toward entities. Plato just pointed this out with previously unknown power and assurance" (ET 38/GA34 51). Nor, however, should we make the opposite mistake by underestimating the ontohistorical importance of the great metaphysicians. For, Heidegger says, the crucial ontohistorical discovery that a great metaphysician focuses and disseminates (let alone the way such a discovery comes subsequently to transform our fundamental understanding of ourselves and our place in the world) "is not self-evident, nor is it simply given to man like a nose and ears, nor does it come to man in his sleep, nor is it the same at all times" (ET 115/GA34 157).

This "nor is it the same at all times" brings us to the second important point behind the later Heidegger's provocative claim that "all metaphysicians think the same." Although he includes "the eternal return of the same" as Nietzsche's "theological" contribution to the history of being (that is, as Nietzsche's endeavor to view the totality of entities from outside and characterize the ultimate way that this totality exists), Heidegger's claim that the series of different ontotheological conceptions of the being of entities *all* think "the same" should not to lead us to imagine the "monotonous" recurrence of something "merely identical." To recognize that Heidegger is not committing such a massive oversimplification, we need to know that for Heidegger: "Sameness implies a relation of 'with,' that is, a mediation, a connection, a synthesis: the unification into a unity. . . . But that unity is by no means the stale emptiness of that which, in itself without relation, persists in monotony" (I&D 25/87). Our worry dissipates, in other words, when we recognize that for two things to be "the same" actually *requires* that they be different. As Heidegger puts it: "The same [*das Selbe*] is not the merely identical [*das Gleich*]. In the merely identical, the difference disappears" (I&D 45/111). Heidegger credits

German Idealism with getting us to pay attention to "the mediation that prevails in unity" (I&D 25/87–8), but it is Derrida who, true to form, gives this claim about "the non-self-identity" of the same its most succinct and provocative rendering: "The other is in the same."[23] Although such assertions sound paradoxical, the distinction they seek to convey is clear enough: Sameness requires likeness in some significant respect (a shared ontotheological structure, for instance), but identity requires likeness in every respect. Heidegger's provocations thus draw attention to the seemingly paradoxical fact that there will always be some *difference* between two things that are "the same."

Finally, Heidegger's assertions that "all great thinkers think the same" and that metaphysics' "transformations vouch for the kinship of the same" also intend to make a third and even subtler point. For these assertions point toward the phenomenological fact that, as Reiner Schürmann recognized, "beneath the epochal differences something shows forth that remains the same."[24] "This same," Heidegger tells us, "is so essential and rich that no single thinker exhausts it" (N1 36/NI 46). Indeed, "Only with difficulty do we bring this same into view in its proper character, and seldom in its full richness" (PR 91/GA10 135). This notion of the "same" is recognizable as one of Heidegger's names for "being as such" (that is, being in its *difference* from the metaphysically conceived being of entities). Hence Heidegger also refers to the same as: "It, being, [*that which is*] *given to thinking/to be thought* [*Daß Es, das Sein*, zu denken gibt]" (N4 228/NII 372). "The same" thus designates a matter that the later Heidegger associates with Parmenides (for whom, famously, "thinking and being are *the same*"); it is one of Heidegger's names for that which gives rise to our worlds of meaning without ever being exhausted by them, a dimension of intelligibility we experience primarily as it recedes from our awareness, eluding our attempts finally to *know* it, to grasp and express it fully in terms of some positive content. Heidegger finds this phenomenon mysterious and compelling enough to give it the Nietzschean title "the *enigma*" (I&D 23–41/85–106; GA15 410–17). This third meaning is the most important for Heidegger because, despite the difficulties involved, this attempt to gain access to the original phenomenological "showing forth" that all metaphysicians name but none "exhausts" ultimately motivates his deconstruction of metaphysical foundationalism. Indeed, we touch here on the idea at the very core of *Heideggerian hope*, for it is his

[23] "Ellipsis," *Writing and Difference*, 295–7.
[24] *Heidegger on Being and Acting*, 118; see also I&D 25/87.

philosophical contention that a non-nihilistic futural understanding of being will come, if it comes at all, from a phenomenological experience and articulation of the continuing epiphanies of that which remains "the same" beneath all change.[25] This mysterious "same" is, in other words, part of Heidegger's own attempt to elaborate an alternative to thinking of being metaphysically as the ontotheological ground of entities (a difficult point to which we will return in the conclusion).[26]

There is thus a sense in which the later Heidegger successfully carries out to the letter (if not the spirit) the deconstructive project famously called for in *Being and Time*: "Taking *the question of being as our clue*, we are to *deconstruct* the traditional content of ancient ontology until we reach into and recover those primordial experiences in which we achieved our first ways of determining the nature of being – the ways that have guided us ever since" (B&T 44/S&Z 22). For, as we will see, Heidegger's deconstruction of metaphysics both grants us access to the phenomenological record of those primordial Western experiences of being and, moreover, allows us to understand the sense in which these original experiences turned out to be historically *determinative* without being *necessary*. In order to follow Heidegger's approach toward this original phenomenological showing-forth, let us investigate the difficulty of bringing this "same" into view by expanding on our previous objection to his understanding of ontotheology.

After considering Heidegger's claim that all the great Western metaphysical systems share this ontotheological structure, the philosopher who has been disabused of a certain naïveté by the poststructuralist revolution will have an obvious question to ask of Heidegger: Why think that all metaphysics has this deep ontotheological structure? If Heidegger is not simply legislating an indefensible claim about the *a priori* structure of metaphysics, then he owes us some account of *how* it happened that these two ways of asking about the "ground" of entities – and hence of postulating the ontotheological "being of entities" to play the role of that ground – became so inextricably linked. Only such an account, moreover, can tell us whether this entanglement of ontology and theology at the

---

[25] See esp. Heidegger's essay "The Turning" (QCT 36–49/GA79 68–77).

[26] Some may worry that the later Heidegger's understanding of the explanatory role played by "being as such" in the history of intelligibility fails to escapes his own charge of ontotheology. From what has been said here, however, it should be clear that such a devastating immanent criticism would be true only if it were the case that Heidegger understands "being as such" metaphysically *in his own distinctive sense of metaphysics*, that is, as an ontological and theological double "ground" for intelligibility. Because that seems highly implausible to me, I leave it to others to advance the critique, should they be so inclined.

heart of metaphysics is a necessary connection, which we had better learn to live with, or merely a fateful historical contingency, to which alternatives can be envisioned.

As I will now show, Heidegger does in fact countenance this "deepest problem" himself, although for the most part only obliquely, under the obscure rubric of "the still *unthought* unity of the essence of metaphysics" (I&D 55/121):

> Where does the essentially ontotheological constitution of metaphysics come from? To take up the question thus posed means, at the same time, to carry out the step back. In this step we now contemplate the essential ancestry of the ontotheological structure of all metaphysics.
>
> (I&D 56/123)[27]

According to Heidegger, investigating this question requires that we take "the step back" (N4 244/NII 390), meaning that we must step back from the particular metaphysical understanding of being implicitly shaping our thinking and try to gain access to that broader phenomenon ("the same") that has made possible the history of remarkably *different* understandings of being. To seek a path leading beyond ontotheology, we need first to step back from the particular epoch of the history of being in the currents of which we otherwise remain immersed. One way to do this, Heidegger suggests, is by specifically investigating the genealogical "ancestry" of "the ontotheological structure of all metaphysics," asking into the origins of metaphysics in hopes of understanding and so loosening the grip it continues to exert on our thinking. Like so much of his account, Heidegger's answer to this question of the origin of metaphysics must thus be drawn from what are for the most part only more or less elaborate "sketches" of the "in-ception" (*An-fang*) of Western philosophy.[28] Nevertheless, taking this poststructuralist skepticism as our point of departure, we will now move beyond the formal account of the metaphysical question by following Heidegger's "step back" and thereby approaching his understanding of what it is that shows forth as "the same" beneath the successive epochal permutations of ontotheology.

---

[27] See also I&D 60/128: "For it still remains unthought by what unity ontologic and theologic belong together." By 1930, Heidegger was already posing an early version of this question: "Why precisely this doubling of whatness and thatness belongs to the original essence of Being is one of the deepest problems [*der tiefsten Probleme*] ... that indeed has hitherto never yet been a problem at all, but something self-evident. This can be seen, for example, in traditional metaphysics and ontology, where one distinguishes between *essentia* and *existentia*, the whatness and thatness of beings. This distinction is employed as self-evidently as that between night and day" (FCM 357/GA29–30 519–20).

[28] The point of Heidegger's hyphenation of "*An-fang*" is to suggest that the "in-ception" of history takes place as a grasping of being "in the fangs" of time (N4 199/NII 335).

To be as clear as possible, this "deepest problem" can be restated as follows. *How did the metaphysical project of "grounding" entities come to have an ontotheological structure?* We will have answered this question once we understand the answers to the three subquestions that constitute it: (Q_1) *From where* – and (Q_2) *With what necessity* – did the first ontotheological fissure in the kernel of metaphysics develop? (Q_3) *How* did this fissure become incorporated into the structure of metaphysics so as to be decisively perpetuated throughout its entire history?

In his difficult but important 1957 lecture "The Ontotheological Constitution of Metaphysics," Heidegger situates his account of metaphysics as ontotheology within the context of ancient Western philosophy in such a way as to answer question Q_1, the question of *whence.* As the first Western metaphysicians investigated the "primordial matter [*ursprüngliche Sache*] of thinking," what Heidegger calls "the primal matter" (*die Ur-sache*), they attempted to put this *prôtê archê* into language (I&D 60/127).[29] Rendering *prôtê archê* as "the first ground," Heidegger shows that it was as a result of this quest for such a first ground that the earliest Western metaphysicians postulated two different kinds of entities to fill the role of the *prôtê archê*; they understood the being of entities in terms of both an ontological "universal and first entity" and a theological "supreme and ultimate entity" (I&D 61/128). In other words, the first Western metaphysicians' pursuit of the *prôtê archê* led them to postulate two very different ways of "grounding" all entities in an understanding of their being. They attempted *both* a bottom-up (or inside-out) proto-ontological "ground-giving," which understood the being of entities by generalizing from an "universal and first entity" in whose being all other entities shared, *and* a top-down (or outside-in) proto-theological "founding," which derived its understanding of the being of entities from an exemplary "supreme and ultimate entity." Here, then, Heidegger provides an historical analysis in support of his thesis that "since the earliest days of Western thought, being has been interpreted as the ground in which every entity as an entity is grounded" (I&D 32/96). Of whom, however, is he thinking?

Several years before *Being and Time*, in his 1924–1925 lectures on Plato's *Sophist*, Heidegger told his students that: "The Greeks asked how the *on* is there in *logos*, or, more precisely: how a *koinonia* in *onta* is possible" (S 354/GA19 512). Here Heidegger is recalling the fact that the

---

[29] With this notion of a "primal matter [*Ur-sache*]," Heidegger draws our attention to the sememes constituting the ordinary word for "cause" (*Ursache*).

ancient Greek attempt to put being (*on*) into language (*logos*) was carried out as search for a *koinonia* amidst *onta*, a unity (or "community") among entities. This is Heidegger's reading of the famous Presocratic search for the *hen* within the *polla*, the One within the Many. One might initially think that this quest for "the One" was solely a proto-ontological endeavor, but in 1941, Heidegger writes: "The *hen* to the *polla* . . . is the One as *koinon*, as [both] the where from [*Woher*] and the common to [*Gemeinsame*] the Many" (EP 2/NII 400–1). In other words, originally *koinon* is ambiguous between "from where" and "in common"; the One is both *that from where* the Many (entities) emerge and *what* the Many (entities) hold *in common*. Such considerations allow us to surmise that when Heidegger recounts the archaic split of the *prôtê archê* into a proto-ontological "universal and first entity" and a proto-theological "supreme and ultimate entity," he is thinking of Thales and his student Anaximander, who, in the course of their pursuit of a *prôtê archê*, can be understood as having first articulated what would later become the ontotheological division.

Heidegger does not directly name these thinkers of the Milesian school as responsible for this proto-ontotheological division of the *koinon* into a *what* and a *from where*. If, however, we remember his explanation that metaphysics operates in an ontological mode when, surveying the totality of entities, the metaphysician tries to isolate their universal ground, the ground which all entities share in common, then it seems clear enough that Thales – with his understanding of water as the universal entity ("the one element") – is best thought of as Heidegger's proto-ontologist. For metaphysics is *ontology* when it "thinks of entities with an eye for the ground that is common to all entities as such" (I&D 70/139), and certainly water plays such a role for Thales, allowing him to understand the being of all entities in its terms.[30] Furthermore, if we recall that metaphysics operates in a *theological* mode when it searches for a "supreme or highest" entity, an entity from which the being of all entities issue or by which their being can be derived and justified, then Anaximander – with his doctrine that "the *archê* is *apeiron*" – is the best candidate for the role of proto-theological thinker. For it is theology: "When metaphysics thinks of the totality of entities as such . . . in regard to the supreme, all-founding entity," the ultimate entity from which all other entities issue and by which their being is thus derived and justified (or, as in Anaximander's case,

---

[30] "The much discussed four substances – of which we say the chief is water, making it as it were the one element – by combination and solidification and coagulation of the substances in the universe mingle with one another" (Thales, in Kathleen Freeman, *Ancilla to the Presocratic Philosophers*, 19).

condemned, judged and found undeserving of its finite existence), even if
that "entity" is Anaximander's *to apeiron,* "the limitless" (I&D 70–1/13).[31]

Thus, in answer to question Q_1 above – namely, *Whence* arose the first
ontotheological fissure in the kernel of metaphysics? – we can say that this
fissure first emerged at the end of the seventh century B.C. in Miletus (on
the west coast of modern Turkey), where the ancient Milesian school of
Presocratic thinkers' quest for the *prôtê archê* led them to understand the
being of entities in terms of both Thales's ontological "universal and first
being" and Anaximander's theological "supreme and ultimate being."
Postponing question Q_2, let us return to question Q_3, namely: How did
this ontotheological division become incorporated into the structure of
Western metaphysics so as to be decisively perpetuated down throughout
its entire subsequent history?

On Heidegger's reading, metaphysics is not explicitly formalized into
a single, unified ontotheological doctrine until Aristotle.[32] In the *Metaphysics,* when Aristotle explicates his own *prôtê philosophia,* he formalizes
the proto-ontotheological ambiguity inherent in the Presocratic conception of the *koinon* (which had already functioned as both the theological
"where from" and the ontological "in common" of entities). Aristotle
explicitly divides this *koinon* into an ontological "*koinotaton*," a universal being "shared in common," and a theological "*katholon (Theion),*" a
being "on the whole, [or] in general (the *Theion)*" (GA9 450, note a).
When assigning Aristotle credit for the inauguration of metaphysics as
ontotheology, however, Heidegger does not overlook Plato's distinctive

---

[31] "The Nonlimited [*apeiron*] is the original material of existing things; further, the source
from which existing things derive their existence is also that to which they return at
their destruction, according to necessity; for they give justice and make reparation to
one another for their injustice, according to the arrangement of Time" (Anaximander,
in Freeman, *Ancilla,* 19). For an analysis supporting this reading of Thales's and
Anaximander's different pursuits of the *archê,* see Kirk, Raven, and Schofield, eds., *The
Presocratic Philosophers,* 88–90, 98–9, 108–17. The fact that *apeiron* cannot easily be understood as an entity (is the indefinite self-identical?) does not prevent Anaximander from
deriving a complex and tragic understanding of the being of all entities from his way of
conceiving it. For more on this point (and more generally on Thales's and Anaximander's crucial roles in the history of metaphysics), see my "Interpretation as Self-Creation:
Nietzsche on the Pre-Platonics," esp. 198–200. As Heidegger saw, moreover, Nietzsche's
own contrasting attempt to *justify* existence, his doctrine of *amor fati,* is also motivated
by his ("theological") conception of eternal recurrence.
[32] "[M]etaphysics represents the beingness [*Seiendheit*] of entities in a twofold manner: In
the first place, the totality of entities as such with an eye to their most universal traits (*on
katholoy, koinon*); but at the same time also the totality of entities as such in the sense of
the highest and therefore divine entity (*on katholoy, akrotaton, theion*). In the *Metaphysics*
of Aristotle, the unconcealedness of entities as such has specifically developed in this
twofold manner (*cf.* Met. Bk. 3, 5, 10)" (P 287/GA9 378).

contribution to its earlier development. On the contrary, he asserts that Aristotle's inaugural act could only have been accomplished atop the ground previously laid by Plato. As Heidegger writes (in 1941): "The distinction between *essentia* and *existentia* was established in the light of history by Aristotle, who – after Plato's thinking had responded to the appeal of being in a way which prepared that distinction by provoking its establishment – first conceptualized the distinction, thereby bringing it onto its essential ground" (EP 4/NII 403). In other words, it is Aristotle who formally articulates the metaphysical distinction between what "later came to be called" *essentia* and *existentia*, and who thereby transforms and "establishes in the light of history" the prior Platonic distinction between "whatness" and "thatness." For, although Plato took over the ambiguity inherent in the Presocratic *koinon*, that distinction itself remained only implicit in his thinking (EP 8/NII 407–8). We will say more about this Aristotelian inauguration of ontotheology after briefly characterizing the sense in which Plato himself "provoked" or "invited" this metaphysical distinction *par excellence.*

In "Plato's Doctrine of Truth" (1940), Heidegger maintains that the ontotheological distinction had already been brought together implicitly in Plato's doctrine of the forms or *ideas.* "Since the interpretation of being as *idea*, thinking about the being of entities is metaphysical, and metaphysics is theological" (PDT 268/GA9 235–6). Here Heidegger seems to be thinking of the middle Plato's doctrine of *ideas*, where the *ideas* are conceived both theologically, as the paradigms that entities only imperfectly instantiate, and ontologically, as the universals common to the many instances of each kind of entity.[33] In Plato's *Symposium*, for example, the *idea* of beauty is both the *paradigm* of beauty, the most beautiful of all that is beautiful, and the *universal* of beauty, that in virtue of which different kinds of beauty (such as beautiful bodies, beautiful artworks, and beautiful laws) all count *as* beautiful. As Heidegger succinctly puts it, Plato's *ideas* explain both the "thatness" and the "whatness" of entities (EP 2–3/NII 401). In a particularly murky passage, he points out that within the ontotheological ambiguity implicit in Plato's doctrine of *ideas*, thatness is subordinated to whatness: "The *idea* brings about presencing, specifically, the coming to presence of what an entity is in any given instance. An entity becomes present in each case in its whatness. . . . That is why for Plato the proper essence of being consists in whatness" (PDT 173/GA9 225).

---

[33] See esp. Plato's *Phaedo*, 73a–77. In an analysis that confirms Heidegger's, David Bostock observes that "the forms are both perfect paradigms and universals. This ambivalent conception is found in all the middle dialogues" ("Plato," in T. Honderich, ed., *The Oxford Companion to Philosophy*, 684).

Plato subordinates thatness to whatness, for he holds that without their respective *ideas*, entities could not exist. In other words, a being's existence is dependent on its *idea*, for it is this *idea* that the being (more or less imperfectly) instantiates, whereas its *idea* is independent of the existence of any of the particular entities that instantiate it. As Aristotle's famous empiricist objection to Platonic rationalism contends, however, Plato cannot say, consistently, that the existence of an *idea* is independent of the entire class of entities which instantiate that *idea*.

Nevertheless, it is Plato's implicit distinction between whatness and thatness that Aristotle explicitly draws and so formalizes – even as he reverses Plato's privileging of whatness over thatness (or of essence over existence, if you will pardon the anachronism) – when Aristotle asserts in the *Posterior Analytics* that "our capacity for discovering *what* a thing is [*ti estin*] depends upon our awareness *that* it is [or *that* it exists, *hoti estin*]."[34] On Heidegger's reading, Aristotle inscribes the ontotheological distinction into the heart of metaphysics when, in order to explicitly differentiate "whatness" from "thatness," he distinguishes between *prôtê* and *deutera ousia* (in the standard translation, "primary and secondary substance").[35] The *prôtê ousia* is Aristotle's answer to "the *hoti estin*," the metaphysical question of "whether something is." Aristotle contends that the *prôtê ousia* is "the This, the singular," the fact "that something is [or exists]." In accordance with Heidegger's understanding of "presence" as the basic characteristic of Western metaphysics here inaugurated, he characterizes what Aristotle describes as a "persisting of something which lingers of itself" as "presence in the eminent and primal sense" (EP 7/NII 406–7). On the other hand, the *deutera ousia* answers Aristotle's question *ti estin*; it describes "*what* something is," which Heidegger renders as "presence in the secondary sense" (EP 7–8/NII 407). For Aristotle, on Heidegger's reading, to be is to be present. Thus we get the claim, implicit in Heidegger and made explicitly by Derrida, that Aristotle here inaugurates a "metaphysics of presence" in which for the next twenty-five hundred years, whatever else changes, the being of entities will be characterized in terms of what Heidegger calls the permanent "presence" (*Anwesenheit*) of those entities (B&T 47/S&Z 25).[36]

---

34 *Posterior Analytics*, 93a28–29 (my emphasis).

35 See Aristotle, *Categories*, 2a11ff.

36 See Derrida, "Différance," *Margins of Philosophy*, 22. I have reservations about Derrida's reading of Heidegger's multiepochal history of being in terms of a single "epoch of the *diapherein*," because Derrida's account subsumes and so obscures the Heraclitean and Parmenidean moments that, as we will see in the concluding section, remain crucial for Heidegger.

Heidegger claims, convincingly in my view, that Aristotle's distinction between *prôtê* and *deutera ousia* constitutes a decisive juncture in
the history whereby Western metaphysics becomes ontotheology. For
it was this very distinction that the medieval Scholastics would treat as
the self-evident difference between *existentia* and *essentia*, "existence" and
"essence." Hence Heidegger's answer to question Q₃ (namely, How did
the ontotheological fissure come to be built into the very structure of the
metaphysical question, and thus decisively perpetuated by the tradition?)
is this: When Aristotle formalizes the difference between thatness and
whatness in his distinction between *prôtê* and *deutera ousia*, the ontotheological fissure first opened up by the Milesian Presocratics and then
implicitly taken up into Plato's doctrine of the *ideas* is made decisive for
the ensuing history of Western metaphysics – "with the help of the subsequent conceptual formulation (of *essentia* and *existentia*) common to
the metaphysics of the schoolmen," the tradition of medieval scholasti-
cism upon which Aristotle's metaphysics would exert such a profound
influence (EP 4/NII 402).

Yet, even as Heidegger thus answers question Q₃ by recounting
Aristotle's inauguration of "metaphysics proper," he cannot help but pose
question Q₂, namely: *With what necessity* did the first fissure in the kernel
of metaphysics develop?

> *Essentia* answers the question *ti estin*: What is (an entity)? *Existentia* says of an
> entity *hoti estin*: That it is. In this distinction a different *estin* is named. Herein
> *einai* (being) manifests itself in a distinction. How can being be divided in this
> distinction? Which essence [*Wesen*] of being shows itself in this distinction, as if
> putting this essence out in the open?
>
> (EP 4/NII 403)

As we have seen, Aristotle's *ti estin* and the *hoti estin* refer to two different
kinds of *estin*, two different ways of understanding what (and how) entities
are, or of understanding the *being* of those entities. Yet, how is this possible?
It is crucial to grasp that again Heidegger is asking a *phenomenological*
question, and thus is looking for a phenomenological rather than a causal
(let alone a metaphysical) explanation. His question should be heard
accordingly as: What is it about the original Western manifestation of
being that allows it to be understood in terms of this distinction between
two different kinds of *estin*? How can phenomenological presencing yield
two such different ways of understanding the ground of entities, ways
which, as we have seen, will *both* be handed down by the metaphysical
tradition, maintained as the "unified ontotheological ambiguity" at the
constitutively fractured core of Western metaphysics?

Heidegger still needs an answer to this question (question Q_2, the question of the *necessity* of the original ontotheological fissure), because his answer to question Q_3 (which showed how Aristotle's distinction between *prôtê* and *deutera ousia* decisively unified and formalized the ontotheological structure of metaphysics) not only leaves question Q_2 unanswered but seems to lead to the kind of regress that makes us despair of ever finding an answer. For, Heidegger's claim that in formalizing the ontotheological structure of metaphysics Aristotle was "thinking the unthought" of Plato (or, further, that Plato himself was thinking that which went "unthought" in the Milesian Presocratics) does not answer the question of whether and in what sense this original fracture itself was *necessary*; it only pushes back the question another step further in time. The missing phenomenological explanation of the original ontotheological split thus remains perhaps the single "deepest problem" inherent in Heidegger's understanding of metaphysics as ontotheology; the very possibility of answering it seems to recede into the mists surrounding the beginnings of Western history.[37] Can we safely conclude, then, that this ontotheological fracture in the core of the metaphysical tradition was merely historical happenstance, an ultimately *arbitrary* – albeit historically determinative – effect of chance?

Despite his interest in thinking of being otherwise than as the double, ontotheological *ground* of entities, Heidegger rejects this response as phenomenologically unsatisfying, for it fails to allow us to understand the presumed logic of the phenomena under investigation. Heidegger's interpretation of the inception of Western metaphysics relies instead on the phenomenologically consistent presupposition that the ontotheological split at the core of metaphysics must have resulted from the way in which being showed itself in the beginning of Western history. As he expresses this realist intuition (in 1961):

Obviously, the twofoldness of the [metaphysical] question about being must result from the way the being of entities manifests itself. Being manifests itself in the character of that which we name ground: Entities in general are the ground in the sense of the basis upon which any further consideration of entities takes place; an entity, as the highest entity, is the ground in the sense of what allows all entities to come into being.

(KTB 340/GA9 449–450)[38]

[37] Cf. Hubert Dreyfus and Paul Rabinow, *Michel Foucault: Beyond Structuralism and Hermeneutics*, 37–41.
[38] Heidegger repeats this crucial claim in various registers, for example, in his later "Introduction" to 1929's "What Is Metaphysics?" (viz., 1949's "The Way Back into the Ground of Metaphysics"): "This ontotheological nature of philosophy proper (*prôtê philosophia*)

Here Heidegger postulates that being originally must have "manifested itself" *as* "ground," and this – as we saw when we explicated the Milesian school of Presocratics – in two distinct senses: the proto-ontological bottom-up "grounding," which understands the being of entities on the *ground-giving* "basis" (*Bodens*) of a basic entity (like Thales's water), and the "grounding" of a proto-theological top-down *founding*, which derives its understanding of the being of entities from a highest entity (such as Anaximander's *apeiron*).

The problem is that if, having uncovered this Milesian bifurcation of the *prôtê archê*, whereby the being of entities is understood in terms of both a proto-ontological "universal and first entity" and a proto-theological "supreme and ultimate entity," we try to take another step back in time by reposing the question of the necessity of this split, asking what it was about the original phenomenological manifestation of being that lent itself to being interpreted as this dual ontotheological ground of entities, we find ourselves running up against the limits of philosophical self-knowledge as it is preserved within the Western tradition. Nevertheless, at one point (c. 1941), Heidegger speculates about *how* the original phenomenological manifestation might have facilitated the ontotheological "distinction between whatness and thatness." His contention is this: Conceived phenomenologically as an "emergence to visibility, presencing has in itself the distinction between the pure proximity of that which lasts and the gradations of [its] remaining" (EP 8/NII 407).

Unfortunately, Heidegger abruptly breaks off and does not explain this speculation at all. The basic idea, however, seems to be that if we examine the emergence of entities into phenomenological visibility, there is an implicit difference between the dynamic *showing* and the more passive *lasting* of those entities – a difference Heidegger will later formalize as that between "presencing" (*Anwesen*) and "presence" (*Anwesenheit*). In other words, in the process whereby entities come into being, linger, and pass away, we can distinguish between their dynamic emerging and disappearing, on the one hand, and the more static aspect of that which lasts, on the other. To take a rather un-Heideggerian example, we could think of a time-lapse film showing the life cycle of a flower. In the stark drama of this "insurrection against nothingness" (EP 1/NII 399), we watch the young plant burst forth into the light, see its stem grow and unfurl,

must be grounded in the way in which the *on* brings itself into the open, namely as *on*.... [I]t is due to the way in which entities have from the very beginning revealed themselves as entities" (P 287–8/GA9 379).

then observe the flower itself open, linger in its openness, partially closing and reopening (as the quick exchange of light and darkness in the
background conveys the succession of days), and, finally, ineluctably, we
watch the flower die and wither away. Here it might seem difficult to discern anything truly lasting in what the time-lapse recording reveals to be
a thoroughly dynamic process. Yet, without the aid of such technological
prostheses to supplement our vision, the exact opposite is much more
likely to be the case: We generally have difficulty noticing anything passing in and out of what seems to be a very static existence; what Heidegger
calls the "*presencing* of presence" is very difficult to detect.

Indeed, when faced with the immediacy of an entity's existence, be
it a flower, a loved one, or we ourselves, it is quite easy to forget that
this entity is caught up in a process of coming-into and passing-out-of
existence. Our phenomenological numbness to the immediate makes it
seem natural to arrest an entity's temporally dynamic ontological manifestation, freezing it into a preconceived permanent presence. (Heidegger
will later advocate the phenomenological comportment he calls "releasement to things," *Gelassenheit zu den Dingen,* in part to help break the
hold of just such preconceptions.) Once this dynamic emergence is mistaken as a permanent presence, the door is open for conceiving it as
a ground in both the ontological and theological senses. In order to
pursue Heidegger's investigation of the historical genealogy of ontotheology any further, however, we would need to reconstruct speculatively
the phenomenological situation of early Western humanity confronting
the seemingly primordial phenomena of the earth below and the heavens
above. For, Heidegger suggests, the "awe" felt by ancient humanity before
the "overwhelming" primordial phenomena of the *earth* and the *heavens*
may very well have disposed them to these particular foundationalisms
(MFL 11/GA26 13). For reasons we will conclude Chapter 1 by investigating, however, Heidegger also contends that this *mythos* preserves a
crucially important understanding of being as "what shows itself in advance and in everything as that which [actively] presences in all [so-called]
'presence'" (PAR 60/GA54 89).[39]

---

[39] Heidegger's conclusions concerning the ontotheological structure of Western metaphysics do not depend on the plausibility of such a speculative account. The strength
of this speculative account, however, is that not only would it allow us to understand
how the metaphysical tradition came to treat being both as a permanent presence and
as the ground of entities, it also would help us to see why the attempt to treat permanent presence as a fundamental ontological ground (of the kind that Heidegger
originally thought his deconstruction would uncover) actually ended up undermining

§5. CONCLUSIONS: BACK TO THE BEGINNING

The conclusion to which Heidegger's painstaking deconstruction of Western metaphysics leads him is this: Although we must suppose that the doubly foundationalist project of ontotheological "grounding" is in fact rooted phenomenologically in some basic aspects of being's original Western self-manifestation, we can nevertheless conclude that this ontotheological project is not historically *necessary*. Why? Because the project of metaphysical "grounding" is *underdetermined*, even by those aspects of being's original self-manifestation from which this project derives. For, as we will now see, these Milesian aspects of the original Western manifestation of being do not themselves exhaust that inceptive self-showing, even in the fragmentary form in which it has been preserved for us by the tradition.

Indeed, it is at precisely this juncture – his deconstruction of metaphysical foundationalism having taken him back to the beginnings of Western metaphysics – that the later Heidegger, rather than trying to take another, diachronic step back in time, as though back behind the "inception" of Western metaphysics, instead makes a lateral or synchronic historical move, turning to other Presocratic thinkers in an attempt to illuminate further aspects of the original self-manifestation of being in the West. In this way, Heidegger's deconstruction of metaphysics clears the way for the recovery of what remains of any original understandings of being which preserve this pre- and extraconceptual phenomenological presencing otherwise than as an ontotheological *ground* of entities.[40] It is for this reason that, as Schürmann suggests, the later Heidegger is concerned to elaborate a synchronic analysis of the multifaceted "clearing"

the plausibility of this precritical ambition. For, as we have seen, our phenomenological numbness to the immediate makes it seem natural to arrest an entity's inherently dynamic manifestation – its "presencing" (*Anwesen*) – freezing this into a preconceived permanent "presence" (*Anwesenheit*), thereby allowing us to conceive of this illusory permanent presence as a kind of fundamental ontological ground. Yet, recall our example of the time-lapse film of the flower: Where is the permanent presence here? A similar line of thought can be found even in Nietzsche's earliest work (see my "Interpretation as Self-Creation," 201–5), and Nietzsche's neo-Heraclitean emphasis on flux may have helped Heidegger come to recognize that there is no ontological content to the notion of permanent presence that would allow it to serve as the fundamental ontological ground for all other entities, leading him to the painful realization that his own earlier quest for a fundamental ontology had been caught up in the ultimately untenable project of metaphysical foundationalism.

[40] *Heidegger on Being and Acting*, 168–81. Schürmann should be credited for recognizing that, for Heidegger, being is a "plural" phenomena. (See also Schürmann, "How to Read Heidegger," 4–6.)

(*Lichtung*) of being at the "inception of its history." About this multi-faceted clearing, Heidegger will conclude that:

> In the inception of its history, being clears itself as emerging (*phusis*) and disclosure (*alêtheia*). From there it acquires the cast of presence [*Anwesenheit*] and permanence [*Beständigkeit*] in the sense of enduring (*ousia*). Thus begins metaphysics proper.
>
> (EP 4/NII 403)[41]

In other words, before being became interpreted in terms of the permanent presence of *ousia* ("substance"), it was thought and named as emergence and disclosure, *phusis* and *alêtheia*. Since *phusis* and *alêtheia* – names given by Heraclitus and Parmenides, respectively, to the original self-manifestation of being in the West – manage to safeguard something of the temporal dynamism inherent in the rapprochement between being and human beings whereby intelligibility happens, Heidegger calls this ontotheological *phusis–alêtheia* couple "the inceptive essence of being" (EP 10/NII 409).[42]

Heidegger's genealogical investigation thus traces the fractured ontotheological core of metaphysics back into the mists surrounding the inception of Western thought. Because *different* aspects of being's self-showing are named and preserved within the textual ruins of Presocratic thought, Heidegger's deconstruction of metaphysics uncovers not just what comes to stand out as the single monolithic ontotheological beginning effected by Thales and Anaximander; it also reveals an historically intervening, but soon forgotten, alternative, namely, the multi-aspectival self-showing of being preserved in the writings of Parmenides and Heraclitus. On Heidegger's account of the Parmenidean and Heraclitean aspects of the inception of Western philosophy, being shows up phenomenologically – and is named by these "basic words" and so caught in the "fangs" of time – not as a "ground" but rather simply *as showing up*. More precisely, "being" is expressed in temporally dynamic, nonfoundational terms by the Heraclitean understanding of *phusis* as a "self-opening unfolding" or "self-blossoming emergence" of phenomenological intelligibility, and by the conception of truth as an active historical "clearing" in which thinking necessarily participates, a conception that Heidegger argues is inherent in the "unconcealment" or "disclosure" of

---

[41] On the temporal dynamism of "*Anwesen*," see Heidegger's critical remarks at WHD 143 (unfortunately elided in the English translation, cf. WCT 237).

[42] In *An Introduction to Metaphysics* (1935), Heidegger already wrote of "the unique and essential relationship between *phusis* and *alêtheia*" (IM 107/GA40 109).

Parmenidean *alêtheia* (IM 14/GA40 20). Within two generations of thought, however, as the history of being took its first formative steps, our earliest metaphysicians made the first few fateful "historical decisions" that we have recounted, and this other Presocratic understanding of being as *phusis* and *alêtheia* was "forgotten," ossified into the "permanent presence" of *ousia* and thus swallowed up into the metaphysics of substance, the self-reifying entrenchment of which would profoundly shape the history of being. The implicit role of thought and the temporal dynamism inherent in the manifestation of being, although preserved in the fragments of Heraclitus and Parmenides, were thereby obscured and subsequently forgotten through a kind of "double-forgetting" (in which we both forget and forget that anything has been forgotten), against which Heidegger mobilizes the anamnetic forces of the deconstruction we have recounted.[43]

It is thus that, his genealogical deconstruction of metaphysics having established that the ontotheological split accomplished by Thales and Anaximander was not historically necessary, the later Heidegger struggles to bring into focus other aspects of being's "inceptive" self-showing, not out of some antiquarian "nostalgia" for a "transcendental signified" (*pace* Derrida) but, rather, in an anamnetic attempt to recover ways of understanding being otherwise than as the dual ontotheological *ground* of entities.[44] Heidegger's hope is that careful philosophical study of such roads not taken might help us envision alternatives to our own metaphysical epoch of "enframing," given that this epoch is rooted, as we have seen, in Nietzsche's *ontotheological* understanding of the being of entities as eternally recurring will-to-power, an ontotheology that preconceives all entities as intrinsically meaningless resources merely awaiting optimization. Thoughtful recollection can help us to envision such alternatives not only negatively, by contesting the necessity of the Nietzschean metaphysics underlying our increasingly homogenized "age of technologically leveled world civilization" (GA13 243), and thereby clearing the conceptual space for ways of understanding being otherwise than in terms of the metaphysics of the atomic age (which Heidegger takes to be fulfilling itself in the almost uncontested spread of the cybernetic paradigm, as we will see in Chapter 2). It also can do so positively, by recovering concrete (albeit fragmentary) historical examples of nonmetaphysical ways

---

[43] On this "double-forgetting" and its relation to Heideggerian "deconstruction," see also B&T 43/S&Z 21, and PAR 71/GA54 104–12.

[44] Derrida, *Of Grammatology*, 20.

of understanding being, the two main aspects of which – namely, the temporal dynamism of Heraclitean *phusis* and the conception of truth as an active disclosure in which thinking implicitly participates inherent in Parmenidean *alêtheia* – Heidegger thinks we can draw on in order to elaborate heretofore unimagined historical paths leading beyond our own late-modern Nietzschean impasse. Here we thus return again to the later Heidegger's central philosophical project, the vision behind his enigmatic call for a "new beginning," which he insisted could emerge only out of a renewed and sustained hermeneutic altercation with the first beginnings of Western thought, a vision we will seek to flesh out repeatedly here in this text.

In the end, then, although I do not expect that my interpretive reconstruction of ontotheology will have purged the notion of all of its strangeness (to do so would be to downplay the great originality of Heidegger's historical understanding of metaphysics), I do hope to have made clear the meaning and significance of Heidegger's claim that metaphysics is ontotheology, to have convincingly demonstrated the centrality of this long-overlooked notion to his deconstruction of metaphysics, and to have at least plausibly conveyed something of the importance of this deconstruction for his larger project. If so, then it is my hope that those who might once have found themselves heading for the door at the mention of ontotheology will, having made it this far, find themselves moved to respond a bit more philosophically instead. (At the very least, Heidegger's opponents should now have a much better sense of their intended target.) Still, I would like to go further than that here.

In contemporary philosophy, there are other meaningful uses of the term "metaphysics," and many self-described "metaphysicians" may not recognize their own endeavors in Heidegger's description of metaphysics as ontotheology. Some of our contemporaries, however, *should* see themselves reflected in his mirror, even if these metaphysicians are once again called *physicists*, as were Thales and Anaximander, whose speculative attempt to grasp all of reality from both the inside out (microscopically, we might say) and the outside in (as if telescopically) these (meta)physicists have inherited (and continue boldly to pursue well beyond the reach of any empirically verifiable results). Rather than debate the proper use of the term *metaphysics*, however, I shall instead try to further convey the plausibility of Heidegger's understanding of metaphysics as ontotheology by showing that, however idiosyncratic that notion may initially seem to be, it in fact casts a deeply revealing light on some of the critical issues that arise at the intersection of Heidegger's thinking and our contemporary world.

Now that we have elaborated the general background and basic contours of the later Heidegger's central philosophical project, we are ready to explore the important implications of this background for some of the great contemporary debates surrounding his work, addressing the pressing topics of technology, totalitarianism, and education. In Chapter 2, we will begin by systematically responding to the main objections that have been raised against Heidegger's critique of our nihilistic, "technological" understanding of being, thereby returning to the controversy surrounding Heidegger's seemingly dystopian criticisms of the contemporary age, which we postponed confronting at the end of Section 2. We needed to wait to address that controversy until now, because Heidegger's incisive critique of technology forfeits a great deal of its force and appeal when it is treated in isolation from the understanding of metaphysics as ontotheology that in fact undergirds and motivates it philosophically. Indeed, *Heidegger on Ontotheology* will seek to show that Heidegger's later thought can be better understood, more sympathetically interpreted, and more robustly defended, all on the basis of the comprehension of his understanding of metaphysics as ontotheology we have achieved here in Chapter 1.

That may sound like a bold claim, but it should not be too surprising at this point, seeing as we have just recounted (albeit in broad strokes) the way in which Heidegger's understanding of ontotheology provides the crucial philosophical background for both the critical and the positive dimensions of his later work. Conversely, then, insofar as the interpretations offered in the next three chapters prove persuasive – not just as readings of Heidegger but also as revealing diagnoses of and suggestive responses to some deep and pressing problems confronting our own world – this will lend Heidegger's understanding of ontotheology, as I have reconstructed it here, that much more force and plausibility. For a first concrete illustration of this claim, let us now turn to address the most formidable criticisms that have been leveled against Heidegger's critique of our "technological" understanding of being, seeing how we can respond to these criticisms once we fully understand the way in which Heidegger's critique of our technological understanding of being follows directly from his account of metaphysics as ontotheology.

2

Understanding Ontotheology as the Basis for Heidegger's Critique of Technology

§6. INTRODUCTION: FROM ONTOTHEOLOGY TO TECHNOLOGY

In Chapter 1, in our reconstructions of Heidegger's understanding of metaphysics as ontotheology (§1) and of ontotheology as the substructural scaffolding of historical intelligibility (§2), it became clear that Heidegger holds Nietzsche's "unthought" metaphysics responsible for our nihilistic "technological" understanding of the being of entities and its devastating historical consequences. Two crucial details of Heidegger's reading merit particular emphasis in this regard: First, that Nietzsche understands the being of entities ontotheologically, as eternally recurring will-to-power (that is, in short, as sheer "will-to-will"), forces coming together and breaking apart with no end other than the self-augmentation by which these underlying forces perpetuate themselves. Second, that it is precisely this ontologically reductive understanding of the being of entities that encourages us late moderns implicitly to understand, and so generally to treat, all the entities with which we deal, ourselves included, as intrinsically meaningless *Bestand*, mere "resources" standing by to be optimized, ordered, and enhanced with maximal efficiency. We will return to explore these details of Heidegger's view shortly, but it should be clear from this outline that *Heidegger's critique of our contemporary age of "enframing" follows directly from his particular understanding of metaphysics as ontotheology.* Amazingly, this basic hermeneutic connection has never adequately been recognized and taken into account, although Heidegger's "critique of technology" is one of the most widely discussed aspects of his later thought.[1]

This hermeneutic oversight generates serious problems, however, because Heidegger's critique of technology, when unknowingly detached from the "ontotheological" background that in fact motivates it, forfeits much of its philosophical force and appeal, and so can easily appear to be motivated extraphilosophically – for example, by Heidegger's supposed "nostalgia" for the preindustrial world of the Black Forest peasant (as critics frequently allege), and so as the reactionary antimodernism of a philosophical "redneck" (as Richard Rorty rather colorfully puts the charge). The problem with such brightly rouged caricatures, in our context, is that they encourage critics to dismiss Heidegger's profound and far-reaching critique of technology as the product of what Andrew Feenberg calls Heidegger's Luddite "technophobia."[2] Of course,

---

[1] I know from experience that referring to Heidegger's "critique of technology" has the potential to mislead some audiences by generating inappropriate expectations concerning what he is up to philosophically and so what we should thus expect from his views. Heidegger certainly developed a "critique of technology"; indeed, he is widely recognized as a founding figure in this increasingly important philosophical domain. But the field Heidegger did so much to open has changed a great deal in the meantime. To wit, the dominant contemporary approach is a *social constructivism* that purports to be resolutely "antiessentialistic" with respect to technology, and so tends to focus its analyses on the social normativity embedded in particular technological devices rather than on the broader effects of technology *per se*. I question the philosophical coherency of this "antiessentialist" approach later, but it is important for those influenced by it to recognize that Heidegger's critique of technology is not primarily concerned with particular technological devices, but rather with ontological *technologization*, that is, with the disturbing and increasingly global phenomenon – manifest with particular clarity in exemplary technological devices like the autobahn and Internet, and so rightly called "technological" – by which entities are transformed into intrinsically meaningless resources standing by for optimization, all on the basis of an unnoticed ontotheology we late moderns have inherited from Nietzsche.

[2] There are, in my view, other problems with Rorty's characterization of Heidegger as a "redneck" ("Taking Philosophy Seriously," 33). Rorty was in attendance when I presented an earlier version of this chapter at the University of Tokyo Center for Philosophy's International Symposium on Pragmatism and Philosophy of Technology in the 21st Century (on 15 December 2003), and I discovered that, as I began to present Rorty's view, I needed to explain to our Japanese audience that the derogatory term "redneck" (not found in their English-to-Japanese dictionaries), which literally refers to a person whose neck has been sunburned repeatedly during manual labor outdoors, has become a broad term of disparagement used by cosmopolitans to denigrate the less sophisticated tastes of those from the country. (When used by those *within* the American South, the term often also connotes racism, suggesting that the use of this stereotype afforded some Southerners a convenient way to make a distinction that the rest of the country, falling back on a widespread stereotype of all white Southerners as "rednecks," tends to ignore.) I suggested that this was an unfortunate choice of words for Rorty, because his important

if Heidegger's ontological critique of technology were just a theoretical excrescence or superstructural symptom of material forces – and so an unwitting ideological testament to that ongoing historical clash between the progressive forces of technological–industrial modernity and the inertial resistances of the premodern era – then his detractors might be right to dismiss this critique of technology as the product of a philosophical "worldview" already rendered obsolete (in advance, as it were) by the apparently inevitable victory of the historical forces it came into existence by resisting. Yet, even if it were correct to characterize Heidegger as a reactionary antimodern (as do such critical theory–informed commentators as Marcuse, Jürgen Habermas, Feenberg, and Robert Pippin)– and I shall argue below that this common characterization misleadingly caricatures Heidegger's actual view in crucial respects – what the use of this caricature to dismiss Heidegger's critique of technology overlooks is the fact, brought home to the United States with startling force on September 11, that political reverberations from the clash between the modern and premodern eras continue to profoundly shake the globe, unsettling Kant's optimistic prognostications concerning humanity's "essential destiny" by calling into question, once again, our long-standing and amazingly resilient liberal democratic faith in the slow but steady historical progress of rational "enlightenment."[3]

Such a neo-Marxian challenge to Heidegger's ontological critique of our technological age of "enframing" has been pressed most formidably by Andrew Feenberg, today's leading critical theorist of technology. Because Feenberg's critique is precise and informed rather than vague and dismissive, and because it also possesses the considerable merit of generally distinguishing the issues most relevant to Heidegger's ontological critique of technology from the larger and more heated controversy surrounding Heidegger's politics (which we will focus on in Chapter 3), I shall address Feenberg's specific objections here in order to frame a more general Heideggerian response. Doing so will allow me to begin

---

work *Achieving Our Country: Leftist Thought in Twentieth-Century America* shows that one of liberalism's great political shortcomings has been our failure to make common cause on economic issues with the poor (in the American South especially), instead allowing the economically disenfranchised members of our society to be coopted by the right-wing ideology of cultural conservatism.

[3] See Kant, "An Answer to the Question: What Is Enlightenment?" *Perpetual Peace and Other Essays*, 41, 44; Habermas, *The Philosophical Discourses of Modernity*, 131–60; and Pippin, *Modernity as a Philosophical Problem*, 117–47. I address these issues further in "Deconstructing the Hero."

to demonstrate concretely the great significance of the previously over-looked fact that Heidegger's understanding of ontotheology undergirds and motivates his distinctive and influential critical perspective.

§7. WHAT'S WRONG WITH TECHNOLOGICAL ESSENTIALISM?

Questioning Technology (1999) is Feenberg's third major work on the criti-cal theory of technology in a decade, and it confirms his place as one of the world's leading philosophers of technology.[4] In an earlier ex-amination of Feenberg's work, I traced out some of the philosophical and political tensions in the legacy of technology critique leading from Heidegger through Marcuse to Feenberg, and concluded that the criti-cal theory of technology Feenberg elaborates in *Questioning Technology* re-mains much more conceptually indebted to Heidegger than Feenberg's own Marcuseanism had allowed him to admit. In response, Feenberg forthrightly acknowledged Heidegger's great influence on his own work, but then went on to stress what he took to be the most basic and impor-tant outstanding difference between his own critical theory of technology and Heidegger's critique of our technological understanding of being, namely, Heidegger's "untenable" *technological essentialism*.[5] On closer in-spection, however, matters are not quite so simple, because technological essentialism turns out to be a rather complex notion. Indeed, if we are to respond to Feenberg's critique of Heidegger, the first thing we need to do is establish the criteria that determine what counts as "techno-logical essentialism." To minimize potential objections, I will adopt the criteria set forth by Feenberg himself. Despite their slightly odd names, Feenberg's criteria succinctly restate and refine three of the major ob-jections that have long been advanced against Heidegger's critique of

---

[4] Feenberg's recent books include *Critical Theory of Technology; Alternative Modernity: The Technical Turn in Philosophy and Social Theory;* and *Questioning Technology.* His *Heidegger and Marcuse: The Catastrophe and Redemption of History* appeared just as my book was going to press.

[5] See my "From the Question Concerning Technology to the Quest for a Democratic Technology: Heidegger, Marcuse, Feenberg," 203–15; Feenberg, "Constructivism and Technology Critique: Response to Critics," 225–37; and Feenberg, "The Ontic and the Ontological in Heidegger's Philosophy of Technology: Response to Thomson," 445–450. In our exchange it became clear that Feenberg adopts Heidegger's diagnosis of the on-tological damage done by our technological understanding of being, but rejects what he takes to be Heidegger's "essentialistic" and so overly "fatalistic," "technophobic," and "totalizing" understanding of technology. These objections will be addressed systemati-cally in what follows.

our technological understanding of being. Responding to Feenberg's objections should thus help to dispel some persistent doubts surrounding Heidegger's critique of technology.

What, then, is *technological essentialism*, and what is wrong with it? The necessary criterion of technological essentialism seems obvious; in order to be a technological essentialist, one needs to ascribe an essence to technology. This criterion is not sufficient for our purposes, however, because it does not tell us what makes technological essentialism *objectionable*. A radical constructivist such as Bruno Latour or Don Ihde might maintain that there is no technology, only particular technologies, and thus that *all* technological essentialisms are unsound; but whether or not that is a coherent position (which I doubt), it is not one Feenberg shares.[6] Feenberg proposes his own "theory of the essence of technology," so the mere belief that technology has an essence cannot be sufficient to qualify one as the kind of technological essentialist to whom he objects. Thus, despite Feenberg's rather incautious claim that: "The basic problem is essentialism," his work shows that the problem is not with technological essentialism as such but, rather, with particular *kinds* of technological essentialism.[7] In fact, Feenberg objects to technological essentialists such as Heidegger, Jacques Ellul, Albert Borgmann, and Jürgen Habermas because each commits himself to at least one of three particular claims about the essence of technology (in Heidegger's case, all three), and these claims render their technological essentialisms unacceptable. Feenberg calls these three offending forms of technological essentialism *ahistoricism, substantivism*, and *one-dimensionalism*. Our next task will be to unpack these three species of technological essentialism with the goal of understanding what they are and why they are objectionable. We will then come

---

[6] It is not clear that the radical constructivists' sloganistic claim – that there is no technology, only technologies – makes sense; in virtue of what are all these different technologies "technologies"? I put this question to Don Ihde (at the International Symposium on Pragmatism and Philosophy of Technology in the 21st Century), and his blunt response was, "I just don't find that question interesting." Ihde later explained that "being able to give that kind of answer is one of the things I really appreciate having learned from Rorty." Yet, most philosophers, committed to reasoned dialogue, would not find such a response satisfactory. Heidegger, for his part, suggests that we should understand the emergence of "technology" in terms of its (more than two millennia) history, as an eventual eclipse of *poiesis*, bringing into being, by one of its species, *technê*, a making which imposes a pre-given form on matter, regardless of its intrinsic potentialities. (On the affinities between Feenberg and the constructivist camp, see *Questioning Technology*, 83–5, and Feenberg's response to the constructivist David Stump in his "Response to Critics.")

[7] *Questioning Technology*, 17.

back to each in turn and ask whether Heidegger holds the objectionable doctrine in question.

So, what is *ahistorical* technological essentialism, and what is wrong with it? As Feenberg explains, an ahistorical technological essentialist is someone who interprets the "historically specific phenomenon [of technology] in terms of a transhistorical conceptual construction." Thus, for example, Max Weber and Habermas understand the essence of technology in terms of "rational control [and] efficiency," while Heidegger allegedly understands the essence of technology as the reduction of "everything to functions and raw materials." What does Feenberg think is illegitimate about such ahistorical conceptions of the essence of technology? The problem is that, in an attempt to "fix the historical flux [of technology] in a singular essence," ahistorical essentialists abstract their understandings of the essence of technology from the "socially and historically specific context" in which particular technologies are always embedded. As a result, not only do these ahistoricist theories fail to understand "the essence of technology as a social phenomenon," but their complete abstraction from sociohistorical context yields an "essentially unhistorical" understanding of the essence of technology that is "no longer credible," and so needs to be replaced by Feenberg's own "historical concept of essence."[8] We will hold off on evaluating this objection and asking whether or not it really applies to Heidegger until the two other objectionable forms of technological essentialism are on the table.

Let us turn, then, to "substantivism," the second form of technological essentialism Feenberg seeks to vitiate and surpass. What is *substantivist* technological essentialism, and what is wrong with it? Feenberg characterizes substantivism as the claim that the essence of technology comes from somewhere beyond us and is thus out of our control. Substantivists from Marx to Heidegger understand technology as "an autonomous force separate from society, . . . impinging on social life from the alien realm of reason." For the substantivist, the essence of technology seems to be shaping history from outside, imposing itself as though from some metaphysical beyond that entirely escapes human control. We can easily understand why Feenberg finds substantivism so objectionable if we recognize that he is a critical theorist who believes that "[t]he fundamental problem of democracy today" is the question of how to "ensure the survival of agency in this increasingly technological universe." The substantivist's belief that

[8] Ibid., vii–viii, 15–17, 201.

the essence of technology escapes human control seems to entail a fatalistic attitude about the historical impact of technology, and this fatalism runs directly counter to Feenberg's attempt to preserve a meaningful sense of agency in our increasingly technological world. For Feenberg, Heidegger's substantivism seems pessimistically to surrender too much human autonomy to the technological order.

It is thus not too great a simplification to say that Feenberg's charge of "substantivism" gives a new name to the old accusation of *fatalism*. Indeed, with this objection to Heidegger's substantivist understanding of the essence of technology, Feenberg develops the critical theoretical charge against Heidegger's thought first advanced by Heidegger's former student, and Feenberg's teacher, Marcuse. In effect, Feenberg appropriates one of Marcuse's most powerful *political* criticisms of Heidegger, the charge that Heidegger succumbed to a "hopeless heteronomism," that is, he lost faith in the Enlightenment understanding of freedom as the capacity for substantive rational self-determination, the ability to direct the ends as well as the means of human life. Hence, Feenberg also expresses this Marcusean criticism in a Marxist register, accusing Heidegger of being a "technological fetishist." In the Marxist vocabulary, fetishism occurs when a "social relation between men" assumes "the fantastic form of a relation between things" (as Marx famously put it). For a Marxist (and we should not forget that "critical theory" is an interdisciplinary, post-Marxian development of Marxism), to *fetishize* something is to detach it from the human labor that produced it while continuing nevertheless to project human meanings on it, thereby mistaking these projections for an independent reality. The fetishist's unconscious anthropomorphic projection endows a humanly created thing with the magical appearance of possessing a *telos* independent of human ends. Heidegger's substantivism "fetishizes" the essence of technology, then, insofar as it treats a human creation as if it were beyond human control.[9]

---

9 See Marcuse, "The Struggle Against Liberalism in the Totalitarian View of the State," *Negations*, 39; Karl Marx, *Capital* (Volume One), in *The Marx–Engels Reader*, 321; and Feenberg, *Questioning Technology*, vii–viii, 101. For Feenberg, Heidegger's technological fetishism is visible in the fact that, in his view, "technology rigidifies into destiny" (14). Here, however, Feenberg overlooks the fact that for Heidegger enframing *is* our "destiny," but it is not necessarily our *fate*. Dreyfus explains this subtle but important distinction as follows: "[A]lthough our understanding of things and ourselves as resources to be ordered, enhanced, and used efficiently has been building up since Plato and dominates our practices, we are not stuck with it. It is not the way things have to be, but nothing more or less than our current cultural clearing" ("Heidegger on Gaining a Free Relation to Technology," 102). This distinction is crucial because, as we saw in Chapter 1, the critical

Finally, Feenberg objects to those technological essentialists who subscribe to what he calls *one-dimensional* thinking, the belief that all technological devices express the same essence. What is wrong with claiming that the myriad diversity of technological devices all express a common essence? The problem, Feenberg explains, is that one-dimensional technological essentialists must either reject or embrace technology wholecloth. There is allegedly no room within one-dimensional conceptions of technology for a fine-grained analysis capable of appreciating both the positive potentials and the deleterious effects of the ever more pervasive rule of technology in our everyday lives. For the critical theorist of technology, however, an uncritical embrace of the totality of technological devices is just as unsound as a technophobic rejection of technology across the board. To charge that Heidegger's ontological understanding of technology is "one-dimensional," then, is to accuse it of being "totalizing" or "indiscriminate," as the criticism has also been advanced in the past. (With the charge of "one-dimensional" technological essentialism, Feenberg develops another critique of Heidegger that can be traced back to Marcuse.)[10]

In sum, then, Feenberg's objections go not to technological essentialism as such but, rather, to three specific kinds of technological essentialisms, namely, the *ahistoricisms* that illegitimately elide technology's embeddedness within sociohistorical currents that continue to shape it, the *substantivisms* that adopt a politically dangerous fatalism by viewing technology as a force completely beyond our control, and the *one-dimensionalisms* that treat all technological devices as of a kind and thereby preclude any balanced critique of technology's benefits as well as its harms. With these three objectionable varieties of technological essentialism laid out before us, we are almost ready to evaluate Feenberg's critique of Heidegger's technological essentialism, asking: Is Heidegger's conception of the essence of technology really unacceptably ahistorical, substantivist, or one-dimensional? In order to answer these questions, however, we need first to understand how Heidegger's critique of "enframing"

force of Heidegger's history of Being comes from his hope for a new historical beginning in which we would *no longer* treat everything as intrinsically meaningless resources awaiting optimization.

[10] Feenberg appropriates this critique from his teacher Marcuse, then applies it back to Marcuse's own "one-dimensional" conception of our "fully administered" society or *technocracy*. Marcuse and Heidegger are indeed remarkably similar on this point, as I show in "From the Question Concerning Technology to the Quest for a Democratic Technology." Feenberg develops this connection in *Heidegger and Marcuse*.

follows from his understanding of ontotheology. Indeed, doing so will help us to vindicate much of Heidegger's ontotheological critique of our contemporary "technological" epoch from the long-standing objections Feenberg sharpens and brings to bear against Heidegger's critique with such forceful clarity.

§8. RECOGNIZING NIETZSCHE'S ONTOTHEOLOGY AS THE ESSENCE OF TECHNOLOGY

What exactly is Heidegger's understanding of the essence of technology? Heidegger's most famous remark, that "the essence of technology is by no means anything technological" (QCT 4/GA7 7), may not initially seem to be of much help. To comprehend his point, however, we need to know that "essence" is an important term of art for Heidegger, a term which he explains in his celebrated 1955 essay "The Question Concerning Technology."[11] This explanation initially seems to suggest that Heidegger's claim that *the essence of technology is nothing technological* is best approached in terms of what we could call, after Wittgenstein, *the paradox of the measure.* Height is not high, treeness is not itself a tree, and the essence of technology is nothing technological. For, that which defines the measure cannot be measured meaningfully by the metric it defines, on pain of circularity.[12] As Heidegger puts the point in *Being and Time:* "If an ordering principle is genuine, it has its own content as a thing [*Sachgehalt*], which is never to be found by means of such ordering, but is already presupposed in it" (B&T 77/S&Z 52). In other words, that which establishes a system (or defines a concept) cannot be grounded by the system it establishes (or the concept it defines), no more than an axiom can be proved by theorems derived from it.

Yet, such analogies, although suggestive, can be a bit misleading, because Heidegger's point is not to uncover conceptual difficulties plaguing concept definition; as Dreyfus astutely observes, Heidegger is simply not trying to provide a fixed definition of the "essence of technology."[13] His goal, rather, is to help us to see that, if we want to understand what

---

[11] De Beistegui goes so far as to claim that "the question of essence . . . drives the entirety of Heidegger's thought and marks the possibility of thought itself" (*Thinking with Heidegger: Displacements*, 88).

[12] Cf. Wittgenstein, *Philosophical Investigations*, ¶50, 25.

[13] As Dreyfus writes, "when he asks about the essence of technology we must understand that Heidegger is not seeking a definition. His question cannot be answered by defining our concept of technology" ("Heidegger on the Connection between Nihilism, Art, Technology, and Politics," 305).

he means by the "essence of technology," then we cannot conceive of "essence" the way we have been doing since Plato (as what *"permanently endures"*), for that makes it seem as if "by the [essence of] 'technology' we mean some mythological abstraction" (QCT 31/GA7 32). Instead, we should think of "essence" as a verb, as the way in which things "essence" [*west*] or "remain in play [*im Spiel bleibt*]" (QCT 30/GA7 31). Indeed, once we conceive of "essence" as a verb rather than a noun, we can see that "the essence of technology" denotes the way technological entities tend to "come to presence" or *happen* for us. Thus, as Heidegger bluntly states in "The Age of the World Picture" (1938), "the essence of technology . . . is identical with the essence of contemporary metaphysics" (QCT 116/GA5 75). In other words, the referent of Heidegger's phrase "the essence of technology" is our current constellation of historical intelligibility, "enframing" (*das Gestell*), an historical "mode of revealing" in which things increasingly show up only as resources to be optimized. Heidegger employs the polysemic term "*Gestell*" to name the ontotheological essence of technology because, by etymologically connoting a *gathering together* ("*Ge-*") of the myriad forms of *stellen* ("to set, stand, regulate, secure, ready, establish," and so on), it succinctly conveys his understanding of the way in which our present "mode of revealing" – a "setting-upon that challenges forth" – forces the "presencing" (*Anwesen*) of entities into its metaphysical "stamp or mold [*Prägung*]" (QCT 16–21/GA7 17–22). This, however, is not simply to substitute etymology for argument, as understandably confused detractors frequently allege. Heidegger uses etymology in order to come up with an appropriate name for our contemporary "mode of revealing," but it is crucial to recognize that the argumentative work in his ontological critique of technology is done by the understanding of metaphysics as ontotheology which quietly undergirds and generates this critique.

In order to remind ourselves of the details of Heidegger's understanding of ontotheology explicated in Chapter 1, let us approach the matter from a slightly different angle. Heidegger, as I understand him, is a great critical heir of the German idealist tradition.[14] His ontological critique of "enframing" builds on the Kantian idea that we implicitly participate in the making-intelligible of our worlds, but maintains that

---

[14] Of course, for Heidegger "critical heir" is a pleonasm, because (as we will see in Chapter 3) the calcified "tradition" is only transformed into a living "heritage" through a critical "reciprocative rejoinder" that updates it, renewing it so that it can speak to the changed needs of the contemporary world.

our sense of reality is mediated by lenses inherited from metaphysics. In effect, Heidegger *historicizes* Kant's "discursivity thesis," which holds that intelligibility is the product of a subconscious process by which we "spontaneously" organize and so filter a sensibly overwhelming world to which we are fundamentally "receptive."[15] For Heidegger, however, this implicit organization is accomplished not by historically fixed cognitive "categories" but, instead, by a changing historical understanding of what and how entities *are*, an ontotheology that is supplied, maintained, contested, and transformed historically by the metaphysical tradition. At the core of this "history of being," as we have seen, the great metaphysicians articulate, focus, and disseminate an ontotheological understanding of the being of entities. When metaphysics succeeds at this ontotheological task, it temporarily secures the intelligible order by grasping it both "ontologically," from the inside out, and "theologically," from the outside in. By uncovering and joining together the dual points at which the

[15] On Kant's "discursivity thesis," see Henry Allison, *Kant's Transcendental Idealism: An Interpretation and Defense*, 65–8. For Heidegger, the "discursivity" (*Diskursivität*) "which belongs to the essence of understanding is the sharpest index of its finitude" (KPM 21/GA3 29–30), and "the understanding of being which thoroughly dominates human existence . . . manifests itself as the innermost ground of human finitude" (KPM 160/GA3 228). In *Being and Time*, Heidegger already implicitly contested the *completeness* of Kant's categories, not with respect to the being of physical nature (for which they are presumed complete) but, rather, with respect to the distinctive being of Dasein, which "becomes *invisible* if one interprets it in a way that is ontologically inappropriate" (B&T 86/S&Z 59). Because Kant extends "dogmatically" the same category mistake made by Descartes (B&T 45–6/S&Z 23–24), interpreting human being in terms drawn from (and perfectly appropriate to) the study of physical nature, "Kant made an essential omission" (B&T 46/S&Z 24). Kant's approach eclipses Dasein's distinctive existential structures (Heidegger prefers "existentials" to "categories" here, precisely because "categories" have come to refer to "characteristics of the being of entities other than Dasein" (B&T 70/S&Z 44), for example, "disposedness" (*Befindlichkeit*), "conversance" (*Rede*), and "understanding" (*Verstehen*), as Wrathall nicely translates these terms. Heidegger, going further, will seek to show that Kant's categories derive from Dasein's *temporalizing* of temporality (KPM 60–1/GA3 86–7; KPM 132–6/GA3 189–95). Heidegger even develops an argument to this effect for the crucial category of substance, contending that our basic idea of the "permanence" of substance derives from the way our experience is conditioned by the sense that it is always "now" (KPM 75–6/GA3 106–8). By 1938, however, Heidegger rightly abandons this "temporal idealism" – which sought to generate intelligibility entirely out of Dasein's self-temporalizing – as radical "subjectivism." (He sometimes also criticizes his earlier approach for being "transcendental," but this is misleading, because he never abandons the search for conditions of the possibility of intelligibility.) Blattner's aptly titled *Heidegger's Temporal Idealism* gives us by far the best critical study of this early project, making a strong case for why it failed and so had to be abandoned. (Although Blattner overlooks Heidegger's aforementioned suggestions from *Kant and the Problem of Metaphysics* [cf. *Heidegger's Temporal Idealism*, 258–61], I think these reinforce rather than undermine his argument.)

ontological and theological "spades turn," the great metaphysicians effectively provide the anchors that suspend Western humanity's changing sense of "reality," holding back the floodwaters of historicity long enough to allow the formation of an "epoch," an historical constellation of intelligibility unified around this ontotheological understanding of the being of entities.

We can thus interpret Heidegger's understanding of the ontotheological structure of Western metaphysics ("the history that we *are*") as advancing a doctrine of *ontological holism*. For, by giving shape to our historical understanding of "what *is*," metaphysics determines the most basic presuppositions of what *anything* is, ourselves included. This, as we saw, is what Heidegger means when he writes that: "Western humanity, in all its comportment toward entities, and even toward itself, is in every respect sustained and guided by metaphysics" (N4 205/NII 343). By explicitly focusing and disseminating an ontotheological understanding of what and how entities *are*, our great metaphysicians establish the most basic conceptual parameters and ultimate standards of legitimacy for their successive historical epochs. Heidegger's ontological holism thus explains *how* these ontotheologies can function historically like self-fulfilling prophecies, pervasively reshaping intelligibility. Put simply, because all entities *are*, as a new ontotheological understanding of *what and how* entities are takes hold and spreads, it progressively transforms our basic understanding of *all* entities.

Nietzsche is the pivotal figure in Heidegger's critique of our technological epoch of enframing because, according to Heidegger's reductive yet revealing reading, Nietzsche's "unthought" metaphysics provides the ontotheological lenses that implicitly structure our own current sense of reality. Let us recall that Nietzsche criticized what he (mistakenly) took to be Darwin's doctrine of "the survival of the fittest" by pointing out that life forms cannot survive by aiming at mere survival.[16] In a changing environment characterized by material scarcity and hence competition, life can survive only by continually overcoming itself, surpassing whatever stage it has reached previously. From the perspective of this inner "will" of life (what Nietzsche calls "will-to-power"), any state of being previously attained serves merely as a rung on the endless ladder of "sovereign becoming." As Heidegger thus puts it, Nietzsche understands "the totality of entities as such" *ontotheologically* as "eternally recurring will-to-power" (or simply "will-to-will"), that is, as an unending

---

[16] See John Richardson, "Nietzsche Contra Darwin."

disaggregation and reaggregation of forces without any purpose or goal beyond the self-perpetuating augmentation of these forces through their continual self-overcoming. Now, our Western culture's unthinking reliance on this Nietzschean ontotheology is leading us to transform all entities, ourselves included, into *Bestand*, mere resources standing by to be optimized, ordered, and enhanced with maximal efficiency. Heidegger is deeply worried that within our current technological constellation of intelligibility, the post-Nietzschean epoch of enframing, it is increasingly becoming the case that: "Only what is calculable in advance counts as being" (TTL 136/USTS 17). For, our technological understanding of being produces a "calculative thinking" (DT 46/G 13) that quantifies all qualitative relations, reducing entities to bivalent, programmable "information" (TTL 139/USTS 22), digitized data ready to enter into "a state of pure circulation" on the Internet.[17] As this historical transformation of beings into intrinsically meaningless resources becomes more pervasive, it comes ever more to elude our critical gaze; indeed, we late moderns come to treat even ourselves in the nihilistic terms that underlie our technological refashioning of the world: no longer as conscious subjects standing over against an objective world (as in the modern worldview Heidegger already criticized in *Being and Time*), but merely as one more intrinsically meaningless resource to be optimized, ordered, and enhanced with maximal efficiency, whether cosmetically, psychopharmacologically, genetically, or even cybernetically.[18]

As this "technological" understanding of being takes hold and spreads, it dramatically transforms our relations to ourselves and our worlds, yet we tend not to notice these transformations, because their very pervasiveness helps render them invisible, a seemingly paradoxical fact Heidegger explains by appeal to his "first law of phenomenology." This "law of proximity" (or "distance of the near") states that the closer we are to something, the harder it is to bring it clearly into view (the lenses on our glasses, for example, or Poe's eponymous purloined letter), and thus that the more decisively a matter shapes us, the more difficult it is for us to understand it explicitly. Eventually, however, Heidegger thinks that either a new understanding of the being of entities will emerge and take hold (perhaps, as Kuhn suggests, out of the investigation of those anomalous entities

---

[17] See Baudrillard's *The Transparency of Evil,* 4; and Dreyfus's important monograph, *Thinking in Action: On the Internet.*

[18] For a wide variety of concrete illustrations of this alarming technological transformation of humanity into resources, see David Shenk, "Watching You," 2–29.

that resist being understood in terms of the dominant ontotheology), or else our conception of *all* entities will be brought permanently into line with this spreading ontotheology. This latter alternative has never yet occurred (because no previous ontotheology succeeded in permanently entrenching itself), yet Heidegger calls it "the greatest danger." He is worried that our Nietzschean ontotheology could indeed become *totalizing*, "driving out every other possibility of revealing" (QCT 27/GA7 28) by overwriting and so effectively obscuring Dasein's "special nature," our defining capacity for world disclosure, with the "total thoughtlessness" of lives lived entirely in the grip of the Nietzschean conception of all entities, ourselves included, as intrinsically meaningless resources on standby to be optimized for maximally flexible use (DT 56/G 25). If Nietzsche's metaphysical "enframing" succeeds in securing its monopoly on the real, and so preemptively delegitimates all alternative understandings of being (deriding them as "non-naturalistic," for example, and thus as irrelevant, ridiculous, nonserious, irrational, and so on), Heidegger thinks this enframing could effect and enforce that double forgetting in which we lose sight of our distinctive capacity for world disclosure *and* forget that anything has thus been forgotten. The danger, as he provocatively puts it, is that we could become so *satiated* by the endless possibilities for flexible self-optimization opened up by treating our worlds and ourselves as resources to be optimized that we could lose the very sense that anything is lost with such a self-understanding (the very idea that entities have "intrinsic meanings," for example, may come to seem like an outdated myth). This helps explain the later Heidegger's strange and seemingly paradoxical claim that the "greatest danger" is to be found in the "authentic need" of "needlessness" (GA79 56), his idea that we live in the age of greatest need precisely insofar as we experience ourselves as not needing anything at all.[19]

[19] Thus we get Heidegger's provocative evocation of the great danger we could call, with a nod to Marx, *the problem of the happy enframer*: "What has long since been threatening man with death, and indeed the death of his own nature, is the unconditional character of mere willing in the sense of purposeful self-assertion in everything [i.e., "will-to-will," Heidegger's shorthand for the ontotheological unity of will-to-power and eternal recurrence]. What threatens man in his very nature is the willed view that man, by the peaceful release, transformation, storage, and channeling of the energies of physical nature could render the human condition, man's being, tolerable for everybody and happy in all respects" (PLT 116/GA5 294). Heidegger's postulation of a great "need of needlessness" may sound strange (he was writing at a time when nuclear energy promised to conquer material scarcity), but he develops here a line of thought long familiar to German philosophy (and not only critical theory), going all the way back to

§9. ADDRESSING FEENBERG'S OBJECTIONS TO HEIDEGGER'S CRITIQUE OF TECHNOLOGY

Now that we have deepened our understanding of the way in which Heidegger's critique of our technological understanding of being follows directly from his views on ontotheology, we are ready to evaluate Feenberg's three specific objections to Heidegger's critique.

A. Ahistoricism?

Let us take Feenberg's first objection first: Is Heidegger an *ahistorical* technological essentialist? That is, does he illegitimately decontextualize his ontological understanding of technology from history? Feenberg alleges that Heidegger's "ontologizing approach" to the history of technology entirely "cancels the historical dimension of his theory," but this seems to me to be the least plausible of the three objections he brings to bear against Heidegger's thought. For, although it is true that the later Heidegger understands technology *ontologically*, it is also the case that he also understands ontology *historically*. Remember that, for Heidegger, the essence of technology is nothing other than an ontotheologically rooted self-understanding that has been repeatedly contested and redefined during the last twenty-five hundred years.[20] Indeed, it was Heidegger who gave us the first historical conception of the essence of technology, and I think Feenberg does better to acknowledge this important conceptual debt while continuing to build on this Heideggerian tradition, rather than seeking to distance himself from Heidegger where there are no good philosophical reasons for doing so. If this is right, however, then how could Feenberg possibly think that Heidegger has

the Hippocratic tradition of diagnosing diseases of which the patient remains blissfully unaware. (See Raymond Geuss, *The Idea of a Critical Theory: Habermas and the Frankfurt School.*) Recall, for example, Kant's historical prediction that "human nature must endure the harshest of evils, which pass in disguise as external well-being," because: "All good that is not grafted onto a morally good character is nothing but illusion and glistering misery" ("Idea for a Universal History with Cosmopolitan Intent," *Perpetual Peace and Other Essays,* 36, 32).

20 This is why I suggested in my first exchange with Feenberg that Heidegger's historical understanding of the "essence" of technology allows his view to avoid the twin excesses of "constructivism" and "essentialism," and that Feenberg actually proposes a similar view when he advocates "an historical concept of essence" in *Questioning Technology*'s concluding chapter. (See *Questioning Technology,* 16, 201; and my "From the Question Concerning Technology to the Quest for a Democratic Technology," 208.)

an ahistorical conception of technology? It is instructive to pinpoint just where Feenberg's reading goes off the tracks.

Critics like Derrida have long questioned Heidegger's epochal account of the history of being. They were not persuaded by the way his account divides the history of our ontological self-understanding into a series of five unified constellations of intelligibility, demarcating the pre-Socratic, Platonic, medieval, modern, and (our own) late-modern epochs. Where Heidegger sees a succession of overlapping but relatively distinct and durable ontological epochs, his critics claimed to observe a much greater degree of ontohistorical flux. As we saw in Chapter 1 (§2), however, the metaphysical tradition's ontotheological understandings of the being of entities unite the deepest and broadest insights attained by each historical epoch, and so constitute an epistemic *Ungrund* between *Grund* and *Abgrund* (IM 3/GA40 5); they are, in other words, nothing more nor less than the dual point at which our sharpest ontotheological spades turn historically. The ontotheological "double groundings" effected by metaphysics are thus neither as secure as those permanent foundations metaphysics always sought would be, but nor are they as shaky as the merely arbitrary constructions Heidegger's postmodern and poststructuralist heirs take them to be, and this helps explain why the history of being Heidegger charts takes the form of a series of relatively durable understandings of what is, rather than either a single unbroken epoch or a continuous flux.[21] Now, like Derrida, Feenberg too questions the "periodization" of Heidegger's history of being, but his objection is more precise: In order to "deny all [historical] continuity and treat modern technology as unique," Heidegger introduces an untenably "sharp ontological break" between modern technology and premodern craft. The problem here, however, is that, although Heidegger does indeed claim that our contemporary technological understanding of being is unique, he does not deny all historical continuity in order to make this claim. Indeed, when we understand, as too few scholars do, what exactly Heidegger thinks is unique about our contemporary historical self-understanding,

---

[21] Even where leading scholars contest the details of Heidegger's account, their own analyses tend to confirm rather than undermine the basic epochal divisions he first discerned. See, for example, Michel Foucault, *The Order of Things*; and Reiner Schürmann, *Broken Hegemonies*, two important works that build on, refine, and extend Heidegger's history of being. (On the relation of Foucault's account to Heidegger's, see Dreyfus and Rabinow, *Michel Foucault*, as well as Dreyfus, "Being and Power: Heidegger and Foucault" and "Being and Power: Revisited.")

then it becomes clear that Feenberg has bought into a widespread misreading when he attributes to Heidegger the "unconvincing" claim that the contemporary age is "uniquely oriented toward control."[22]

According to Heidegger's understanding of the ontotheological "ground" of enframing, the ontological "reduction [of all entities] to raw materials" is *not* "in the interests of control." Why not? Because in our post-Nietzschean age there is increasingly no subject left to be doing the controlling. The subject, too, is being "sucked up" into "the standing reserve" (QCT 173/GA7 55)![23] This late-modern dissolution of the subject (fragmented into component forces by the analyses of Darwin, Nietzsche, and Freud) is unknown to prior historical epochs, and it makes our contemporary epoch unique in Heidegger's eyes, but he still explains this ongoing development historically. Put simply, the transformation of modernity's vaunted subject into just another intrinsically meaningless resource awaiting optimization results from the fact that we late-moderns have turned the practices developed by the moderns for objectifying and controlling nature back *onto ourselves*.[24] Once modern subjects dominating an objective world begin treating *themselves* as objects, the subject/object distinction itself is undermined, and the subject is thereby put on the path toward becoming just another resource to be *optimized*, that is, "secured and ordered *for the sake of flexible use*."[25]

For Heidegger, this passage from Cartesian modernity to Nietzschean late modernity was already clearly visible in 1955, in the portentous transformation of employment agencies into "human resource" departments (QCT 18/GA7 18; cf. N3 250/NII 333). In fact, Feenberg, despite this misreading, has now taken this basic Heideggerian point on board. In a recent essay on "Modernity Theory and Technology Studies," Feenberg observes with grim irony that contemporary "societies are unique in de-worlding human beings in order to subject them to technical action – we

---

[22] See Feenberg, *Questioning Technology*, 15, 16. See also Trish Glazebrook, "From *Phusis* to Nature, *Technê* to Technology: Heidegger on Aristotle, Galileo, and Newton."

[23] *Questioning Technology*, 15, 178. In Feenberg's more recent "Modernity Theory and Technology Studies: Reflections on Bridging the Gap," he again attributes to Heidegger "the familiar complaint about modernity's obsession with efficiency and control." (Feenberg would be right if he were distinguishing "modernity" from "late modernity," rather than using modernity the way he does here, as a synonym for the contemporary age.)

[24] Even Levinas, perhaps the most outspoken post-Heideggerian critic of Heidegger, appropriates Heidegger's insight that, in our current "mutation in the light of the world," "*the subject is eliminated from the order of reasons*" (*Humanism of the Other*, 59).

[25] See Spinosa, Flores, and Dreyfus, "Skills, Historical Disclosing, and the End of History: A Response to Our Critics," 188 (my emphasis).

call it management." As Feenberg here seems to recognize, Heidegger presciently described an alarming ontological trend that now appears disconnected from our actual sociohistorical reality only to those who are not paying close enough attention. Indeed, we will see in Chapter 4 that the contemporary technologization of the university, with its would-be reduction of teachers and scholars to online "content providers," and its "growing marginalization of . . . part-time" teachers in the name of efficiency and "flexibility," merely extends, and so crystallizes, the underlying logic whereby modern subjects become late-modern resources.[26] Whether or not one accepts the perspicacity of Heidegger's analysis, however, it should be clear that his ontotheological critique of our technological understanding of being does not suffer from the ahistoricism Feenberg attributes to it. Let us turn, then, to one of Feenberg's more telling objections, namely, the charge that Heidegger's understanding of technology suffers from a politically dehabilitating substantivism.

B. Substantivism (or Fatalism)?

We saw earlier that Feenberg is moved to reject technological substantivism, the belief that the essence of technology is outside of human control, because of the politically dangerous fatalism such a belief seems to entail.[27] Of course, a philosopher, *qua* philosopher, cannot reject a philosophical doctrine solely because of its political consequences. Distressing political implications should lead us to subject a philosophical doctrine to especially relentless critical scrutiny, but ultimately such philosophical

---

[26] See Derrida, "The University Without Condition," *Without Alibi*, 226.

[27] According to Feenberg, Heidegger is fatalistic because he ignores the bottom-up perspective of those "enrolled" within technological networks and so misses their "subjugated wisdom," which teaches that technologies can be appropriated from below, diverted away from the fixed ends for which they were originally designed. Heidegger, however, would not deny that specific technological designs can be subverted in this way. The crucial question is whether such "ontic" subversions could ever culminate in an ontological transcendence of the technological mode of revealing. As I show later, the later Heidegger did believe in such a possibility, he just did not believe it could be accomplished by willfully steering the course of technological development from within. Already in 1940, Heidegger criticizes his contemporary age's call for the Nietzschean *Übermensch*, the idea (which Heidegger sees exemplified in the work of Ernst Jünger) that: "What is needed is a form of mankind that is from top to bottom equal to the unique fundamental essence of contemporary technology and its metaphysical truth; that is to say, that lets itself be entirely dominated by the essence of technology precisely in order to steer and deploy individual technological processes and possibilities" (N4 117/NII 165–6). Feenberg can himself be understood as advocating just such a voluntaristic, "superhuman" Nietzschean strategy.

scrutiny must seek to determine whether or not the doctrine in question is true. If a philosophical doctrine turns out to be true, moreover, then either we have to accept its political consequences, however disturbing (as will often be the case when it turns out to have been merely our unreflective judgments, or *prejudices*, that were being disturbed), or else we have to work politically to bring about a change in the world that would subsequently falsify the offending doctrine. The problem with Heidegger's substantivism, as Feenberg presents it, is that the truth of the doctrine would seem to preclude the latter, activist option: If Heidegger's substantivism is right that it is not within our power to transform the essence of technology, then neither can we change the world so as subsequently to gain control over the essence of technology.[28] In fact, if Feenberg were correct about Heidegger's substantivism, this would place us before a strict *aporia* (that is, a "necessary impossibility"), because, as Dreyfus points out, we cannot stop trying to take control of the essence of technology; the endeavor may be both impossible and unavoidable. Insofar as "enframing" has a hold on us, "the drive to control everything is precisely what we do not control."[29] Nevertheless, as Dreyfus points out, "this is a situation about which something can be done – at least indirectly."[30] This Heideggerian caveat, which holds that our actions could *indirectly* transform the essence of technology, is crucial, it seems to me, for vindicating Heidegger's substantivism against what I take to be Feenberg's most powerful objection.

For, Feenberg is right that if Heidegger thought we had no hope of ever transcending our technological understanding of being, then his insights would lead only to fatalistic despair. Fortunately, Heidegger's position is more complex than the many otherwise insightful critics of his "quietism" (from Schürmann and Olafson to Marcuse, Habermas, Wolin, and Feenberg) allow. To see this, it helps to recall, with Dreyfus, that Heidegger's primary "concern is the human *distress* caused by the *technological understanding of being*, rather than the *destruction* caused by

---

[28] If substantivism is right that we cannot control the essence of technology (and clearly this is meant as the time-independent claim that the essence of technology is out of our control now and forever, because it would not otherwise be objectionable), then there is no non-question-begging way to say that we could change the world such that we *could* control the essence of technology.

[29] See Dreyfus, "Heidegger on the Connection between Nihilism, Art, Technology, and Politics," 307–10. On Heidegger's alleged "fatalism," see also Young's insightful discussions in *Heidegger, Philosophy, Nazism*, 188–91, and *Heidegger's Later Philosophy*, 83–90.

[30] "Heidegger on the Connection between Nihilism, Art, Technology, and Politics," 305.

specific technologies." Heidegger thus approaches technology not as "a *problem* for which we must find a *solution* [which would be a technological approach], but [rather as] an *ontological condition* that requires a *transformation of our understanding of being.*"[31] From the Heideggerian perspective, then, the most profound philosophical difference between Feenberg and Heidegger concerns the level at which each pitches his critique of technology. Feenberg's strategy for responding to the problems associated with the increasing rule of technocracy takes place primarily at what Heidegger would call the "ontic" level, having to do with our ordinary, everyday experience with entities, rather than the ontological level, which concerns our underlying understanding of the being of those entities. The problem with Feenberg's strategy is that such everyday ontic actions and decisions almost always take place within the fundamental conceptual parameters set for us by our current ontology, otherwise these actions would tend not to make sense to ourselves or to others. The crucial question, then, is this: Can ontic political decisions and resistances of the type Feenberg puts his faith in ever effect the kind of ontological change Heidegger seeks?

Ontologically, Heidegger is more of a realist than a constructivist; our understanding of the being of entities is something to which we are fundamentally receptive, something that (as we saw in Chapter 1) we discover rather than create. We cannot just fabricate and legislate a new ontology. Thus, as Dreyfus nicely puts it: "A new sense of reality is not something that can be made the goal of a crash program like the moon flight."[32] So, does Heidegger deny that our ontic decisions could ever build up enough steam to effect an ontological transformation? No; in fact, Heidegger explicitly recognized this possibility. As he wrote in the late 1930s:

"World–historical" events are capable of assuming a scale never seen before. [The unprecedented magnitude of these events] at first speaks only to the rising frenzy in the unbounded domain of machination and numbers. It never speaks immediately for the emergence of essential decisions. But when, within these "world historical" events, a coming-together of the people sets itself up – and partly establishes the people's existence according to the style of these events – could not a pathway open here into the nearness of decision? Certainly, but with the supreme danger that the domain of this decision will be missed completely.
(CP 68/GA65 98)[33]

---

[31] Ibid.
[32] Ibid., 310.
[33] The context of this passage is philosophically and politically problematic: philosophically, because here Heidegger is still naively committed to the metaphysical project of

In other words, it is possible that a confluence of ontic political struggles could open the space for a reconfiguration of our ontological self-understanding, but only if we are aware of the true radicality of this endeavor, the fact that it requires a fundamental transformation in the nature of our existence, not merely the redistribution of power or the realignment of particular interests. As Dreyfus's famous example of Woodstock is meant to illustrate, it is possible that practices marginalized by our technological understanding of being (radical egalitarianism and *fraternité*, pagan sensibilities, an ethic of care, and so on) could make use of technological means (such as electronic instruments, sophisticated sound systems, and the most advanced methods of mass marketing and social organization) in order to become central to our self-understanding, radically transforming our sense of what is and what matters.[34] Although Feenberg's own project is clearly inspired by the structurally analogous Paris events of May 1968 in which he personally participated, he is extremely wary of this revolutionary aspect in Heidegger's thinking because of the political direction in which it took Heidegger himself.[35] One question is thus: Just how different are Feenberg and Heidegger on this point? Do we not have Feenberg's own position if we replace Heidegger's politically dangerous Nietzschean–Wagnerian hope for a revolutionary *Gesamtkunstwerk*, a work of art that would transform our entire ontological self-understanding in one fell swoop, with the more modest hope that a "convergence" of differently situated political microstruggles could evolve into a counterhegemony capable of permanently subverting our contemporary *technocracy*?[36] If so, then this is a move I believe we should

establishing a new historical ground for entities (by "deciding" on a new understanding of the being of entities); politically, because Heidegger not only connects this metaphysical project with the "people" (*Volk*), but even asserts the "singularity" of this folk's "origin and mission," grounding this "destiny" in "the singularity of Be-ing itself" (CP 67/GA65 97). This nationalistic philosophical appropriation of the Jewish trope of the chosen people, sometime between 1936 and 1937, is undeniably troubling. Nevertheless, the "supreme danger" Heidegger is thinking of here is clearly instantiated by the National Socialists, who have gathered a movement but failed utterly, in Heidegger's view, to appreciate its true philosophical potential.

34 See Dreyfus, "Heidegger on the Connection between Nihilism, Art, Technology, and Politics," 311; and Dreyfus, "Heidegger on Gaining a Free Relationship to Technology," 106.

35 See Andrew Feenberg and Jim Freedman, *When Poetry Ruled the Streets: The French May Events of 1968*.

36 A "technocracy," according to Marcuse, is a political state in which "technical considerations of imperialistic efficiency and rationality supersede the traditional standards of profitability and general welfare"; it is his name for the postfascist form totalitarianism took after World War II. (See Marcuse's "Some Social Implications of Modern

join Feenberg in making, out of a sober, post-Heideggerian respect for the important differences – in such politically consequential matters as attitude and approach – which tend to go along with the dangerous fantasy of instantaneous and total revolutionary change, as opposed to the more patient, progressivist commitment to the slow but steady work of progressive transformation (which accepts as its melancholy mantra, "Two steps forward, one step back"). For, Heidegger's own short-lived embrace of a Nietzschean–Wagnerian, total-revolutionary view seems to have played a role in desensitizing him to the real violence and human suffering ushered in by the pseudorevolution of 1933.[37] Nonetheless, Heidegger's

---

Technology" [1941], *Technology, War, Fascism*, 41; my "From the Question Concerning Technology to the Quest for a Democratic Technology"; and cf. Feenberg's *Questioning Technology*, 4.)

[37] In an unpublished 7 March 1933 letter to Maria Scheler, Heidegger writes: "Hitler once said: 'Terror can only be broken up by way of terror.' If you have really observed the gruesome activities of communism during the past years, you will not be surprised about the kind of violent behavior [*des Anstürmens*] going on today. And it is up to *us* now to support the buildup, and to clean up and clarify and make the goals and measures [to be taken] effective ones. The 'political' [attitude] of the youth that serves the *polis* is a new reality and the beginning of a new inner greatness for our people. The old concepts, even good ones included, of what is 'spiritual' do not have enough relevance here anymore. [For the rather alarming concept of "spirit" Heidegger favors circa 1933, see GA16 289–98, discussed in Chapter 4.] Take a look at the life of a young human being, Horst Wessel, and you will see how in the midst of a dark reality both heart and mind are preserving each other in their need to recast themselves. It has been a long time since we have had to listen to the internal drift of our German reality and act accordingly." (Heidegger's letter is preserved in the Max Scheler archives at the University of New Mexico.) Such privately expressed sentiments are revealing (showing clearly, for example, that Heidegger bought into the Nazi demonization of communism). They further undermine that already discredited exculpatory narrative which had Heidegger joining the Nazi movement only reluctantly, and in May, but, just as importantly, they reinforce his claim that he joined the party in order to try to redirect it philosophically (a point addressed in Chapter 3). Such private correspondence needs, of course, to be read alongside Heidegger's public philosophical statements. Compare, for example, the remarks on "revolution" in his first (and most sympathetic) *Nietzsche* lecture course, begun in 1936: "The public and common representation of Nietzsche is as a revolutionary figure who negated, destroyed [*zerstört*], and prophesied.... But what is essential in the revolutionary is not that he overturns as such; it is rather that in overturning he brings to light what is decisive and essential. In philosophy that happens always when those few momentous questions are raised" (N1 20/NI 28). Near this course's conclusion, Heidegger adds: "The more clearly and essentially a decisive inquiry traces the history of Western thought back to its few essential stages, the more that history's power to reach forward, seize, and commit grows.... The greater a revolution is to be, the more profoundly must it plunge into its history" (N1 203/NI 234–5). Such quotes show that even when Heidegger was at his most Nietzschean, he was attempting to effect a "revolution" *philosophically*, by articulating the history of being whose "few essential stages" we have been reconstructing. (Although some may also be disturbed by the violence of

critique of our optimistic faith in gradual change is right about at least this much: The mere fact that the hands of the clocks keep turning does not mean that history is moving toward any sort of deeper ontological transformation.

When confronted with this proximity to Heidegger, Feenberg falls back on two widespread misinterpretations of Heidegger. According to the first misreading (influentially disseminated by Habermas), Heidegger asserts the absolute heterogeneity of the ontic and ontological levels of analysis, then effectively retreats from the former into the latter. Although Feenberg is correct that many Heideggerians do ascribe such a bizarre *heterogeneity thesis* to Heidegger, I find such a thesis simply untenable as an interpretation of Heidegger, for his philosophical methodologies, both early and late, not only assume but positively presuppose that the ontic and the ontological remain interconnected. Yes, the ontological fundamentally *conditions* the ontic (with the important implications mentioned below), but Heidegger also recognized, as many Heideggerians do not, that our only access to the ontological is *through* the ontic, and that what makes an ontological interpretation convincing (or not) is the revealing light it throws back on such shared ontic phenomena.[38] Second, Feenberg adopts Michael Zimmerman's influential claim that the later Heidegger rejected his own earlier insight into the possibility of an active human role in ontohistorical transformation and withdrew into a fatalistic "quietism" in response to the failure of his own political activism in the 1930s.[39] This received view is misleading, however, because (as we will see in Chapters 3 and 4) the later Heidegger continued quietly to develop and refine the underlying philosophical project that initially led him to join the National Socialist movement in 1933, rather than abandoning this project after the war, as is almost universally supposed.

If Heidegger steadfastly advocates the eventual goal of ontohistorical transformation, while Feenberg seeks to "reverse-engineer" a possible

Paris, May 1968, in which Feenberg participated, it seems clear that such violence against repressive political authorities in the name of inclusion is quite different from violence by such authorities in the name of exclusion, the *closing of ranks* celebrated in the infamous *Horst Wessel Lied*, the Nazi anthem, whose lockstep unity Heidegger celebrates in 1934, as we will see in §20.)

[38] I develop this argument in Chapter 5 of "The End of Ontotheology: Understanding Heidegger's Turn, Method, and Politics," esp. 317–30.

[39] See Feenberg, "The Ontic and the Ontological in Heidegger's Philosophy of Technology: Response to Thomson"; this thesis is proposed by Habermas in *The Philosophical Discourses of Modernity*, and prominently developed by Zimmerman in *Heidegger's Confrontation with Modernity*.

means to achieving this goal (through a confluence of "democratizing" ontic struggles over technological design), this should also lead us to wonder, I think, how much Heidegger and Feenberg really differ on the truth of substantivism. For his part, Feenberg himself wavers back and forth on the substantivism question, a tension in his view that reflects a fundamental difference between the Marcusean and Heideggerian positions he synthesizes. Feenberg vacillates between a voluntaristic, Marcusean, May 1968, "Progress will be what we want it to be" view, which exalts the human capacity to control our future through strategic interventions in the process of technological design, on the one hand, and, on the other, a more "substantivist" Heideggerian view, which suggests that although we cannot directly *control* the historical direction in which technology is taking us, we can nevertheless impact the future in small ways by learning to recognize, encourage, and support technological democratizations when they occur, while hoping that these (and other) ontic political interventions might yet indirectly foster an ontological transformation.[40] The Marcusean position has the surface appeal of all heroic existential voluntarisms, but it ignores the very issue that led Heidegger to develop his ontological approach, indeed the precise reason that Marcuse discipled himself to Heidegger before the war: However important, democratization without a corresponding ontological transformation will just end up replicating and reifying the technological understanding of being.[41] If, as is the case for Heidegger, Feenberg's goal is not simply democratic control *for the sake of control*, if, rather, his endeavor is indeed "prefigurative," that is, if its goal is "to open up a possible future" other than "enframing" or "technocracy," then what this suggests, in my view, is that Feenberg's projected democratization of technological design needs to be incorporated

[40] *Questioning Technology*, 22. We could recast this subtle but important difference by suggesting that Feenberg would agree with Michael Heim's view that: "Philosophy should be projecting possibilities, as part of a team of scientists, technicians, artists, designers, people who are coming from different areas, *to create* future environments," whereas, sharing Heidegger's more realist intuition, I would instead say that we should seek *to disclose* the constituent elements of such future environments. (See Heim, "Heidegger Online," 29, my emphasis.)

[41] My insistence on this point remains one of the basic differences between our ways of understanding Marcuse's debt to Heidegger. (Cf. my "From the Question Concerning Technology to the Quest for a Democratic Technology" with Feenberg's *Heidegger and Marcuse*. I develop another concrete example of this same problem in "Ontology and Ethics at the Intersection of Phenomenology and Environmental Philosophy," showing how a failure to understand the *ontological* roots of environmental devastation undermines the otherwise well-intentioned efforts of a number of Nietzschean and Husserlian ecophenomenologists.)

into a larger pedagogical project aimed at the level of what the Greeks called *paideia*, the Germans *Bildung*, that is, an *educational* project specifically envisioned to encourage the recognition, cultivation, and development of humanity's distinctive world-disclosing skills, one important species of which will be those skills necessary for making appropriate democratizing interventions in the technological design process.[42] I shall develop the pedagogical reforms I take to be necessitated by Heidegger's ontotheological critique of "enframing" in detail in Chapter 4, and so will only say a bit more about the goal of this pedagogical project as we evaluate Feenberg's final objection.

C. One-Dimensionalism?

Is Heidegger's technological essentialism one-dimensional? Does he believe that all technological devices express the same essence? In "The Question Concerning Technology," Heidegger explicitly denies that "enframing, the essence of technology," is "the common genus of everything technological" (QCT 29/GA7 30). A great deal of confusion seems to have been generated by a widespread failure to recognize that, in seeking to understand the essence of technology, Heidegger is not trying to fix the extension of the term; he is not seeking to determine what is and what is not a member of the class of technological devices.[43] Heidegger does not conceptualize technology's essence in terms of the commonalities shared by the hydroelectric plant, the autobahn, the cellular phone, the Internet, and so on, the way a Platonist might conceive of the essence of trees as the genus uniting "oaks, beeches, birches, and firs."[44] Strictly

---

[42] *Questioning Technology*, 108. Spinosa, Flores, and Dreyfus's groundbreaking work, *Disclosing New Worlds: Entrepreneurship, Democratic Action, and the Cultivation of Solidarity* concludes by issuing a similar call (see esp. 171–3), and Feenberg has embraced this suggestion in his "Modernity Theory and Technology Studies."

[43] See Dreyfus, "Heidegger on the Connection between Nihilism, Art, Technology, and Politics," 305.

[44] The Platonist conceives of the essence of the different species of trees in terms of the abstract idea of "treeness," but Heidegger does not analogously conceptualize the essence of the diversity of technological devices by abstracting toward a kind of "technicity" [*Technik*] or "machination" [*Machenschaft*]. Instead, the reverse is closer to the truth: Heidegger believes that our technological devices – like all entities in our current historical clearing – tend to show up in terms of our "technological" ontotheology, and thus as intrinsically meaningless resources merely awaiting optimization. Indeed, by 1938, he recognized that "Machination itself . . . is the essential swaying of being as such [*die Wesung des Seyns*]" (CP 89/GA65 128), that is, that what technological devices share in common is their ontological mode of revealing (an understanding of being rooted in Nietzsche's metaphysics of "constant overcoming," and so his ontotheology of "eternally

speaking, then, Heidegger's understanding of the essence of technology is *orthogonal* to the question of whether or not all technological devices express the same essence. Nevertheless, the question of whether Heidegger is a technological one-dimensionalist remains; and the answer, I think, is a qualified yes. Why? Because, as we have seen, Heidegger holds that *the essence of technology is nothing less than the ontological self-understanding of the age.* Insofar as we implicitly adopt the Nietzschean ontotheology undergirding enframing, *everything* in the contemporary world will tend to show up for us as reflecting the essence of technology, technological devices being only particularly perspicuous cases. In this limited sense, then, Heidegger does seem to be a kind of technological one-dimensionalist. So, do the negative consequences Feenberg attaches to this position obtain in Heidegger's case? Not unless Heidegger's understanding of the essence of technology forces him globally to reject technology. This, then, is the crucial question: Does Heidegger's one-dimensionalism force him to reject technology *in toto*?

Now, Heidegger is obviously no fan of technology; he seems, for instance, to have had a visceral reaction to the sight of his neighbors "chained hourly and daily to their television" sets (DT 50).[45] Even on the personal level, however, Heidegger seems to have been capable of distinguishing between those technological applications which serve, and those that undermine, the cause of phenomenology, the endeavor to go back "to the things themselves!" For example, when watching a television show a friend put together to showcase the art of Paul Klee, Heidegger was appalled by the way the images framed on the television screen moved over the paintings randomly and forced the eye away from one piece and on to the next prematurely, "hindering an intensive, quiet viewing as well as a lingering reflection, which each single work and the relations within it deserve." On the other hand, Heidegger deeply appreciated the way a televised soccer match revealed its subject, raving publicly about the "brilliance" of Franz Beckenbauer it had showcased. Such anecdotes, of course, do not get us to the crux of the issue. For, however "technophobic" Heidegger may have been personally (for good reasons, in at least some cases), it is clear to careful readers of his work

---

recurring will-to-power"). Heidegger thus maintains that: "The bewitchment by technicity and its *constantly self-surpassing progress* is only *one* sign of this enchantment, by which everything presses forth into calculation, usage, breeding, manageability, and regulation" (CP 87/GA65 124, first emphasis mine).

[45] Thirty years earlier (in 1928), moreover, Heidegger pictured technology as rampaging across the globe "like a beast off its leash" (MFL 215/GA26 279).

that he does not philosophically advocate any monolithic rejection of technology.[46] (That should not be too surprising, since the philosophical implications of Heidegger's thinking often far exceed the rather narrow conclusions he himself drew from them.)

In our earlier debate, I reminded Feenberg of Heidegger's phenomenological description of a massive freeway interchange on the autobahn. Here, in 1951, Heidegger treats the autobahn in terms of what he calls a "thing thinging," that is, as an entity that has come into its own and is thus, in this case, capable of reflecting back to us the ontological self-understanding of the age (PLT 152–3/GA7 155). In response, Feenberg forthrightly acknowledged that in these passages on the autobahn bridge, "Heidegger discusses modern technology without negativism or nostalgia and suggests an innovative approach to understanding it." Nevertheless, Feenberg countered, Heidegger's "defenders have to admit that the famous highway bridge passage is the one and only instance in his whole corpus of a positive evaluation of modern technology."[47] Feenberg may well be right about this; Heidegger's brief phenomenological meditation on the autobahn interchange as a paradigm reflecting our ontological self-understanding seems to be the only "positive evaluation of modern technology" to be found in his work. Nevertheless, is not this single, carefully thought-out exception sufficient to prove that Heidegger does not reject technology wholecloth?

In his meditation on the autobahn interchange, Heidegger's concern is not to valorize this technological paradigm but, rather, to help us recognize that – as the Internet now makes plain for all to see – we are increasingly treating our world and ourselves as a kind of "network of long distance traffic, paced as calculated for maximum yield" (PLT 152/GA7 155).[48] Indeed, the only thing making this a "positive evaluation," as Feenberg rightly puts it, is the fact that Heidegger, in his phenomenological description of the autobahn interchange, is attempting to get us to notice the presence of "the divinities" that linger in the background of even our most advanced technological constructions (PLT 153/GA7 155). When he refers to the presence of the divine, Heidegger is evoking those meanings which cannot be explained solely in terms of human will, and thereby encouraging us to attend to that preconceptual

---

[46] See Heinrich W. Petzet, *Encounters and Dialogues with Martin Heidegger*, 149–50, 210; and Feenberg, *Questioning Technology*, 151.

[47] "Constructivism and Technology Critique: Response to Critics," 225–6.

[48] For an analysis of freeway interchanges as reflections of the self-understanding of the age, see David Brodsly's *L.A. Freeway: An Appreciative Essay.*

phenomenological "presencing" on which all of our interpretations rest, a "presencing" which (as we saw at the end of Chapter 1) will be a prime source of what Dreyfus aptly characterizes as any "new paradigm . . . rich enough and resistant enough to give a new meaningful direction to our lives."[49] Like his meditation on the place of "earth" in the work of art, Heidegger's resacralization of the simple and inconspicuous "thing" (*Ding*) reminds us that the "conditioned" (*bedingt*) has its roots in the "unconditioned" (*unbedingt*), the finite in the infinite, and thus suggests that we should adopt a very different attitude toward our world, a *Grund-stimmung* much more reflective and thankful than the thoroughgoing instrumental reasoning characteristic of our technological mode of re-vealing.[50] Indeed, as Dreyfus has argued, Heidegger is convinced that

[49] "Heidegger on the Connection between Nihilism, Art, Technology, and Politics," 311. As possible sources of such a new paradigm, Dreyfus stresses those "marginal practices" that have not yet been completely "mobilized as resources," "such as friendship, back-packing in the wilderness, and drinking the local wine with friends" (310). I would add to Dreyfus's view, and the similar Kuhnian suggestion advanced earlier, that for Heidegger a crucial role will be played by "being as such," a phenomenon we can learn to experi-ence as a preconceptual "presencing" and extraconceptual excess that existing practices never exhaust.

[50] In "The Origin of the Work of Art" (1935), Heidegger maintains that for a great artwork to *work*, that is, for it to "gather and preserve" a meaningful "world" for its audience, it must maintain an essential tension between this *world* of meanings and something he calls "earth." *Earth*, on his analysis, both sustains this meaningful world and resists being interpretively exhausted by it, thereby allowing the artwork quietly to maintain the sanctity of the uninterpretable within the very world of meanings it conveys. "Earth," in other words, is one of Heidegger's names for "being as such," that phenomenological presencing that gives rise to our worlds of meaning without ever being exhausted by them, a dimension of intelligibility we experience primarily as it recedes from our awareness. Heidegger contends, nevertheless, that we can get a *sense* for the "earth" from great works of art like Vincent van Gogh's painting of the peasant shoes, in which, in the worn opening of one shoe and in the hole in the sole of the other, thick dark paint conveys the insides of the shoes, interior spaces we cannot see because they are hidden by what the painting conveys: not just the visible exterior of these shoes, but the entire *world* of the peasant. Admittedly, Heidegger's poetic way of putting these crucial points makes them rather easy to miss: "From out of the dark opening of the worn insides of the shoes the toilsome tread of the worker stares forth. . . . In the shoes vibrates the silent call of the earth, its quiet gift of the ripening grain [i.e., "earth" makes "world" possible] and its unexplained self-refusal in the fallow desolation of the wintry field [i.e., it is also constitutive of earth that it resists world]" (PLT 33–4/GA5 19). On Heidegger's reading, van Gogh's painting reveals the very "truth" of the work of art, the essential tension in which "earth" simultaneously makes possible and resists being fully expressed by "world." (We should not allow the long-standing debate about whether van Gogh painted a peasant's shoes or his own – Heidegger notes in the 1960 Reclam edition of the lecture that we cannot tell "to whom they belong" – to obscure the point of his analysis.)

we should be *grateful* for our technological understanding of being; for, without this ontological clearing, "nothing would show up *as* anything at all, and no possibilities for action would make sense."[51]

We enter into what Heidegger calls a "freeing claim" when we pass from a recognition of the devastation done by our technological understanding of being to a sense of gratitude for this, our historical clearing (QCT 26/GA7 26).[52] Heidegger believes that we need to recognize our technological understanding of being – which reduces being to *nothing* (dissolving it into Nietzsche's "permanent becoming") – as the way "being as such" shows itself to us, now, within our own epoch of "enframing." This may sound paradoxical, but one of the later Heidegger's definitive insights is that being shows itself to us *as* nothing. For Heidegger, this is not an insignificant realization, but quite the contrary. For, to recognize our current constellation of intelligibility *as* the way being as such happens for us is to recognize our ongoing ontological receptivity in addition to our active role as disclosers of what-is. If we can incorporate an appropriate sense of this receptive spontaneity into our practices, he suggests, we can learn to relate to things with a phenomenological comportment open to alterity and difference on the ontological as well as the more fashionable ontic level, a comportment through which Heidegger believes we can begin to experience and disclose the constituent elements of a post-technological ontology (as we saw in Section 5).[53]

That may sound a bit mysterious, but in his 1949 essay "The Turning," Heidegger unequivocally states that he is not advocating anything as ridiculous as the abandonment of technology. In the postnihilistic future Heidegger worked philosophically to help envision and achieve, "Technology," he repeats, "will not be done away with. Technology will not be struck down, and certainly it will not be destroyed"

---

[51] Dreyfus, "Heidegger on the Connection between Nihilism, Art, Technology, and Politics," 307. I am indebted to Julian Young for the former point; see his insightful *Heidegger's Philosophy of Art*, 107.

[52] As Young explains, "Heidegger's account of the turning that we need to make ... for all its sound and fury, is, in fact, best read as plotting a middle way between the complaisant endorsement of modern technology, on the one hand, and the Luddite demand for a return to the cave, on the other" (*Heidegger's Later Philosophy*, 83).

[53] See also Young's admirably clear and succinct account in *Heidegger's Later Philosophy*, 75–7. I would, however, resist Young's interpretive thesis that: "A technological disclosure of B/being is something possessed by every species of humanity, is the way things show up in every historical epoch all of the time" (76). I understand the broader point Young is making (viz., that each epoch's understanding of the being of entities shows being as such), but his way of formulating this thesis downplays that which, I argued earlier, makes our "technological" understanding of being *unique*, namely, the self-objectification that dissolves the subject into the resource pool.

(QCT 38/GA79 69). It is thus hermeneutically inexcusable to continue to confuse Heidegger with a Luddite longing nostalgically for a return to a pretechnological society.[54] In his famous *Der Spiegel* interview (given in 1966), Heidegger reiterates that the technological world must be "superceded, in the Hegelian sense [that is, incorporated at a higher level], not pushed aside" (Q&A 63/A 107).[55] As we saw, technological devices will tend to express the essence of technology, insofar as they remain products of an understanding rooted in Nietzsche's ontotheology. Yet, as Feenberg (building here on the work of Foucault) shows persuasively, some of these devices can be subverted, reappropriated, or redesigned so as to be used in the struggle against this ontotheology. In addition to Feenberg's examples of online user groups networked together in order to share information and so empower isolated individuals who would otherwise tend to be marginalized by increasingly dehumanizing corporate bureaucracies (examples with which Feenberg presciently anticipates the formation of MoveOn.com, Meetup.org, and other online networking operations transforming the political scene by empowering grassroots political organizations), we also could think, for instance, of the work of artists such as David Byrne, whose popular "Envisioning Emotional Epistemological Information" installations use PowerPoint software in order to make art that challenges, from within (as it were), the already overwhelming acceleration of information being amassed and circulated by our technologies. Such technological subversions (or, more precisely, "sublations") *must* be possible, if Heidegger's point about *superceding* technological devices (in the Hegelian sense of incorporating them into a post-"technological" understanding of being) is to have any meaning.[56]

---

54 Indeed, "[t]he first thing Heidegger does in the important 1949 essay 'The Turning' is to dispose of Luddism" (Young, *Heidegger's Later Philosophy*, 75). This is important politically as well as hermeneutically, because Eduardo Mendieta is surely right to emphasize Don Ihde's thesis (from *Technology and the Lifeworld* and *Bodies of Technology*) that: "Retreat to a pretechnological time, or a pristine form of technology, are essentially regressive and conservative agendas that are as pernicious as those that seek to eliminate the use of all technology" (Mendieta, "Bodies of Technology," 97).

55 For Hegel, "transcending" (or "sublating," *Aufheben*) "is at once a negating and a preserving" (*Phenomenology of Spirit*, 68/*Phänomenologische des Geistes*, 80). Heidegger, of course, fully realizes this: "Sublated does not mean done away with, but raised up, kept, and preserved in the new creation" (PT 51/GA9 63).

56 I address Foucault's influence on Feenberg in "From the Question Concerning Technology to the Quest for a Democratic Technology." Most important here is Foucault's conviction that "the connections among and the uses made of the local systems of subjection," when viewed "from below," show how specific "technologies of power . . . have been and are invested, colonized, used, inflected, transformed, displaced, extended . . . and modified." Foucault, like the technological constructivists he helped inspire, encourages

Feenberg and other critics may continue to object that Heidegger does not provide enough actual guidance about *how* to transcend our current technological understanding of being, but we will see that this objection too has been exaggerated when we develop Heidegger's surprisingly specific pedagogical suggestions concerning how we can inculcate the requisite world-disclosing skills (in Chapter 4). Heidegger, however, can no longer be accused of a reactionary rejection of technological devices, and even less of wanting to reject the essence of technology, which, he says in no uncertain terms, would be madness, "a desire to unhinge the essence of humanity" (N4 223/NII 365).[57]

It is, finally, important to point out that another widespread and closely related criticism of Heidegger is misguided as well. Put simply, Heidegger did not believe that our technological understanding of being could be transcended though a phenomenological practice disconnected from sociohistorical reality. It will doubtless surprise those who have been taken in by a one-sided stereotype to hear that when Heidegger was devoting a great deal of thought to the question of the relation between "the work of art and the power plant," he spent "several days visiting power plants under the direction of professors from technical colleges."[58] The fruits of such phenomenological labors are undeniable. When Heidegger looked out at the autobahn interchange and the power plant on the Ister and found words that powerfully describe those fundamental transformations in our self-understanding that are only now becoming obvious with the advent of the Internet, word processing, genetic research, and

---

us to focus on "the actual instruments that form and accumulate knowledge," but he is also, like Heidegger, sensitive "above all" to the dangers resulting from the fact that these technologies of power "are invested or annexed by global phenomenon" (*Society Must Be Defended*," 29–34).

[57] In an important later work, "the Memorial Address" (1955), Heidegger seeks to take his audience performatively through a "turning" whereby they come to recognize that although technology is ubiquitous, its meaning remains mysterious. He believes recognizing that the ontological impact of technology remains concealed even though our worlds are saturated with technological devices, and thus that *technology reveals itself in a way that conceals its meaning*, helps facilitate the crucial insight that enframing *is* the way "being as such" reveals itself for us – viz., by "concealing" or "withholding" itself (as we noted with respect to his analysis of "earth"). "Where the danger is, the saving power also grows," then, because that which makes possible our technological understanding of being – and every other understanding of being (without being exhausted by these successive understandings of the being of entities) – is a pretheoretical source of intelligibility which simultaneously elicits and defies full conceptualization, a "mystery" which, as we saw in Chapter 1, Heidegger thinks is key to understanding ourselves otherwise than in the terms established by enframing's reductive ontotheology.

[58] See Petzet, *Encounters and Dialogues*, 145–6.

cloning, his was not what W. H. Auden called "The dazed uncompre-
hending stare/Of the Danubian despair."[59]

Still, we may be able to help head off further misunderstandings by emphasizing that Heidegger's critique of our "technological" understanding of being is not focused primarily on particular *technological devices* but,
rather, on a progressive *technologization* of intelligibility, an ontologically
reductive transformation of all entities into intrinsically meaningless resources on standby for optimization.[60] Heidegger's frequent description
of this "enframing" as a "technological" understanding of being reflects
his insight that exemplary technological devices – such as the autobahn,
the hydroelectric dam, the airport, and, we must now add, the Internet –
show themselves, when studied with the appropriate phenomenological
sensitivity and rigor, to be revealing expressions of the disturbing historical direction in which our underlying ontotheology seems to be taking
us (QCT 116/GA5 75). In other words, Heidegger's critique of technology is focused on identifying the ontotheological grounds of an ongoing
transformation of intelligibility, the effects of which reach far beyond

[59] For a more detailed argument to this effect, see Dreyfus and Spinosa, "Highway Bridges
and Feasts: Heidegger and Borgmann on How to Affirm Technology."

[60] In other words, Heidegger's critique of our "technological understanding of being" is
not meant to help us sort *good* from *bad* technological devices and designs (although
Heidegger is not without a few suggestive remarks on this score – such as his interesting
but problematic idea that we should not allow ourselves to become *addicted* to technological devices – which I develop in "From the Question Concerning Technology to the
Quest for a Democratic Technology"). Feenberg's own sorting of technological devices
is guided primarily by "ontic" rather than "ontological" considerations; he is concerned
with which devices enhance democratic agency rather than with which devices (or relationship to those devices) might promote a non-nihilistic understanding of being. Of
course, these ontic and ontological considerations could turn out to be mutually rein-
forcing, such that those devices which expand the arena of democratic decision making
also serve the cause of ontohistorical revolution (and vice versa), although Heidegger
never relinquished his own long-standing doubts on this score (Q&A 54/A 96). Indeed,
Heidegger would agree with the general intuition guiding Feenberg – viz., that devices
that help us expand our possibilities are to be preferred over devices that narrow our
range of free decisions – only if this expansion of possibilities is done *not* in order to increase *optimization* but, rather, for the sake of ontohistorical revolution. That may sound
unlikely *prima facie*, but I believe Heidegger's call for us to learn to practice comportmental attunements receptive to other, non-Nietzschean ontological self-understandings
could appeal even to "happy enframers," on the grounds that learning such a comportment (in which we experience the being of entities as being richer than we are capable of
ever doing full justice to conceptually) will enrich their lives by increasing the density of
their experience. That is an appeal the happy enframer would appreciate, even though
(I argue in Chapter 4) successfully learning such a comportment would ultimately help
them to transcend the very Nietzschean ontotheology with which they had previously
thought themselves happy.

the domain of technological entities. He will thus remain convinced that the appropriate treatment of this problem (which we will focus on in Chapter 4) needs to address its ontotheological roots, and not just its technological symptoms.

§10. CONCLUSIONS: VINDICATING HEIDEGGER'S CRITIQUE

To sum up, then, Heidegger appears to be a technological essentialist, but of a largely unobjectionable variety. For, as we have seen, he rejects ahistoricism entirely, and the forms of one-dimensionalism and substantivism he accepts lack these doctrines' usual negative implications. Indeed, Heidegger's substantivism offers an indirect response to Feenberg's political objection, a response driven by a more thorough and plausible philosophical analysis than the voluntaristically motivated objection, and Heidegger's one-dimensionalism clearly does not force him into any global rejection of technology. His rather limited technological essentialism thus does little to discredit his profound ontological understanding of the historical impact of technology.[61] Thus, although the main charges frequently leveled against Heidegger's critique of technology are succinctly consolidated and advanced by Feenberg's objections that Heidegger's understanding of the essence of technology ("enframing") is ahistorical, substantivist (or *fatalistic*), and one-dimensionalism (or *indiscriminate*), we have seen that either these objections are persuasively countered (as with the charges of ahistoricism and substantivism), or else the impact of the criticism is greatly softened (as in the case of one-dimensionalism), once we appreciate the way in which Heidegger's critique of enframing follows from his philosophical understanding of the way the ontotheology we late moderns have inherited from Nietzsche continues implicitly to shape and circumscribe our experience. This conclusion not only helps vindicate Heidegger's groundbreaking critique of technology, it also provides further evidence for the overarching thesis I have sought to establish thus far, namely, that Heidegger's understanding of ontotheology provides the crucial philosophical background motivating much of his later thought. Hence, treated in isolation from

---

[61] Although Feenberg's rhetoric sometimes obscures this fact, his important critical theory of technology clearly has learned a great deal from the ontological and phenomenological subtleties found in Heidegger's work (as he forthrightly acknowledged in our earlier exchange), and there is every reason to suppose that Feenberg and future philosophers of technology will continue to find in Heidegger's reflections a challenging and rewarding source of philosophical inspiration.

this understanding of ontotheology, some of the later Heidegger's main philosophical views – such as the famous critique of "enframing" examined here – can indeed seem quite arbitrary and indefensible. When such views are recognized as following directly from Heidegger's understanding of ontotheology, however, their full philosophical depth and significance begins to emerge with new clarity.

By recognizing the great importance of the later Heidegger's long-overlooked views on ontotheology, we have been able to answer some long-standing objections to the later Heidegger's complex and controversial critique of technology. Still, some of the strongest support for Heidegger's critique of technology comes from the revealing light this critique casts on our own current crisis in higher education. We will examine this connection in Chapter 4, elucidating Heidegger's critique of the technologization of higher education and developing his insightful pedagogical suggestions for how we can move from diagnosing to actually addressing the problem. Yet, because the development of Heidegger's philosophical views on education was deeply entangled with his appalling decision to join the National Socialist movement in 1933, we will need to examine this political dimension of his thought carefully before seeking to critically appropriate and build upon any of his pedagogical views. The justification for yet another treatment of these complex and controversial political matters is not merely negative, however. I think we can reach a philosophically more satisfying understanding of this highly controversial issue by approaching it on the basis of the insight gained thus far into his critique of ontotheology. If this is right, moreover, it too will reinforce my overarching thesis that Heidegger's views on ontotheology are crucial for understanding his later thought. In any case, the furious debates that raged over the "Heidegger controversy" throughout the 1990s seem only to have entrenched the polarized standoff between the prosecution and defense, so the time may well be ripe for an attempt to recast the matter in another light, one which will illuminate not only the terrible mistakes of the past (Chapter 3), but also the real needs of the future (Chapter 4).

3

Heidegger and the Politics of the University

§11. HEIDEGGER AND NATIONAL SOCIALISM

A. Introduction

It is unfortunate but in retrospect undeniable that Heidegger's brief but very public tenure as the first Nazi Rector of Freiburg University in 1933–1934 helped cast an early sheen of intellectual legitimacy over the brutal regime that, less than a decade later, earned everlasting historical infamy for Auschwitz and the other horrors of the Shoah.[1] The question for many of us, then, is this: How do we come to terms with the fact that the man who was probably the greatest philosopher of the twentieth century threw the considerable weight of his thought behind what was certainly its most execrable political movement? This profoundly troubling juxtaposition has haunted intellectuals for seventy years, generating a secondary literature of singular immensity. Although the debates carried on in this literature are multifaceted and complex, an historical examination of this "Heidegger controversy" shows that it has long had the character of a trial, both before it actually became one and after Heidegger himself was no longer alive to stand trial.[2] An "accuse or

---

[1] One of the terrible ironies here is that Heidegger, because of his international fame as the author of *Being and Time* (1927), helped to intellectually legitimize the National Socialist movement in the early 1930s, despite the basic truth behind Gadamer's blunt assertion that "the real Nazis had no interest in us at all" (*Gadamer in Conversation*, 128). In *Heidegger's Crisis: Philosophy and Politics in Nazi Germany*, Hans Sluga substantiates Gadamer's controversial statement about the role of philosophy in the rise of the Third Reich.

[2] Q&A and HC collect many of the primary texts at the heart of the controversy over the significance of Heidegger's Nazi affiliation. The best succinct introduction to the

excuse" dichotomy still structures the field of competing interpretations, obliging scholars to take sides, as though with either the prosecution or the defense. Unfortunately, this adversarial logic increasingly dominates the public sphere in the West, its common spectacle of talking heads talking past one another working to obscure the fact that in complex matters the truth is usually located between the opposing extremes, and so is unfit for the polemical purposes of demagogues on either side. Such a binary polarization has long diminished the signal-to-noise ratio of the so-called Heidegger case by putting the juridical imperative to either condemn or exonerate before the hermeneutic necessity first to understand.

One of our main goals here in Chapter 3, accordingly, is just to understand something of the relationship between Heidegger's philosophy and his politics. (Throughout, "politics" is a convenient shorthand for what Wolin characterizes less euphemistically as Heidegger's "short-lived, though concerted, partisanship for Hitler's regime.")[3] Recently, scholars such as Michael Zimmerman, Hans Sluga, and Domenico Losurdo have done invaluable work situating Heidegger within the broader context of the many German intellectuals who implicitly contributed to or actively collaborated with the rise of the (self-proclaimed) National Socialist Workers' Party, but such approaches tend not to focus on what I take to be the most direct connection between Heidegger's philosophy and his politics, which is precisely what those of us particularly

---

philosophical issues is Dreyfus, "Heidegger on the Connection between Nihilism, Art, Technology, and Politics." The two most important in-depth treatments remain the formidable critique advanced by Wolin in *The Politics of Being: The Political Thought of Martin Heidegger* and the strong defense mounted by Young in *Heidegger, Philosophy, Nazism.* Safranski's *Heidegger: Between Good and Evil* is less philosophical but provides a balanced narrative. On the specific philosophical views responsible for Heidegger's attempt to transform the university, see Crowell's "Philosophy as a Vocation: Heidegger and University Reform in the Early Interwar Years," Milchman and Rosenberg's "Martin Heidegger and the University as a Site for the Transformation of Human Existence," de Beistegui's *Heidegger and the Political: Dystopias,* and below. On Heidegger and the Shoah, see Berel Lang's *Heidegger's Silence* and Agamben's *Remnants of Auschwitz: The Witness and the Archive.* I provide a synoptic treatment of the historical debate in "The End of Ontotheology," 246–367.

3 "Karl Löwith and Martin Heidegger – Contexts and Conversations: An Introduction," in Löwith, *Martin Heidegger and European Nihilism,* 7. Wolin believes Heidegger's "disillusionment with Nazism dates from the moment when the movement abandoned its original revolutionary élan – the Röhm purge of June 1934 – and consolidated itself qua regime" (*Heidegger's Children,* 67). New historical evidence, however, challenges this view (see note 91).

interested in Heidegger find most important – and troubling.[4] I will thus adopt a narrower approach here by addressing the following two linked questions.

Q₁, *Did Heidegger's politics stem directly from his philosophy?*

Q₂, If so, *did Heidegger learn anything philosophically from (what he called) his terrible "political mistake"?*

Although we cannot investigate all the myriad connections that have been proposed to obtain between Heidegger's philosophy and politics, nor the many possible lessons he might have learned subsequently from these supposed connections, I believe we can say enough to answer "yes" to both questions nevertheless.[5] Indeed, I shall devote much of Chapter 3 to developing what I take to be the most convincing affirmative answer to Q₁, to establishing, in other words, the most direct connection between Heidegger's philosophy and his politics.[6] This will then allow us to address Q₂ within the purview of Q₁, thereby showing as precisely as possible at least one important lesson that Heidegger learned from this connection between his thought and National Socialism.

Of course, because I seek to establish a direct relationship between Heidegger's philosophy and his politics, my interpretation is likely to run afoul of the aforementioned controversy – despite the fact that Heidegger himself affirmed just such a connection in no uncertain terms (a point to we will return in Section 14).[7] For, in order to deflect the many precipitous attempts to use Heidegger's politics simply to dismiss his thought outright (a move no serious critic makes today), Heideggerians have become accustomed to rigidly separating Heidegger's philosophy from his politics. Even eminent thinkers such as Rorty, Schürmann, Jean-François Lyotard, Pöggeler, and Olafson employ this strategy, thereby seeking to

---

4 See Zimmerman's *Heidegger's Confrontation with Modernity*, Sluga's *Heidegger's Crisis*, and Losurdo's *Heidegger and the Ideology of War*.

5 Here the most significant and provocative works include Derrida's *Of Spirit: Heidegger and the Question*, Lacoue-Labarthe's *Heidegger, Art, and Politics: The Fiction of the Political*, Dallmayr's *The Other Heidegger*, Young's *Heidegger, Philosophy, Nazism*, Rickey's *Revolutionary Saints: Heidegger, National Socialism, and Antinomian Politics*, and Bambach's *Heidegger's Roots: Nietzsche, National Socialism, and the Greeks*.

6 Only in this way will we seek to address what Dreyfus calls "the central question," namely, "to what extent was Heidegger's support and then rejection of National Socialism a personal mistake compounded of conservative prejudices, personal ambition, and political *naïveté*, and to what extent was his engagement dictated by his philosophy?" ("Mixing Interpretation, Religion, and Politics: Heidegger's High-Risk Thinking," 19). For, by establishing a direct connection between Heidegger's philosophy and politics, I do not purport to completely explain (let alone justify) his terrible political decision.

7 See Löwith, *My Life in Germany Before and After 1933*, 60.

insulate Heidegger's important philosophical achievements from what he later called his life's "greatest stupidity."[8] Gadamer, however, is right to observe of the claim that Heidegger's "political errors have nothing to do with his philosophy," that: "Wholly unnoticed was how damaging such a 'defense' of so important a thinker really is."[9] As a defensive strategy, moreover, such a move is fatally flawed, for it accepts the major premise of the most devastating political criticisms of Heidegger: The idea that Heidegger's politics are unrelated to his thought forms the basis of the accusations that his politics represent arbitrary *decisionism* (Wolin), careerist *opportunism* (Pierre Bourdieu), and even the fundamental *betrayal* of his philosophy (Marcuse).[10] Here, however, both prosecution and defense fail to do justice to the philosophical integrity of Heidegger's work. The ongoing publication of his *Complete Works* makes it increasingly obvious that Heidegger regularly invoked his own philosophical views as justifications for his political decisions, and, as a result, even long-embattled Heideggerians are beginning to realize that a firm separation of Heidegger's politics from his philosophy is no longer tenable. Thus Rorty recently supplemented his well-known counterfactual argument that Heidegger's politics are philosophically irrelevant (because,

---

[8] See Schürmann, *Heidegger on Being and Acting*, 3; Rorty, "Taking Philosophy Seriously," 32; Lyotard, *Heidegger and "the Jews,"* 59; Olafson, *Heidegger and the Ground of Ethics*, 13–14; and Pöggeler's comments in the "Concluding Discussion" of Harries and Jamme, eds., *Martin Heidegger*, 247. Although these thinkers give us slightly different versions of the thesis that Heidegger's politics have at most a merely contingent or adventitious relation to his philosophy, Norris is right that this "last-ditch saving strategy" should be understood in terms of its usefulness for dealing with the "crude *ad hominem* abuse" which has been an all-too-common feature of what Dreyfus calls "the journalistic chatter surrounding Heidegger's political past" (Norris, *What's Wrong with Postmodernism*, 222–3; Dreyfus, "Mixing Interpretation, Religion, and Politics," 17).

[9] "Back from Syracuse?," 428.

[10] Wolin, *The Politics of Being*, 52; Bourdieu, *The Political Ontology of Martin Heidegger*, 70–3; Olafson, "Heidegger's Politics: An Interview with Herbert Marcuse," 99–100; and Marcuse, "The Struggle Against Liberalism in the Totalitarian View of the State," *Negations*, 41. For Bourdieu, it is Heidegger who, aided by insecure Heideggerians seeking to prove they are *really* philosophers, represses the fact that Heidegger's "philosophy is political from beginning to end" (*The Political Ontology of Martin Heidegger*, 96). According to Bourdieu's reductive "socioanalysis," Heidegger's repressed "id, his unthought – that of an 'ordinary university professor' – and the entire train of social phantasms [generated by Heidegger's position in the academic field] . . . led around by the nose this small bearer of a cultural capital . . . whose 'fixed assets' were in danger." See Bourdieu, "Back to History: An Interview" (HC 277). Against Bourdieu, however, Randall Collins shows that "the intellectual field is not homologous to the social and political field," but has its own imminent and irreducible logic (*The Sociology of Philosophies*, 1019 note 41). On this point, see also Dreyfus and Rabinow, "Can There Be a Science of Existential Structure and Social Meaning?"

Rorty imagined, Heidegger could have lived a politically blameless life and still written essentially the same philosophical works).[11] Tellingly, Rorty now judges that "Heidegger's books will be read for centuries to come, but the smell of smoke from the crematories – 'the grave in the air' – will linger on these pages."[12]

As Rorty poignantly suggests (the interjected quote is from Paul Celan's powerful "Death Fugue"), another question haunts the two we will focus on here, and it is perhaps the most vexed: What was Heidegger's relationship to Nazi anti-Semitism, and so to the Shoah? My first sentence in this section expresses the general view I take on this disturbing issue. Many edifying details from the exculpatory narrative long disseminated by Heidegger and his most loyal followers – for example, that Heidegger became Rector of Freiburg reluctantly, and did so only in order to use his fame to protect his Jewish colleagues, students, and the academic freedom of the university – have been seriously compromised by the facts. We now know, for instance, that Heidegger occasionally resorted to strategic uses of anti-Semitism in the service of his academic political goals, and that this led (after a letter from Heidegger containing a derogatory reference to "the Jew Fraenkel" was leaked to Karl Jaspers) to Heidegger's indefinite loss of his teaching license and his subsequent hospitalization for depression.[13] At the same time, however, even Heidegger's

---

[11] "On Heidegger's Nazism," *Philosophy and Social Hope* (originally published as "Another Possible World," *London Review of Books*, 8 February 1990). Few Heidegger scholars find Rorty's edifying "other possible world" plausible, since it denies the existential intertwinement of life and thought Heidegger himself always insisted on before 1933. In the end, Rorty comes to the unlikely conclusion that "Heidegger was only accidentally a Nazi" ("Philosophy as Science, as Metaphor, and as Politics," 23).

[12] "A Master from Germany," 2. The title of Rorty's review of Safranski draws attention to the fact that the original title of Safranski's book (*Ein Meister aus Deutschland*) is an oblique reference to Celan's most famous poem, "Death Fugue," where Celan says that "death is a master from Germany" and evokes "the grave in the clouds" of ash hanging over the death camps. (See Paul Celan, *Poems of Paul Celan*, 60–3; cf. Wolin, "Review of *Martin Heidegger: Between Good and Evil*, by Rüdiger Safranski.")

[13] In letters to Jaspers in 1950, however, Heidegger mentions his sense of "shame" when thinking of Jaspers's Jewish wife, refers to "the worst evil [that] set in with the vile persecutions," and says that "from year to year, as more viciousness came out, the sense of shame also grew over having here and there, directly and indirectly, contributed to it.... Then came the persecution of the Jews, and everything fell into the abyss" (HJC 185, 189). The full context of this politically important correspondence deserves to be carefully unpacked. Before 1934 Heidegger and Jaspers were "comrades-in-arms" in the project to revolutionize the university, but they remained permanently estranged afterward owing to Heidegger's unwillingness to apologize to Jaspers for the letter mentioned in the text below (which also contained a politically threatening allusion to Jaspers's "liberal democratic circle of Heidelberg intellectuals" [HJC 209]). Nevertheless, Jaspers would finally

critics acknowledge that he publicly condemned the "biologistic" racial metaphysics behind the Nazi "final solution" to Marx's "Jewish question," and that he did help some Jewish colleagues and students.[14] Moreover, although Heidegger never made the kind of public apology for which Marcuse and others long called, he did not in fact remain "silent" on the Shoah. A 1949 lecture proclaimed "the manufacture of corpses in the gas chambers and the death camps" to be "in essence the same" as mechanized agribusiness (GA79 27), that is, more and less obvious symptoms of our nihilistic, "technological" understanding of being. Such a proclamation may be "scandalously inadequate" (as Lacoue-Labarthe writes), but the point is that, for Heidegger, the inhumanly rational mentality capable of devising such a horribly efficient network of technological processes for the "mass production of corpses" (Arendt) – factories for stripping human beings of all their potentially reusable resources (from fillings to hair), murdering them *en masse*, then reducing them to ashes (Celan's "graves in the air"), a process by which thirty thousand innocents could be, and were, murdered in a single twenty-four-hour period in the Auschwitz death camps alone – appears to be a particularly vivid and horrifying fulfillment of the underlying metaphysical logic that "liquidates" human beings by reducing them to *Bestand*, "resources," mere "items of material available for the manufacture of corpses [*Bestandstücke eines Bestandes der Fabrikation von Leichen*]" (GA79 56).[15] Of course, until

conclude in 1966 that Heidegger expressed "the usual clichés about '"the international [Jewish conspiracy],' etc., but without inner-conviction. He was no 'anti-Semite'" (HJC 281 note 5). See also Q&A 15–22; Ott, *Martin Heidegger: A Political Life*, 190; Safranski, *Martin Heidegger*, 272–3; and Sheehan, "'Everyone Has to Tell the Truth,'" 30–44.

[14] See Wolin, *The Politics of Being*, 4–6; and Safranski, *Martin Heidegger*, 248–75, which also shows the notorious and persistent rumor that Heidegger barred Husserl from Freiberg's library to be completely false.

[15] On the Heidegger–Marcuse relation, see my "From the Question Concerning Technology to the Quest for a Democratic Technology." On the philosophical significance of Heidegger's deliberately provocative remark, see Young, *Heidegger, Philosophy, Nazism*, 181–7; and Agamben, *Remnants of Auschwitz*, 73–86. Lyotard observes that this "'program' of extermination . . . [was] carried out in the manner of an industrial cleanup operation" (*Heidegger and "the Jews,"* 81, 84), and Shirer reminds us that German corporations competed for the contracts to build the gas chambers, registering numerous patents for horrifically efficient devices directly inspired by the technological advances Henry Ford pioneered in conveyor-belt-driven production lines (*The Rise and Fall of the Third Reich*). Arendt went so far as to doubt that such a "mass production of corpses" could even be called "murder" (*The Origins of Totalitarianism*, 139). Certainly this was a different form of murder than history, innumerable atrocities notwithstanding, had ever witnessed before; as Edith Wyschogrod explains: "What is unprecedented in the new phenomenon [of "man-made mass death . . . epitomized in the names 'Hiroshima' and 'Auschwitz'"] is

the notoriously secretive Heidegger archives all come to light, it is only
reasonable to expect this troubling issue to continue to animate and
inform the Heidegger controversy. For the current range of views, one
need only compare the undeniably important but diametrically opposed
treatises on the subject by Wolin and Julian Young.[16] Neither critic nor
defender, however, maintains that Heidegger's decision to join the Nazis
can be explained by anti-Semitism.

To find the philosophical explanation for Heidegger's terrible political
decision, we need instead to turn to what I take to be the most immediate connection between his philosophy and politics, namely, his long-
developed philosophical vision for a radical reformation of the university.
For, as I shall show here, Heidegger's philosophical views on higher education were largely responsible for his decision to become the first Nazi
Rector of Freiburg University. In 1933, Heidegger seized on the National
Socialist "revolution" as an opportunity to enact the philosophical vision
for a radical reformation of the university that he had in fact been developing since 1911. The full depth and significance of this fact only begins
to become clear, however, when we understand Heidegger's complex but
politically crucial view of the relationship between philosophy and the
other academic disciplines, his proposed research program driven by that
view, and the transformations in this research program suggested by his
later insights into ontotheology. These are the tasks that will occupy most
of Chapter 3. If I am right, moreover, that Heidegger's long-developed
philosophical vision for a radical reformation of the university provides
the most compelling affirmative answer to Q_1, showing *how* Heidegger's
politics stem from his philosophical views, then this helps us bring Q_2,
the question of what Heidegger might have learned from this connection, into much sharper focus. For reasons that will now become clear, I
shall henceforth refer to Q_2 – the question of *what Heidegger learned* – as
"the Confucian question."

that the means of annihilation are the result of systematic rational calculation" (*Spirit in
Ashes: Hegel, Heidegger, and Man-Made Mass Death*, ix–x). This "industrialization of death"
is what Heidegger has in mind when he breaks his notorious "silence" in order to assert
that "Agriculture is now a mechanized food industry, the same thing in its essence as the
production of corpses in the gas chambers and the extermination camps." "This statement," as Lacoue-Labarthe observes, is both "scandalously inadequate" and "absolutely
correct" (*Heidegger, Art, and Politics*, 34, 36). On this difficult topic, see also Elisabeth De
Fonteney, "'In Its Essence the Same Thing,'" 236–45; Lyotard, *Heidegger and "the Jews,"*
83–9; and Lang, *Heidegger's Silence*, 16–19.
16 Wolin's *The Politics of Being* and Young's *Heidegger, Philosophy, Nazism* remain indispensable
works.

B. The Confucian Question

An ancient proverb ran, "He who learns but does not think is lost." Confucius added, "He who thinks but does not learn is in great danger."[17]

If this proverb's exhortation to thinking sounds paradigmatically Heideggerian, Confucius's wise rejoinder helps raise that haunting political question: What, if anything, did Heidegger *learn* from his appalling misadventure with Nazism? Heidegger told *Der Spiegel* that he reached his infamous political decision "by way of the university." If, as I believe, Heidegger's philosophical views on higher education were largely responsible for his decision to become the first Nazi Rector of Freiburg University in 1933, then one of our Confucian questions becomes: Did Heidegger learn from what he later called his "life's greatest stupidity" and transform the underlying philosophical views that helped motivate this "political mistake"?[18]

The only scholars to address this question, Pöggeler and Derrida, both think so. We will examine their interpretations in Section 16, once we are in a better position to evaluate them. Obviously, we need to understand Heidegger's early views on university education before we can decide whether or not he changed these views after the war. This task is complicated, however, by the fact that Heidegger's early work on the university turns out to be less philosophically homogenous than previously supposed. Because, as Aristotle observed, "The best way to study politics and other matters is to trace things back to their beginnings and observe their growth," our first major goal will be to reconstruct the development of Heidegger's views on higher education during the period between 1911 and 1933. Proceeding chronologically, we will try to do justice to the most politically significant aspects of these views without claiming to exhaust them. Along the way, we will sketch the later Heidegger's mature philosophical understanding of the genuine task of university

---

[17] *The Analects of Confucius*, II.11, 91 (translation modified). It is hard to know how much Heidegger might have learned from Confucius. As Pöggeler rather pointedly asked (and we should hear the political echo of his question), "Why Heraclitus and Lao-Tzu? Why not Isaiah and Confucius?" ("West–East Dialogue: Heidegger and Lao Tzu," in Parkes, ed., *Heidegger and Asian Thought*, 66). Did Heidegger read Confucius? Paul Hsiao says "an engagement" took place, but his evidence is merely anecdotal ("Heidegger and Our Translation of the *Tao Te Ching*," *Heidegger and Asian Thought*, 93, 96).

[18] See Heidegger, "Only a God Can Save Us" (HC 103); Petzet, "Afterthoughts on the Spiegel Interview" (Q&A 72); Crowell's "Philosophy as a Vocation," 256 (among the first works to emphasize this important connection); and Petzet, *Encounters and Dialogues with Martin Heidegger*, 37.

education (which will then be developed in greater detail in Chapter 4). With both goals accomplished, we will be able to determine whether Pöggeler and Derrida are right that Heidegger's mature work represents a philosophically significant departure from his politically compromised earlier views on university education, or whether, on the contrary, Heidegger never abandoned the main philosophical views that led him to throw his philosophical weight behind the National Socialist movement in the early 1930s.[19]

Of course, even if Heidegger learned nothing from his failed "bid to become the *Führer*, not merely of Freiburg University, but of German higher education as a whole," we could still learn from him.[20] For one thing, as Confucius remarked, the vigilant student can learn from the bad example as well as the good. At the same time, however, Confucius warned students to be wary of spending too much time with these bad examples, lest they become bad examples themselves. In our context, this warning brings to mind the damning judgment Jaspers issued to the postwar "de-Nazification" committee at Freiburg University, to the effect that Heidegger was a politically dangerous teacher, a mystagogue and corrupter of the young.[21] If we take the worry that there is something

---

[19] See Aristotle, *Politics*, 1252a25–6. Heidegger's official entrance into Nazi politics came not in May 1933, with his assumption of the Rectorship (as he and apologists have long maintained), but rather in March, when he joined "the Cultural–Political Working Community of German University Teachers, a kind of National Socialist group within the German Academic's Association" (Safranski, *Martin Heidegger*, 235; see also Chapter 2, note 37, above).

[20] Milchman and Rosenberg, "Martin Heidegger and the University as a Site for the Transformation of Human Existence," 91.

[21] Ironies abound here. Not only was Jaspers Heidegger's main "comrade-in-arms" in their ambitious project to revolutionize the university in the years leading up to Heidegger's assumption of the Rectorate (see note 13 earlier), but Jaspers wrote Heidegger on 23 August 1933 to say that reading Heidegger's Rectorial Address "affected me again like a new, but at the same time obvious truth.... [Y]our address has genuine substance ... [making] this address the only document of an actual academic will and one which will last." Jaspers assures Heidegger of his "trust in your [Heidegger's] philosophizing," and even writes: "I cannot do otherwise than find the new constitution right," referring to a constitution that instituted the two main *Gleichschaltung* (or political realignment) measures of "radically assimilating university structures to the Führer principle and in subordinating the university to political supremacy." The editors of their correspondence rightly conclude that in 1933, Jaspers, like Heidegger, "seems to agree with [the institution of] the Führer principle within the university," that Jaspers too was convinced that "the moment is decisive for the future of the university" (as Jaspers wrote in July 1933), and that "with the new regime, a rational renewal of the university could be carried out under certain conditions, insofar as it ordered what leading scholars prompt it to do, but, if the regime doesn't listen, the final downfall of the university is imminent." Jaspers does, however, want to be sure to hold the new leaders "responsible for their mistakes," and, more generally, to counter "the increasing misuse

politically dangerous about Heidegger's philosophical views on university education as our point of departure (which also means the point we will seek to move beyond), this is not out of deference to Jaspers's dubious and hypocritical judgment, nor to demonize Heidegger and so provide another edifying discourse for our Western liberal good conscience. Rather, it is simply because Heidegger's views on the university constitute the troubling domain in which his philosophy most directly intersected with his politics. Indeed, when one cuts through the haze of hermeneutic distortions surrounding the "Heidegger controversy" and critically examines Heidegger's concrete political interventions circa 1933, it becomes clear that these consist almost entirely in attempts to transform the German university and, through it, Germany itself. Thus, as Miguel de Beistegui keenly observes, "to understand Heidegger's entrance onto the stage of politics, to throw any significant light on his action and his declarations as a prominent figure of the early stages of Nazi Germany would primarily amount to clarifying his conception of science, of the university as an institution and of its relation to the nation as a whole."[22] Let us thus take up this task.

§12. HEIDEGGER'S EARLIEST VIEWS ON UNIVERSITY EDUCATION (1911)

Focusing on Heidegger's early work (1911–1929), scholars such as Theodore Kisiel, John van Buren, Steven Crowell, and Alan Milchman

---

of freedom" across the board through "the exclusion of those who fail." (See HJC 36, 149–50, 254, note 4; the editors summarize Jaspers's unpublished "Theses on the Question of University Renewal." See also Pöggeler, *The Paths of Heidegger's Life and Thought*, 46–8.) Indeed, Jaspers clearly influenced Heidegger's views; when Jaspers addressed the subject of "education" in his 1930 treatise, *Man in the Modern Age*, he contended that: "Today the burning question is whether it will be possible, out of the sources of contemporary life . . . to establish a new community of popular educators, workers, employees, and peasants . . . a community which, transcending occupation and party, will bring together human beings as such . . . once again to become a nation," a nation "conformable with *Volk* in the genuine sense of the term" (113, 118). In 1945, however, when Heidegger had Jaspers's opinion solicited (assuming his old ally would be a friendly witness), Jaspers rendered the judgment to Freiberg's de-Nazification committee that led to the revocation of Heidegger's teaching license (until 1951): "Heidegger's mode of thinking, which seems to me to be fundamentally unfree, dictatorial and uncommunicative, would have a very damaging effect on students at the present time. . . . I think it would be quite wrong to turn such a teacher loose on the young people of today" (quoted by Ott, *Martin Heidegger*, 339). The irony is only compounded here by the striking (if no doubt unintentional) likeness Jaspers's judgment bears to the infamous indictment that convicted Socrates.

[22] *Heidegger and the Political*, 33.

and Alan Rosenberg show that Heidegger's radical critique of the university significantly antedates the rise of the National Socialist "revolution."[23] In the early 1930s, the rise of Nazism provided Heidegger with the opportunity to attempt to realize his long-developed philosophical vision for a radical reformation of the German university. Although this ambitiously conceived attempt was quickly aborted, the project itself has its roots in Heidegger's very earliest work.

In 1911, while still studying theology at Freiburg University, the twenty-two-year-old Heidegger published a short but ambitious article, "Toward a Philosophical Orientation for Academics," in the conservative Catholic journal *The Academic*. Here Heidegger, already highly critical of the academic status quo, employs what would become one of his trademark distinctions in order to differentiate the current state of affairs in "philosophy" from a more genuine "thinking." "Philosophy," he begins, is "in truth a mirror of the eternal," but "'Thinking' can no longer let itself be constrained by the eternally immobile limits of logical propositions." When thinking accepts the yoke of formal validity and so forces itself merely to string propositions together, the result, Heidegger presciently warns, is that mere "connoisseurship in philosophical questions which has already become a sport." The young Heidegger sees signs of hope, however, for even among those philosophers who seem content to do no more than seek to solve logical puzzles, "occasionally – despite so much smug self-consciousness – the unconscious longing breaks out for fulfilled, fulfilling answers to the ultimate questions of being, questions which suddenly flash up, and then lie unresolved, like lead weights, in the tortured soul deprived of goals and ways" (TPOA 496–7/GA16 11).[24]

This 1911 invocation of the "ultimate questions of being" (*Endfragen des Seins*) clearly anticipates Heidegger's famous "question of being" (*Seinsfrage*).[25] Unfortunately, Heidegger inadvertently complicated the interpretation of this early article when he neglected to schedule it – or

[23] See the important works by Kisiel, *The Genesis of Heidegger's* Being and Time, xiii; Crowell, "Philosophy as a Vocation," 255–6 (my interpretation builds on this groundbreaking essay); Milchman and Rosenberg, "Martin Heidegger and the University," 77, 80–6; van Buren, *The Young Heidegger: Rumor of the Hidden King*, 352–7; and de Beistegui, *Heidegger and the Political*, 42–63.

[24] Cf. Pöggeler, *The Paths of Heidegger's Life and Thought*, 8.

[25] Here Heidegger calls for reposing traditional questions concerning the ultimate meaning of being; sixteen years later, *Being and Time* famously opens with an attempt to "reawaken" the question of the meaning of being in general (B&T 1/S&Z 1). In 1907, Heidegger began his formative reading of Franz Brentano's *The Manifold Senses of Being in Aristotle*; see his "My Way to Phenomenology" (T&B 74/ZSD 81).

any of the seven other contributions he made to *The Academic* between 1910 and 1912 – for inclusion in his supposedly "*Complete Works*" (*Gesamtausgabe*). This editorial oversight has now been rectified, but Hugo Ott, who first brought these early publications to the attention of scholars, interpreted Heidegger's omission of his *Jugendschriften* rather melodramatically, as a deliberate "suppression" of the Catholic origins to which, Ott misleadingly claimed, Heidegger later came back full circle. This reception history is significant because John van Buren, the only scholar to interpret this early piece in terms of Heidegger's critique of the university, too closely follows Ott's interpretive overemphasis on Heidegger's Catholicism. Van Buren interprets Heidegger's early article as an expression of "ultraconservative Catholicism," thereby ignoring the subtle but important means by which Heidegger, a young scholar in a professionally precarious position, signals the distinctiveness of his own views, and so also their ambivalent distance from the ideology of the Catholic authorities allowing his work to appear.[26],[27]

For it is true that the young Heidegger, still hoping for a career as a professor of theology, pays homage in this early article to the pedagogical need for fulfilling *answers*, and thus to the need for "a more thorough apologetic education," which, he implies, could supply such answers. At the same time, however, Heidegger suggests that these fulfilling answers can arise only through a pursuit of the ultimate *questions* of being. Indeed, what makes the "apologetic education" he calls for "more thorough" is precisely the ontological questioning he seeks to move to the center of the theology curriculum. Such philosophical studies provide

---

[26] See Ott, *Martin Heidegger*, 384; Ott's "Preface" to "Heidegger's Contributions to *Der Akademiker*," 481–5; and van Buren, *The Young Heidegger*, 122–9, 355. Van Buren's incisive characterization of Heidegger's position as "revolutionary conservatism" (125) strikes much closer to the mark. Heidegger's essays for *The Academic* have now been published in GA16.

[27] In 1910, the Catholic church began requiring clerics to swear an "oath against modernism" (see Young, *Heidegger, Philosophy, Nazism*, 28). Read a bit against the grain (but in the direction his thought was moving), the proclamation with which Heidegger opens this 1911 essay – namely, that philosophical thinking "can no longer let itself be constrained by the eternally immobile limits of logical propositions" – also suggests (as though hiding his own ambivalence in plain sight) Heidegger's unwillingness to agree ahead of time that the results of his philosophical investigations will stay within the boundaries set by papal fiat. Insofar as this is right, it reinforces my claim, pace Ott and van Buren, that the young Heidegger is already more ambivalent about Catholicism and modernism than his explicit remarks suggest. Further support for this reading can be found in Robert Vigliotti's "The Young Heidegger's Ambitions for the Chair of Catholic Philosophy and Hugo Ott's Charge of Opportunism."

"a solid foundation" (*eine gründliche Fundamentierung*) for "theological knowledge." In effect, Heidegger presents the philosophical pursuit of the "ultimate questions of being" as a necessary prerequisite to the discovery of fulfilling theological answers. This, then, is the "philosophical orientation" he advocates: Theological answers should be grounded in ontological questioning.

In order to motivate this unlikely call for his conservative Catholic colleagues to recognize the pedagogical primacy of ontological questioning and transform the university curriculum accordingly, Heidegger implies that this transformation is made necessary by distinctively modern pedagogical problems. If theology is to continue providing the "goals and ways" without which modern "students lose themselves in the face of all the various things which distract, interest, and mobilize them," then the theology curriculum must encourage students to pursue the ultimate questions of being. Otherwise, Heidegger emphasizes (with a bit of Nietzschean word-play), the "estranging entanglements" (*Fremdverwicklung*) of the modern world will alienate students from their "personal development" (*Eigentwicklung*). Heidegger's word-play has a serious intent. *Eigentwicklung* connotes the "unfolding of that which is one's own," a coinage which allows him to raise obliquely, in an antimodern journal, the problem at the center of modern philosophy of education debates: the famous *Bildungsfrage*, the question of how education can best serve the "cultivation" or "development" of essential human capacities. What is more, Heidegger implicitly *answers* this *Bildungsfrage* when he suggests that ontological questioning will help students stay focused on developing that which is most their own and thereby avoid the alienating entanglements of the modern world. Here we thus witness a crucial moment in the development of Heidegger's critique of higher education – the first appearance of a general strategy for university reform he will never subsequently abandon – namely, his attempt to answer the *Bildungsfrage* by yoking pedagogical reform to ontological questioning (TPOA 496–501/GA16 11–14).

Although the young Heidegger makes the important suggestion that ontological questioning will answer the *Bildungsfrage*, he is not yet able to say much about *how* it will do so. He admits that "this fundamental demand [that academics should help students develop that which is their own] includes, along with its great inner worth, *the entire difficulty of how adequately to fulfill it*" (TPOA 496–7/GA16 11, my emphasis).[28] The

---

[28] Complaining that the *Bildung* ideal had degenerated into a belle-lettrist concern with the cultivation of taste, Heidegger will tend to resist using the word in a nonpejorative

Bildungsfrage thus remains a "problem" that academics "must face up to all the more energetically." It is important to observe, however, that the young Heidegger's suggestions for a solution to the problem of *Bildung*, although meager, are markedly *individualistic*. Indeed, he throws almost the entire task of self-development back onto the students themselves: "Young minds search, driven by an inner, magical urge for truth," and must be allowed the "justified egoism" of developing that which is their own. The sole philosophical guidance Heidegger offers at this point consists in his recommendation of several introductory philosophy texts along with the stern advice that only intensive personal study will allow students to acquire the philosophical background necessary for a genuine appropriation of the theological tradition. Only "an undaunted, unceasing activity on one's own part" will allow students to "secure" the philosophical "preknowledge" necessary for appropriating the theological tradition's "treasure of truths." "One only possesses truth in a genuine sense when one has made it one's own in this way." Pace Ott and van Buren, I submit that such calls for the individual to personally reappropriate the living core of the tradition put Heidegger closer to Protestantism than to "ultraconservative Catholicism."[29]

If we step back, then, we can see that Heidegger's earliest critique of university education is marked by a series of unstable tensions: He situates himself politically as a conservative Catholic but provides strategic advice that sounds programmatically Protestant; he writes as a theologian, yet

---

sense until 1941, when (as we will see in Chapter 4) he seeks to recover its "true or genuine" meaning by reconnecting it to the Platonic conception of *paideia*.

[29] Most readings of Heidegger's earliest work tend to overlook this strong individualistic streak, a testament to his formative early encounters with Luther and Kierkegaard (but see Guignon's excellent "Introduction" to the *Cambridge Companion to Heidegger*; Alastair Hannay's *Kierkegaard: A Biography*, 357–8; and Bambach's *Heidegger, Dilthey, and the Crisis of Historicism*, 201–2) as well as evidence of the influence of German Idealism, the *locus originarius* of the modern *Bildungsfrage*. Terry Pinkard glosses *Bildung* as "the self-determining self-cultivation and inwardly motivated love of learning and education" (*Hegel: A Biography*, 427). This rather telegraphic gloss suggests the telling lack of a synonym for *Bildung* in present-day English, despite Stanley Cavell's droll observation that Emerson's now obsolete "'upbuilding' ... virtually pronounces *Bildung*" (*This New Yet Unapproachable America*, 9). "Building" and "*Bildung*" are not etymologically related, however, so this phonetic resemblance is merely fortuitous. (See Geuss, *Morality, Culture, and History*, 45, note 9; Geuss points out that *Bildung* comes from *Bild*, "sign or image," whereas "building" comes from "a completely different Indo-European root having to do with 'dwelling.'") Although there is no single word in current English usage for the polysemic *Bildung* (indeed, Pinkard's gloss leaves out such important meanings as *formation, constitution, culture*, and *training*), "education," properly understood, comes closest, as we will see when we explore Heidegger's mature understanding of these crucial terms in Chapter 4 (§19A).

makes a case for philosophy as a necessary prerequisite to theology; he fulminates against the philosophical establishment while calling for more students to take up "serious philosophical studies"; and, finally, he criticizes the prevalence of "subjective opinions, personal moods and wishes" in contemporary "life-philosophy," but then basically leaves it up to individual students to direct their own philosophical development. Given these tensions, it is not too surprising that this early piece advances only a few crucial steps "Toward a Philosophical Orientation for Academics." It remains an important document nonetheless because Heidegger gives up neither the ambition its title expresses, nor the idea, first advanced here, that the best way to provide the academy with such a "philosophical orientation" involves yoking pedagogical reform to ontological questioning.

Indeed, Heidegger will flesh out this very strategy as he continues to work "Toward a Philosophical Orientation for Academics" over the next two decades, finally beginning to present his own substantive vision for a philosophical reorientation of the German academy as a whole in 1927. Before he can develop this positive philosophical vision for radical university reform, however, he will have to work through some of the tensions that characterize this early piece. As it turns out, Heidegger's philosophical studies will soon supplant the theology they were meant to supplement, and his youthful individualism will hold out only a few years longer against his growing sense that Germany is undergoing an historical crisis to which the philosopher is called on to respond. To see this, let us skip ahead seven years.

§13. TO EDUCATE THE NATION (1918 TO 1924)

On 7 November 1918, Heidegger writes to Elisabeth Blochmann from the Western Front. From his meteorological weather service station, the young Army corporal has just had a bird's eye view of Germany's defeat in World War I. As he confronts the obvious uncertainty of the postwar future, Heidegger first articulates his fateful ambition "to educate the nation," sharing with Blochmann his "unshakable" certainty that Germany now needs the kind of spiritual leadership only a philosophical education can provide:

What shape life generally will assume after this end, which was bound to come and is now our only salvation, is uncertain. Certain and unshakable is the challenge to all truly spiritual persons not to weaken at this particular moment but to grasp resolute leadership and to educate the nation toward truthfulness and a genuine valuation of the genuine assets of existence.

On returning to his teaching duties at Freiburg later that month, Heidegger thus adopts an optimistic view of the German defeat, which he now sees as the opportunity for a philosophical "new beginning." His hope is that the "outward deprivations" of the war's aftermath will serve the cause of *genuine* education (in other words, *Bildung*) by encouraging students to renounce distracting external entanglements and develop those inward and authentic "assets of existence" that no defeat can take away.[30] Heidegger's optimistic interpretation of Germany's defeat is a bit idiosyncratic, but his intellectual trajectory – a postwar return to an earlier pedagogical concern with *Bildung* – coincides with a much broader current of the German *Zeitgeist.*

Following the defeat of World War I, Germany was felt to be in the grip of a profound historical crisis. Prominent German intellectuals had presented the war as a struggle for the "spiritual and intellectual leadership [*geistige Führung*] of the world," a struggle that Germany – because of its ostensibly unique spiritual character, its deep "inwardness" (*Innerlichkeit*) – was both entitled and destined to win.[31] Thus, many reacted to Germany's surrender with disbelief and denial. A common response was to explain away the German defeat by invoking the fateful legend of the "stab in the back," the idea that Germany's political leaders had betrayed the military by surrendering just as the tide of the war was turning (a myth Hitler later mobilized to great effect to both help win over the support of the military and further discredit the political leadership of the Weimar Republic, who were linked to this phantasmic betrayal). A more interesting reaction, from our perspective, occurred when such a refusal to admit defeat combined with a sense that the historical crisis the war represented had not yet been resolved. The result was a dramatic rationalization of Germany's defeat as merely a lost battle in a much larger war – on the grandest scale, a war over the meaning of Western history itself – indeed, a lost battle the hidden virtue of which had been to render visible this larger, more important war.[32]

---

[30] See Safranski, *Martin Heidegger,* 86; and Jeff Collins, *Heidegger and the Nazis,* 22–30. One might think Heidegger exhibits a rather portentous insensitivity to the human suffering surrounding him here. As a lower-middle-class student who attended private schools thanks only to academic scholarships, however, Heidegger has long made a virtue of socioeconomic necessity, and this helps explain his rather optimistic idea that material "deprivation" could help serve the cause of a new and genuine *Bildung.*

[31] See Young, *Heidegger, Philosophy, Nazism,* 13–15 (and, for his exposition of the great influence of these "ideas of 1914" on Heidegger's politics, 13–51). See also GA16 285–308.

[32] Cf. Heidegger (in 1934): "And yet the historical meaning of this tremendous event, which we call 'World War [i.e., WWI],'" lies beyond the question of guilt and guiltlessness, and

Giving this grandiloquent interpretation a popular-philosophical expression, Oswald Spengler's *The Decline of the West* became incredibly influential. Published in 1918, it sold an astounding six hundred thousand copies by 1920, quickly spreading into every corner of the intellectual world its neo-Nietzschean prognosis that the spiritual energies of the occident were declining into an enervating cultural senescence, and issuing forth a resounding summons for heroic German leadership (epitomized in his famous call for a "Caesar with the soul of Christ"), a leader capable of reversing this historical slide into nihilism.[33] Although Heidegger was never an uncritical supporter of Spengler, he was sympathetic to the "tragic" Nietzschean view of historical decline underwriting Spengler's synoptic narrative, and the political energies mobilized by the Spenglerians undoubtedly served Heidegger's own agenda for radical educational reform. For, as the tidal wave of German postwar discontent spread, "discussions and plans were everywhere for the reform of Germany's educational system," and even prominent academics felt impelled to situate themselves with respect to Spengler's hypothesis of cultural decline and his ensuing call for heroic politicospiritual leadership.[34]

It was as an early intervention against precisely this Spenglerian agenda for educational reform that, in the winter of 1918, an ailing Max Weber delivered his famous Munich lecture, "Science as a Vocation" (*Wissenschaft als Beruf*). "Science" is a notoriously misleading translation of the German *Wissenschaft*, which refers much more broadly to the *knowledge* embodied in the humanities as well as the natural and social sciences. Weber's title could thus be rendered "Knowledge as a Calling" but, despite the "calling"

beyond the question of imperialism or pacifism. With the determination of the victor and the defeated, the essential decision has not at all been made, because the decision is spiritual. This decision is of importance for the conviction and comportment of all peoples. The World War is for *every* people the great test of whether it will be able to transform this event itself in a spiritual and historical manner. The World War is the question posed to each of the individual peoples, whether they are willing to rejuvenate themselves in this event or whether they will become old because of it" (GA16 299).

33 According to Germany's historical self-mythologization (which the Nazis drew on and amplified), "the German people consists essentially of ... men-at-arms. . . . [T]hese men-at-arms or aristocratic warriors elect their king, but his only function is to settle disputes and juridical problems in peacetime. . . . It is only in times of war – when a strong organization and one power are needed – that they elect a *leader*, and his leadership obeys very different principles and is absolute" (Foucault, "*Society Must Be Defended*," 148, my emphasis).

34 According to Pöggeler, Heidegger lent his support to this "tragic" view of history when he lectured on *The Decline of the West* in 1920 (*The Paths of Heidegger's Life and Thought*, 38). See Spengler, *The Decline of the West*, 36–40; Safranski, *Martin Heidegger*, 92; and van Buren, *The Young Heidegger*, 354.

in its title, Weber's lecture stoically embraced a "disenchanted" professionalization of the German academy, advocating what we now call (with unintended irony) *vocationalism*, in which the "calling" or mission of education has been replaced with the pragmatic necessity of training students for a job (typically a "vocation" in name only). Seeking to puncture the "romantic" illusions of the contemporary "youth" who "crave a leader and not a teacher," Weber takes direct aim at Spengler's Nietzschean demand that intellectuals should assume politicospiritual leadership of Germany, directly address issues of ethics, character, and values in order to answer questions about what really matters, and thereby help rescue the nation from its growing sense of meaninglessness. Relying on an absolute fact/value dichotomy, Weber classifies all such attempts to determine "what matters" as value judgments that, as such, have no place within the halls of the university. For Weber, conflicting value judgments ultimately come down to a collision of incommensurable "worldviews," a "struggle" between competing "godheads" (as he memorably puts it), and the university lectern is no place for "prophets dispensing sacred values." Instead, Weber concludes pragmatically, academics should confine themselves to the "stern seriousness" of sober "analyses and statements of fact" and so "set to work and meet 'the demands of the day.'"[35]

Thus, from the margins of the academy, Spengler had issued a dramatic Nietzschean call for a heroic intellectual response to the historical crisis, and Weber, from a leading position within the university, countered with a resolute refusal to forsake scientific objectivity in order to answer this call. The competing positions in the debate over university reform were thereby established. Those influenced by Spengler wanted academics to intervene actively in cultural politics, whereas Weberians sought to isolate the university from the political turbulence of the times.

It is no coincidence that Heidegger begins his own lectures in 1919 with some "preliminary remarks" on "Science and University Reform," then gives a lecture course the following semester "On the Nature of the University and Academic Study." In both cases it is clear that Heidegger is grappling not only with the general Spenglerian *Zeitgeist*, but with Weber's iconoclastic response in particular. Gadamer, one of Heidegger's students at the time, would later attest: "This inner-worldly asceticism of a

---

[35] See Weber, "Science as a Vocation," *From Max Weber: Essays in Sociology*, 131, 148–9, 151–2, 155–6. Weber's defense of value-free scholarship was not politically neutral, of course, but favored the postwar political status quo, the representative government of the Weimar Republic Weber had himself influenced.

value-free science which is then perfected by a certain kind of decision-ism, we found it majestic but impossible. Heidegger felt that too. . . . One saw [Weber] as a symbol of a kind of scientific life with which we could not identify."[36] I submit, however, that Heidegger's attitude toward Weber's "majestic but impossible" scientific ideal is more complex than Gadamer's retrospective remark suggests. Heidegger does reject as unrealistic We-ber's idea that academic researchers could *maintain* a "purely theoreti-cal objectivity," but he nevertheless appropriates this Weberian vision of value-free science as a kind of regulative ideal, a goal to be constantly pursued if only occasionally attained. As Heidegger assures his students in 1919, "a purely theoretical objectivity is possible" (TDP 174/GA56–57 206).[37]

Heidegger reaches this compromise position by defending the view (later developed in *Being and Time*) that: "The theoretical world is not always there, but is accessible only in a constantly renewed divesting of the natural world" (TDP 179/GA56–7 211).[38] The life of science cannot be isolated from the rest of one's life, nor *should* it be; the "theoretical life" must be "constantly renewed" by being reconnected to the "experi-ential" life-context from which it arises. Theory neither can nor should be permanently extricated from practice.[39] Moreover, "the scientific man does not stand in isolation" in a further sense; the practices that support and nourish theory are not merely individual but depend on a *community*

---

[36] "Interview: The 1920s, 1930s, and the Present: National Socialism, German History, and German Culture," in Gadamer, *On Education, Poetry, and History: Applied Hermeneutics,* 140.

[37] (Translation of TDP emended, in accordance with the corrected, second edition of GA56–57.) Heidegger's lecture notes for "On the Nature of the University and Aca-demic Study" have been lost, but this volume includes the complete collection of Oskar Becker's incomplete student notes. See also Heidegger's "Comments on Karl Jaspers' Psy-chology of Worldviews" (P 35–6), in which he affirms Weber's adoption of the fact/value distinction for "the historical sciences of culture," but resists prematurely extending this distinction to other domains of knowledge.

[38] In *Being and Time*, Heidegger develops this insight in terms of that "transformation" (*Umschlag*) whereby "hands-on" (*zuhanden*) equipment implicitly encountered in holis-tic contexts of practical use becomes "deworlded" and so transformed into "on hand" (*vorhanden*) objects explicitly accessible to theoretical cognition.

[39] The young Heidegger seems to have been personally exemplary in this respect. After Max Horkheimer met him in 1920, he wrote: "I know now that Heidegger is one of the most significant personalities ever to have spoken to me. Do I agree with him? How could I, when all I know about him for certain is that for him the motive to philosophize does not spring from intellectual ambition or a preconceived theory, but everyday afresh out of his own experience" (Horkheimer's 30 November 1921 letter quoted by Rolf Wiggershaus, *The Frankfurt School: Its History, Theories, and Political Significance,* 45).

of practitioners. In order for science to become fully embodied in "the *habitus* of a personal existence," an individual's scientific practices must be supported by "a community of similarly striving researchers." Indeed, to understand the historical emergence of the university as an institution, Heidegger maintains, we need to view it as an "objective expression" (or organic outgrowth) of the interlocking practices developed by a mutually supportive scientific community.[40] Here we observe another important development in Heidegger's philosophical views on the university: The individualism that characterized his views on education in 1911 is supplemented in 1919 by a new emphasis on the individual's relation to the scientific community – supplemented, but not yet supplanted. For although Heidegger proclaims that the university community has a common, unifying goal – namely, "to awaken and heighten the life-context of scientific consciousness" – he also insists that such a scientific consciousness can only be "authentically realized" if it "grows from an inner calling" of the individual researcher (TDP 4–5/GA56–57 76).

As Heidegger adopts Weber's famous language of the individual *called* into the scientific community, he appropriates the Weberian ideal of theoretical objectivity he seemed to Gadamer to reject. To "authentically realize" one's "scientific consciousness," Heidegger explains, means *attaining*, however episodically, this "purely theoretical objectivity." Describing this "realization" of scientific objectivity in terms of a series of progressive stages, Heidegger postulates a hierarchy of modes of "theoretical comportment," a progression that culminates in the Weberian ideal of "absolute veracity." Heidegger even goes so far as to tell his students that Weber's "'vocational question' stands at the entrance to the theoretical life-context: Can I maintain myself in the disposition to absolute veracity?" Heidegger thus appropriates Weber's ideal of value-free science, but only after reromanticizing it, presenting the struggle for "theoretical objectivity" as a Herculean labor to be heroically pursued, and urging this ongoing struggle for scientific objectivity with the bold Nietzschean motto of an "*education for truthfulness*" (TDP 179–80/GA56–57 212–13).

If we step back again, then, we see that Heidegger tries to answer *both* the romantic Spenglerian–Nietzschean call for intellectuals to help revitalize Germany by providing heroic spiritual leadership *and* the ascetic

---

[40] I return to this Husserlian point below. For Heidegger's views on the institutional history of the university, see also GA61 72–3; GA16 286–297; and de Beistegui's *Heidegger and the Political*, 35–62.

Weberian demand that academics should maintain the sober discipline required for theoretical objectivity. In effect, he accepts the Nietzschean–Spenglerian call for heroic intellectual leadership, but characterizes this leadership in terms of a modified Weberian view of the task of science. The result of this unlikely union of Spengler and Weber is a kind of *romantic asceticism*, an unstable mix to be sure, and one in which the starkest tension in Heidegger's views on education during the early 1920s stands clearly revealed. Not surprisingly, this tension will be short-lived. By the end of the decade, the romantic Nietzschean longing for meaning will have driven out the sober asceticism of the Weberian quest for a rigorous, value-free science.

If Heidegger nevertheless exhibits a surprising proximity to Weber during the early 1920s, these remarkable similarities stem not only from their mutual belief in the importance of scientific objectivity (or *Sachlichkeit*, the same hard-nosed trait that attracted the young Carnap to Heidegger), but also from a shared opposition to Spengler himself.[41] Of course, Heidegger's reasons for criticizing Spengler are the very opposite of Weber's; for Heidegger, Spengler is insufficiently "radical," a mere "vulgarization" of Nietzsche (as he later puts it). Still, given Heidegger's growing Nietzscheanism, and what would come from it between 1929 and 1933, some of Heidegger's sober, Weberian-sounding pronouncements during the early 1920s are simply startling. "So long as it remains true to itself," Heidegger writes in 1920, "philosophy is not called to save or redeem the age" (GA59 170). Turning Spengler against Spengler (and thus against the various neo-Kantians, worldview philosophers, and

---

[41] On the young Carnap's admiration for Heidegger, see Michael Friedman, *A Parting of the Ways: Carnap, Cassirer, and Heidegger*, esp. 12–18. On the subject of Spengler, even Heidegger's seemingly most laudatory remarks are not without a strong critical undercurrent. His general tactic is to use Spengler's popularity to help motivate the problem of historical nihilism, but then to present this problem according to his own philosophical understanding. Thus, for example, Heidegger welcomes Spengler's "consequential" diagnosis of the problem while rejecting Spengler's "dilettantism in fundamental issues and conceptual *habitus*" (OHF 29, 44–5/GA63 37, 56–7). By 1929, however, when Heidegger's own philosophical standing is secure, he will no longer maintain even this pretense of respect. Hence Heidegger writes in 1929–1930 that Spengler's sensationalistic "diagnoses and prognostications" about the *Decline of the West* offer merely an "illusory appeasement," because Spengler's "philosophy of culture does not grasp us in our contemporary situation" (FCM 75/GA29–30 112). Wolin discerns an unreferenced quotation of Spengler's collectively narcissistic "we want ourselves" in Heidegger's Rectorial Address (*The Politics of Being*, 86), but this too is best understood as Heidegger's attempt to appropriate philosophically a popular Spenglerian sentiment. In 1942, Heidegger will explain his objection to Spengler's "vulgarization" of Nietzsche's metaphysics as an objection to the *biologism* of the Nazi ideology (PAR 113/GA54 167–8).

life-philosophers vying to supply Germany with the kind of spiritual leadership for which Spengler called), Heidegger contends ironically that the real historical "decline" is visible in the very demand that philosophy should issue in the "developed doctrine" of a culture-serving "worldview" (GA61 50, 74).[42] Between 1921 and 1923, Heidegger further declares that it is not for the philosopher to "write a system" or "program" for "university reform" (GA63 19), and even insists that serious philosophical discussions of university reform must reject "pseudoreligiosity" and the appeal of "prophethood and the allure of the leader [*Führerallüren*]" (GA61 46–7, 69–70), sober Weberian warnings Heidegger will ignore – along with his earlier admonition against "external entanglements" – to his own detriment between 1929 and 1933.[43]

To summarize briefly the central features of Heidegger's mature views on university education (the main subject of Chapter 4), let us address the question that will seem obvious at this point: What happened to these sober Weberian analyses from the early 1920s? Why did Heidegger so soon discard his own good advice? As the decade drew to a close, Heidegger seems to have concluded that Weber had thrown out the stereo along with the styrofoam, so to speak. For, in rejecting Spengler, Weber also was rejecting two crucial, interrelated aspects of the legacy of Nietzsche, on the one hand, and the German Idealists and Wilhelm von Humboldt, on the other, namely, the struggle against nihilism (inherited from Nietzsche), and the philosophical vision of a distinctively German university (the legacy of German Idealism and Humboldt). Indeed, one has to realize that from the German perspective, Weber played the role of an intellectual collaborator: He presents the invading forces of "rationalization" rhetorically as American and French, then firmly counsels his audience to lay down their arms, as it were, and accept as an irreversible historical fact that these forces of rationalization have now rendered "fictitious" not just the reality but the very idea of the modern German university.[44] What exactly was Weber thus giving up that Heidegger wanted to retain? The answer, I take it, is the ideal of the German university as a place in which life and research are harmoniously integrated, a dynamic communal institution with a shared sense of its own substantive, unifying mission.

[42] See Crowell, "Philosophy as a Vocation," *passim*; and Bambach, *Heidegger, Dilthey, and the Crisis of Historicism*, 213.

[43] In apparent disgust, Heidegger adds a striking exclamation in parentheses: "One writes today about the *Führer* problem!" (GA61 70; cf. GA63 30–3).

[44] Cf. Fritz Ringer, *The Decline of the German Mandarins*.

On the medieval model of the university, the task of higher education was to transmit what was thought to be a relatively fixed body of knowledge. The French preserved something of this view; universities taught the supposedly established doctrines, whereas research took place outside the university in nonteaching academies. The French model was appropriated by the German universities that preceded Kant, in which the state-sponsored "higher faculties" of law, medicine, and theology, which trained (what we would call) "graduate students" to assume official posts as doctors, lawyers, priests, and so on, were separated from the more independent "lower" faculty of philosophy, which was responsible for educating the "undergraduates." Kant personally experienced *The Conflict of the Faculties* of philosophy and theology (after publishing *Religion within the Limits of Reason Alone*), and his subsequent argument that it is in the best long-term interests of the state for the "philosophy faculty" to be "conceived as free and subject only to laws given by reason" helped inspire Fichte's and Schleiermacher's philosophical elaborations of an "indigenous [German] alternative to the French model." At the heart of these proposals for the new University of Berlin, which Humboldt successfully institutionalized in 1810, was the "scientific" view of research as a dynamic, open-ended endeavor. Research and teaching would now be combined into a single institution of higher-learning, with philosophy at the center of a new proliferation of academic pursuits.[45]

From the beginning, however, one of the major problems concerned how the modern university could maintain the unity of community, structure, and purpose distinctive of the medieval university and thought to be definitive of the *uni*versity as such. German Idealists like Fichte and Schelling believed that this unity would follow organically from the interconnected *totality* of the system of knowledge. But this faith in "the system" proved to be less influential on posterity than Schleiermacher and Humboldt's alternative, "humanist" ideal, according to which the university's unity would come from a shared commitment to the educational formation of character. Here Humboldt's seminal idea was to

---

[45] See Kant, *The Conflict of the Faculties*, 43; Haskins, *The Rise of Universities*; Theodore Ziolkowski, *German Romanticism and Its Institutions*, 218–308; Crowell, "Philosophy as a Vocation," 257–9; Wilhelm von Humboldt, *Die Idee der deutschen Universität*, 377; and de Beistegui, *Heidegger and the Political*, 35–9. Schelling famously held that the university did not need a philosophy department at all, since philosophy was at the core of every discipline (see Schelling's *Lessons on the Method of Academic Studies*, cited by Derrida in "The Principle of Reason: The University in the Eyes of Its Pupils," 4).

link "objective *Wissenschaft* with subjective *Bildung*"; the university would be responsible for forming fully cultured individuals, a requirement Humboldt hoped would serve to guide and unite the disciplines despite the new freedom of research. In historical actuality, however, neither the German Idealists' reliance on the underlying unity of the scientific subject matter nor Humboldt's emphasis on a shared commitment to the educational formation of students succeeded in unifying the university community cohesively enough to prevent its fragmentation into increasingly specialized disciplines.

As we will see in Chapter 4, Heidegger's own mature vision of a reontologization of education *combines* (his versions of) these two strategies. The university community he envisions will be unified *both* by (1) the mutual recognition among this community that its members are all committed to the same formal pursuit, the ultimately revolutionary task not simply of understanding what *is*, but of investigating the ontological presuppositions implicitly guiding all the various fields of knowledge, *and* by (2) its shared commitment to forming *excellent* individuals, where "excellence" is understood in terms of a kind of ontological perfectionism, in which students learn to develop their distinctive capacity for world-disclosing as they participate in the advancement of science by learning to question the sciences' guiding ontological presuppositions. Heidegger's view of the relation between philosophy and science thus plays a crucial role in both strands of his dual strategy for reunifying the university, and we will turn our attention to the main philosophical details of this radical research program in the next section. In my view, Heidegger never gives up his belief that ontological education, by restoring substance to the notion of excellence and in so doing teaching us "to disclose the essential in all things," could finally succeed in "shattering the encapsulation of the sciences in their different disciplines and bringing them back from their boundless and aimless dispersal in individual fields and corners" (Q&A 9/GA16 111). Despite some important refinements, his later views, we will see, maintain this dual strategy with remarkably consistency.

Although Heidegger did not elaborate the major features of this positive vision of a reontologization of higher education until 1927, important seeds of his mature view can already be found in his work on university education during the early 1920s. As we have seen, these early views contain a surprising and unstable mix of Nietzschean and Weberian elements. It is, however, the quieter presence of a more familiar influence that helps tip the balance in Nietzsche's favor. For, against Weber, Heidegger adopts the conclusion of Husserl's "Philosophy as Rigorous Science" (1910): Only

Wissenschaft can close the divide between science and meaning that science itself has opened.[46] Already in 1919, Heidegger rejected Weber's overly rigid separation of life and *Wissenschaft* when he began outlining his own long-term plan for "*genuine* university reform":

> The renewal of the university means a rebirth of genuine scientific conscious-ness and life-contexts. But life-relations renew themselves only in a return to the genuine origins of the spirit; as historical phenomena, they require...the in-ner truthfulness of a value-replete, self-cultivating life. Only life, not the noise of overhasty cultural programs, makes "epochs."
>
> (TDP 4/GA56–57 4–5)

This early vision of university renewal relies on a seemingly vitalis-tic, neo-Nietzschean notion of "value-replete, self-cultivating life," but Heidegger unpacks this appeal to "life" in terms of "the vitality of genuine research...through which alone the scientific researcher has any effect." Kisiel glosses Heidegger's point as "philosophy...must cut through... extant theoretical structures in order to find the...'vital impetus' which motivates" each scientific discipline. Here Kisiel underemphasizes the romantic-Nietzschean dimension of Heidegger's project (ignoring, for example, Heidegger's politically ominous call for a "genuine revolution-izing of the spirit"), but he nicely anticipates the Husserlian arguments developed in *Being and Time*, in which – as Heidegger elaborates and re-fines his early vision of philosophy as the "genuinely *primordial* science [Ur-*wissenschaft*] from which the theoretical itself takes its origin" (TDP 81/GA56–7 96) – Husserl's influence temporarily pushes Nietzsche into the background of Heidegger's thought.[47] Thus Husserl's subtle but pro-found impact on Heidegger's project for a philosophical revitalization of the university can indeed already be detected in 1919, and not only in the way Kisiel recognizes.

Husserl's "phenomenological–constitutive consideration" analyzed the way objects are constituted within the temporal flow of experience.[48] Applying this Husserlian approach to a larger scale, Heidegger sought in 1919 to understand the way scientific practices congeal over time around new objects of research, thereby establishing new disciplines or trans-forming old ones. Recognizing that such scientific practices can take years to "genetically consolidate" themselves into new object domains

---

[46] "Only science can definitively overcome the need that has its source in science" ("Phi-losophy as a Rigorous Science," *Phenomenology and the Crisis of Philosophy*, 140–1).

[47] Kisiel, *The Genesis of Heidegger's* Being and Time, 63. On the rhetoric of spiritual revolu-tion, see Zeev Sternhall, *Neither Left Nor Right: Fascist Ideology in France*.

[48] See Husserl, *Ideas Pertaining to a Pure Phenomenology and to a Phenomenological Philosophy, Third Book*, 117; Dermot Moran, *Introduction to Phenomenology*, 166.

and institutions, Heidegger proclaims this "the task of a *whole generation*." Although the Nietzschean rhetoric of Heidegger's early vision for a re-vitalization of the university is dramatic, he follows Husserl (and the Nietzsche of the second *Untimely Meditation*) by counseling patience and a commitment to the long-term view.[49] Before "*genuine* university reforms" can be expected, Heidegger writes, the new scientific life-contexts emerging within the university must be given at least a generation of "peace and security" in which to "mature." By 1924, however, Heidegger's patience for a gradual, progressive revitalization of the academy is already wearing thin:

> The situation of academic disciplines [*Wissenschaften*] and the university has become even more questionable. What happens? Nothing. One writes brochures on the crisis of the academic disciplines, on science as a vocation.... Today there is even a specialized body of literature on the question, "How should things be?" Nothing else happens.
>
> (OHF 27/GA63 32–3)[50]

Heidegger seems to realize here that his Nietzschean romanticization of Weber's ascetic scientific ideal is not actually doing much to revitalize the university. Rather than give up the project, however, Heidegger will

---

[49] Here as elsewhere the early Heidegger seeks to appropriate and deepen contemporary "life-philosophy" (which he associates with Dilthey, Scheler, and Jaspers, three of his major influences at the time) by reconnecting the movement with its Nietzschean roots, and the influence of Nietzsche's second *Untimely Meditation* is particularly obvious. (For the impact of this early work of Nietzsche's on *Being and Time*, see Guignon, *Heidegger and the Problem of Knowledge*, 228.) Here Nietzsche calls for educational reform in terms of a return to "life," predicting a "generation" that will face the difficult task of becoming "ripe" for such reforms (*On the Advantage and Disadvantage of History for Life*, 61–64). Heidegger appropriates Nietzsche's language and thought when he tells his students that: "The much discussed university reform is completely misguided and a total misunderstanding of all genuine revolutionizing of the spirit.... We are not yet ripe for *genuine* reforms in the realm of the university. And becoming ripe for this is the matter of an *entire generation*" (TDP 4/GA56–57 4). The following semester, in "On the Nature of the University and Academic Study," Heidegger again borrows from Nietzsche's second *Untimely Meditation*, appropriating Nietzsche's call for the "'eternal youth' of the theoretical man" (TDP 180–1/GA56–57 214). Thus, *pace* the received view, there can be no doubt that Nietzsche is already in the background of Heidegger's thoughts on education in 1919. Indeed, the influence of Nietzsche and Husserl work together in this regard; compare Husserl's view that: "These men [the worldview philosophers] ... who want to have their system and want it soon enough to be able to live by it, are in no way called to this task.... [A worldview] is to be judged as the habitus and accomplishment of the individual personality, whereas *science is to be judged as the collective task of generations of scholars*" ("Philosophy as a Rigorous Science," 143, my emphasis).

[50] The antepenultimate sentence of this quote, in which Heidegger denigrates brochures on "science as a vocation" (*Beruf der Wissenschaft*), is an obvious swipe at Weber, and so an indication that Heidegger is already casting off his own earlier Weberianism by 1924.

conclude that more active steps need to be taken in order to restore the university to its leading role within the nation.

Heidegger's seemingly unshakeable confidence that he is destined to be a leader of the generation that will transform the university is less surprising if one recalls the way Husserl groomed Heidegger to play just such a dangerous role. In "Philosophy as a Rigorous Science," Husserl presented phenomenology as a "revolution in philosophy" that would "prepare the ground for a future philosophical system." As Heidegger became Husserl's heir apparent during the 1920s, he increasingly saw it as his appointed task to develop – atop the ground cleared by Husserl's phenomenological revolution – that "systematic fundamental science of philosophy, the port of entry to a genuine metaphysics of nature, of spirit, of ideas" for which Husserl himself had called. Unfortunately, in Heidegger's very fidelity to this incredibly ambitious Husserlian project, he would fail to take to heart Husserl's prophetic warning of a "great danger." Because the "spiritual need of our time has, in fact, become unbearable," Husserl cautioned, "*even a theoretical nature will be capable of giving in to the force of the motive to influence practice more thoroughly than his theoretical vocation would permit.*"[51] To see how Heidegger fell prey to the very dangers both he and Husserl previously had discerned, we need only turn to Heidegger's early magnum opus, *Being and Time* (1927), in which he develops his positive views for radical university reform.

§14. RESTORING PHILOSOPHY TO HER THRONE AS THE QUEEN OF THE SCIENCES (1927–1934)

It has long been known that in 1936, at a time when Heidegger had no reason to try to cover his political tracks, he told his former student Karl Löwith that his philosophy and politics were indeed "essentially" connected; the "concept of historicality [presented in ¶¶72–77 of *Being and Time*] was the basis of his political engagement."[52] Scholars still disagree, however, about whether this formal framework did (Löwith, Wolin, Fritsche) or did not (Guignon, Olafson) give Heidegger reason to join the Nazis.[53] Although there is certainly no *necessary* connection between the concept of historicality and Nazism (as Guignon and Olafson

[51] "Philosophy as a Rigorous Science," 75, 116–17 note f, 140, 173 (my emphasis).
[52] Löwith, *My Life in Germany Before and After 1933*, 60.
[53] See ibid., 73–81; Wolin, *The Politics of Being*, 53–66; Fritsche, *Historical Destiny and National Socialism in Heidegger's* Being and Time, 216–24; Guignon, "History and Commitment in the Early Heidegger," 130–42; and Olafson, *Heidegger and the Ground of Ethics*, 13–14.

persuasively show), Heidegger's understanding of authentic historicality clearly did play a crucial role in "bridging" the divide between philosophy and politics (as Wolin and Sluga argue), encouraging and informing Heidegger's attempt to "seize the moment."[54] This is not simply because *Being and Time*'s discussion of authentic historicality already philosophically appropriates concepts that would soon become highly charged Nazi *philosophemes*, such as "struggle" (*Kampf*), "people" (*Volk*), "community," "fate," and "destiny" (B&T 436/S&Z 384–5).[55] Even more important here is the philosophical content such concepts helped give to the notion of "authentic historicality" *as Heidegger himself understood it*. Put simply, but in the terms of authentic historicality, Heidegger "chose" Nietzsche as his "hero" (B&T 437/S&Z 385) and so sought an historically appropriate way to carry on Nietzsche's struggle against nihilism.[56] The eagerness with which Heidegger answered Spengler's Nietzschean call for radical university reform in 1933 followed from his sense that it was his philosophical "fate" – and so his role in focusing the "destiny" of his generation (B&T 436/S&Z 384) – to combat the growing problem of historical meaninglessness "by way of the university" (Q&A 53/A 95).

There can thus be little doubt that the concept of authentic historicality presented in ¶74 of *Being and Time* provides the general philosophical framework in terms of which Heidegger understood his decision to join the National Socialist "revolution" in 1933. I submit, nonetheless, that if one is interested in the specific philosophical motives that justified, in

---

54 See Wolin, *The Politics of Being*, 52; Sluga, *Heidegger's Crisis*, 23–8; and my "The End of Ontotheology," 317–30. Olafson maintains that: "The conception of political society Heidegger developed in his Nazi period was not dictated by the theses of *Being and Time*," and he "rejects the idea that Heidegger's Nazism derives from his political thought" ("Heidegger's Thought and Nazism," 271, 279). In both cases, however, Olafson's terms ("dictates," "derives") set the bar too high for what counts as a meaningful relation between philosophy and practice. As Dreyfus shows (in "Could anything be more intelligible than everyday intelligibility?"), *Being and Time* presupposes a neo-Aristotelian understanding of practical wisdom as operating beyond the domain of principles – and so outside the space of possible "derivations" of praxis from theory – without, for that reason, being "decisionistic" in the objectionable sense of *arbitrary*, let alone "blind and uninformed," as Wolin alleges (*The Politics of Being*, 52).

55 Such rhetorical and historical affinities, although striking in retrospect, also can be quite misleading (as in Fritsche's *Historical Destiny and National Socialism*). Still, they are sufficient to undermine Olafson's claim that Heidegger's conception of historicality "cannot be assigned any particular political complexion" ("Heidegger's Thought and Nazism," 288 note 12).

56 On Heidegger's choice of Nietzsche as his "hero," see Christopher Fynsk, *Heidegger: Thought and Historicity*; and my "The End of Ontotheology" and "Deconstructing the Hero."

Heidegger's mind at least, the actual political initiatives he attempted to enact in 1933 as the Rector of Freiburg University, then the philosophical rubber really hits the political road much earlier in *Being and Time*, in ¶3. For it is here, without naming Kant, that Heidegger appropriates Kant's implicit rejection of the declaration – issued by the "higher faculty" of theology (but anticipated in Locke's image of the empiricist "underlaborer" and echoed in the neo-Kantian call to replace ontology with epistemology) – that philosophy's relation to the other sciences should be that of a "train-bearer" (who follows behind, straightening out the tangles), rather than a "torch-bearer" (who goes first, lighting the way).[57] Explicitly reversing this humble view, Heidegger insists that philosophy "must run ahead of the positive sciences, and it *can* do so" (B&T 30/S&Z 10). Despite its great political importance, Heidegger's attempt to fulfill Husserl's Kantian ambition to restore philosophy to her throne as "the Queen of all the sciences" has been largely overlooked in the secondary literature surrounding the Heidegger controversy, and so is worth examining in some detail in this connection. Doing so, moreover, will enable us to discern a further, heretofore unnoticed connection between "authentic historicality" and Heidegger's politics.

For Heidegger, every scientific discipline with a discrete subject matter is a *positive science*. The term "positive science" conveys his claim that scientific disciplines each rest on an ontological "posit," that is, a presupposition about what the class of entities it studies *is*. Biology, for example, seeks to understand how living beings function. As biologists successfully accomplish this important task, they allow us to understand in ever greater detail the *logos* of the *bios*, the order and structure of living organisms. Nevertheless, Heidegger asserts, biology proper cannot tell us what life *is*. Of course, the biologist must have some understanding of what "life" is, simply in order to be able to pick out the appropriate entities to study. Heidegger maintains, however, that this ontological understanding of "the kind of being which belongs to the living as such" is normally a presupposition rather than a result of the biologist's empirical investigations (B&T 30/S&Z 10).[58] Heidegger makes the same point with respect to the

---

57 See Kant, "To Perpetual Peace: A Philosophical Sketch," *Perpetual Peace and Other Essays*, 126, and his "Preface to the First Edition," *Critique of Pure Reason* (esp. Avii–Axii).

58 This distinction between the "presuppositions" and "results" of science might seem problematic; is not the understanding of what "life" *is* (which the biologist presupposes) subsequently tested (and so confirmed or refuted) by empirical investigation? Heidegger adamantly rejects such a view, because: "These ontological foundations can never be disclosed by subsequent hypotheses derived from empirical material, . . . they

social and human sciences. Psychology, for example, can tell us a great deal about the functioning of consciousness, the *psychê*, but, notoriously, it cannot tell us what consciousness *is*. Analogously, the discipline of history (*Being and Time*'s "historiography") greatly increases our understanding of historical events, yet historians cannot tell us what history *is*.

Let us be clear: Heidegger is not claiming that biologists cannot distinguish organic from inorganic entities, that psychologists are unable to differentiate between conscious and nonconscious states, or that historians cannot tell historical events from nonhistorical ones. His point, rather, is that in making just such fundamental conceptual differentiations, biologists, psychologists, and historians are always already employing an ontological understanding of what the entities whose domain they study *are*. Indeed, no science could get along without at least an implicit ontological understanding of the beings it studies.[59] Simply to *do* historiography, historians must be able to focus on the appropriate objects of study, which means they must already have some understanding of what makes an historical event "historical." In order to distinguish the entities from the past destined for museums from those headed for junk heaps, for example, historians rely on an ontological understanding of what makes an entity *historical,* a sense for what Heidegger calls the "historicality" of the historical (B&T 31/S&Z 10). Likewise, botany relies on an ontological understanding of "the vegetable character of plants," physics on "the corporeality of bodies," zoology on "the animality of animals," and anthropology on "the humanness of humanity" (QCT 118/GA5 78).[60] Heidegger's list could be expanded indefinitely because he believes that *every* positive science presupposes such an ontological posit, a background understanding of the *being* of the class of entities it studies.[61]

are always 'there' already, even when the empirical material simply gets collected. If positive research fails to see these foundations and holds them to be self-evident, this by no means proves that they are not basic or that they are not problematic in a more radical sense than any thesis of the positive science can ever be" (B&T 75/S&Z 50).

[59] As David Cerbone nicely puts it, "any inquiry presupposes some understanding or conception of what is being investigated; otherwise, any would-be investigation amounts to nothing more than blind groping" ("World, World-Entry, and Realism in Early Heidegger," 410).

[60] In *Being and Time*, Heidegger includes "history, nature, space, life, Dasein, language, and the like" as examples of the ontological posits that "corresponding scientific investigations may take as their themes" (B&T 29/S&Z 9). See Trish Glazebrook, "Heidegger on the Experiment," 256.

[61] In *Being and Time*, in a list of disciplines that seek to study Dasein, Heidegger puts "'political science'" in scare-quotes (B&T 37/S&Z 16), apparently to indicate his reservations concerning whether this field of research has even advanced to the level of a

By thus extending Husserl's claim about the "naïveté" or "inadequacy" of the *natural* sciences to the *positive* sciences in general, Heidegger thinks he has found a way to fulfill Husserl's grand ambition to deliver "the systematic fundamental science of philosophy."[62] How exactly does Heidegger propose to restore philosophy to her throne as the queen of the sciences? The core of his argument can be broken down into three steps, the first of which we have just reconstructed. Building on this first claim that all the positive sciences presuppose an ontological posit, Heidegger declares, second, that there is a basic difference between these positive sciences and the "science" of philosophy:

Ontic sciences in each case thematize a given entity that in a certain manner is always already disclosed *prior* to scientific disclosure. We call the sciences of entities as given – of a *positum* – positive sciences.... Ontology, or the science of being, on the other hand, demands a fundamental shift of view: from entities to being.

(P 41/GA9 48)[63]

The positive sciences all study classes of entities, so Heidegger also refers to the positive sciences as "ontic sciences." Philosophy, on the other hand, studies the being of those classes of entities, making philosophy an "ontological science" or, more grandly, a "science of being." Heidegger's second claim, in other words, is that philosophy studies precisely that which the positive sciences take for granted: their ontological posits. The subject matters of the positive sciences and of philosophy are thus distinguished by what Heidegger calls "the ontological difference," that is, the

(normal) science. In his 1942 *Parmenides* lectures, Heidegger follows up on this issue, pursuing the ontological question of the *politicality* of the political by examining the way "the *polis* is essentially related to the being of entities" (PAR 89/GA54 133). In so doing, he anticipates the important work of those post-Heideggerian philosophers and political theorists concerned with precisely this ontological question of "the political," such as Ernesto Laclau and Chantal Mouffe, *Hegemony and Socialist Strategy: Towards a Radical Democratic Politics*; Claude Lefort, *Democracy and Political Theory*; Philippe Lacoue-Labarthe and Jean-Luc Nancy, *Retreating the Political*; and William E. Connolly, *The Ethos of Pluralization*.

62 See Husserl, "Philosophy as a Rigorous Science," 116–17 note f, and 85: "All natural science is naïve with regard to its point of departure." Heidegger's generalization assumes that the human and social sciences (and not just the natural sciences) can achieve agreement on their guiding ontological presuppositions (and so not simply perpetuate a kind of permanent ontological confusion or else follow a succession of more or less superficial trends). This assumption follows, as we will see, from Heidegger's idea that each historical epoch is unified by the fundamental ontology (or, later, ontotheology) it implicitly shares. (Cf. Dreyfus, "Heidegger's Hermeneutic Realism.")

63 The quote is from "Phenomenology and Theology," a lecture Heidegger delivered the same year *Being and Time* was published (1927).

difference between "entities" (*Seienden*) and the "being of entities" (*Sein des Seienden*). Positive sciences study entities of various kinds, while philosophy studies the being of those kinds of entities (GA27 223).[64] Here, then, we have the first two steps in the argument whereby Heidegger seeks to restore philosophy to her throne. First, each positive science presupposes an understanding of the being of the class of entities it studies, and second, the science of philosophy concerns itself with precisely these ontological posits.

The crucial third step in Heidegger's argument is his claim that the positive sciences' ontological posits *guide* the scientists' actual investigations. As he writes in 1927: "Philosophy . . . does of its essence have the task of directing all . . . the positive sciences with respect to their ontological foundations" (P 53/GA9 65). For, these ontological "basic concepts determine the way in which we get an understanding beforehand of the area of subject-matter underlying all the objects a science takes as its theme, and all positive science is guided by this understanding" (B&T 30/S&Z 10).[65] Heidegger's point, I take it, is that a scientist's ontological understanding of what the class of entities she studies *are* impacts not only *what* she studies (which is fairly obvious) but also *how* she studies it (which is perhaps less so). When, for example, contemporary biologists proceed on the basis of an ontological understanding of life as a "self-replicating system," the entities whose functioning they seek to understand will include not only those self-replicating beings now thought to populate the plant and animal kingdoms but also such entities as computer viruses, nanotechnology, "electric fish," and other forms of so-called artificial life. To study such artificial life will require, in turn, new modes and models of investigation, such as the observation of "living systems" entirely confined to complex computer simulations.[66]

Although this is not a fanciful example, it may seem slightly atypical in that here biology's guiding ontological posit (namely, that "life *is* a self-replicating system") has been rendered explicit, whereas Heidegger holds that normally such posits function only as presuppositions in the background of a science's investigations. Anticipating Thomas Kuhn,

---

[64] Here I am reconstructing views Heidegger presents in his 1928–1929 lecture course, *Einleitung in die Philosophie* (GA27 223).

[65] As Heidegger writes in "Phenomenology and Theology": "Whatever is discloses itself only on the grounds of a preliminary (although not explicitly known), preconceptual understanding of what and how such an entity is. Every ontic interpretation operates on the basis, at first and for the most part concealed, of an ontology" (P 50/GA9 62).

[66] See Margaret Boden, ed., *The Philosophy of Artificial Life*.

however, Heidegger recognizes that such ontological posits often enter into the foreground of scientific discussion during a crisis in the normal functioning of that science. Indeed, *Being and Time* contends that the "real movement of the sciences" occurs when such crises unsettle the normal "relationship of the questioning of positive research to the matters themselves questioned," leading the sciences to subject their guiding ontological understandings to "a revision which is more or less radical and lucid with regard to itself" (B&T 29/S&Z 9).[67] During such a crisis, a science often puts its guiding ontological understanding of the being of the class of entities it studies into question, usually settling the crisis only by revising its previous ontological understanding. Those who explicitly recognize and take part in such ontological questioning and revision are doing *philosophy*, Heidegger says, whether or not they happen to be employed by a philosophy department (GA27 226). It is in this sense, I submit, that we need to take Heidegger's provocative but widely misunderstood and so highly controversial claim that science as such "does not think," a view Heidegger espoused throughout his life.[68]

For Heidegger, philosophy is essentially the activity of ontological questioning (although later he will usually call this activity "thinking" in order to distinguish it from metaphysics).[69] In his 1928–1929 lectures, *Introduction to Philosophy*, he says that "philosophy is not the knowledge of wisdom [*Erkenntnis der Weisheit*]. . . . Philosophy is philosophizing [*Philosophieren*]." In a twist on the standard etymology of the word "philosophy,"

---

[67] In *Being and Time*, Heidegger's examples of positive sciences that are either passing through or on the verge of a "crisis" in their guiding ontological understandings include biology, history, literature, mathematics, physics, and theology (B&T 29–30/S&Z 9–10).

[68] Well into the 1960s, Heidegger maintains his view that: "*Science does not move in the dimension of philosophy*; but, without knowing it, science relies on this dimension. For example: Physics moves in space and time and movement. What movement is, what space is, what time is cannot be decided by science as science. Therefore science does not think" (Q&A 83/A 24). In 1965, Heidegger says that "one must demand that physicists first reflect on metaphysical ideas. . . . Of course, physicists can do this only if they are prepared to go back to the underlying suppositions of physics, and beyond this, to what remains and continues to be standard in this domain as *acceptio* [i.e., unquestioned assumptions of the discourse, such as the assumption of "homogenous space" inherent in the modern natural scientific conception of "nature"], even when the physicist is unaware of it" (ZS 57, 30/Z 74, 37; see also ZS 75–6, 122–4/Z 97–8, 159–61).

[69] One might object that Heidegger later refers to his own practice as "thinking" rather than "philosophy," because he comes to equate the latter with metaphysics once he carries out his deconstruction of the ontological tradition. Still, both *philosophy* (earlier) and *thinking* (later) refer to the activity of ontological questioning; it is just that, as we will see, *what* this ontological questioning is supposed to uncover shifts dramatically, from a fundamental ontology to a series of epochal ontotheologies.

Heidegger unpacks *philia* as "a genuine friendship which, in its essence, struggles [*kämpf*] for that which it loves" and *sophos* as "an instinct for the essential," and so defines *philosophizing*, the active practice of philosophy, as the struggle to employ one's sense for the essential (GA27 35, 21–22).[70] By "essence" Heidegger means the ontological presupposition or "posit" that guides a positive science. Heidegger can thus say that: "When we speak of the sciences . . . we will be speaking not against but for them, for clarity concerning their essence" (WCT 14/WHD 49).[71] One is "philosophizing" whenever one explicitly examines and seeks to clarify the ontological understanding that normally guides a science implicitly, but that can come into question during a period of scientific crisis. Thus, biologists as well as philosophers of biology were philosophizing insofar as they explicitly questioned the ontological understanding of what life *is* during the recent debate over "artificial life." To say that the positive sciences, as such, do not "think" simply means that they do not, as positive sciences, question their guiding ontological presuppositions. As Heidegger puts it: "The researcher always operates on the foundation of what has already been decided: The fact that there are such things as nature, history, art, and that these things can be made the subject of consideration" (B&T 30/S&Z 10).

Of course, scientists do occasionally engage in such potentially revolutionary ontological questioning but, when they do, they are (by Heidegger's definition) doing philosophy, not research. Thus, because quantum mechanics engaged in such revolutionary questioning, Heidegger did in fact recognize that "the present leaders of atomic physics, Niels Bohr and [Werner] Heisenberg, think in a thoroughly philosophical way" (WT 67/FD 51).[72] Conversely, philosophy is "only alive and actual" when engaged in the ontological questioning at the center of such scientific crises (GA27 226). That is, philosophers (and others) *philosophize* only by doing the potentially revolutionary work of

[70] Cf. Nietzsche, *The Pre-Platonic Philosophers*, 7–9.
[71] Heidegger immediately adds: "This alone implies our conviction that the sciences are in themselves positively essential. However, their essence is frankly of a different sort from what our universities today still fondly imagine it to be. In any case, we still seem afraid of facing the exciting fact that today's sciences belong in the realm of the *essence* of technology, and nowhere else." Here the later Heidegger expresses his conviction that the sciences take over their guiding ontological posits from the Nietzschean ontotheology underlying our "technological" understanding of being.
[72] *Being and Time*'s examples also include the debate between formalists and intuitionists over the ontological status of mathematical entities and the conflict in biology between mechanists and vitalists over the nature of life. (See also N3 6/NI 476–7.)

questioning and clarifying the ontological presuppositions that guide the natural, social, and human sciences. Hence, Heidegger proclaims in 1928, the Husserlian idea of a "scientific philosophy" is like the concept of a "circular sphere," that is, not simply redundant, for as a sphere is more circular than any circle, so "philosophizing" is "more scientific than any possible science" (GA27 17–18, 221). Indeed, strictly speaking, "philosophy is *not* science, . . . but rather the *origin* [*Ursprung*] of science."[73] Science "springs from" philosophy in a way that resembles the emergence of normal science from revolutionary science, namely, through an eventual routinization and procedural exploration of the ontological insights gained philosophically during a period of revolutionary science, a time of crisis and decision over the ontological posits that normally guide the positive sciences.

To practice philosophy so conceived, Heidegger explains in *Being and Time*, is "to interpret entities in terms of the basic constitution of their being" (B&T 30/S&Z 10). By focusing on a positive science's guiding ontological presuppositions, philosophy explicitly interprets the being of the domain of entities a positive science studies. In so doing, philosophy can clarify the ontological posits of the positive sciences and so transform and guide the course of their future development.[74] Thus, Heidegger writes:

Laying the foundations for the sciences in this way is different in principle from the kind of "logic" which limps along behind, investigating the status of some science as it chances to find it, in order to discover its "method." Laying the foundations . . . is rather a productive logic – in the sense that it *leaps ahead*, as it were, into a particular region of being, discloses it for the first time in its constitutive being, and makes the structures acquired thereby available to the positive sciences as lucid directives for their inquiry.

(B&T 30–1/S&Z 10, my emphasis)

Here Heidegger is employing *Being and Time*'s well-known distinction between a "leaping ahead" that "liberates" and a "leaping in" that "dominates" (B&T 158–9/S&Z 122), a distinction that for Heidegger marks the difference between authentic and inauthentic methods of pedagogical

---

73 Heidegger reaffirms this view in 1966, proclaiming that: "Phenomenology is more of a science than natural science is" (ZS 211/Z 265).

74 The only exception Heidegger makes to this rule concerns the positive science of theology, in which the guiding ontological posit is accessible and verifiable only through faith, not through secular phenomenological analysis (see B&T 30/S&Z 10 and PT). This, I take it, is what Heidegger means by his oft-repeated, provocative assertion that "philosophical theology" is oxymoronic, a "square circle" or "wooden iron."

"being-together" (*Mitsein*), respectively. The point of using this distinction here, I take it, is that philosophy should guide the sciences not by
imposing preexisting standards on them from outside but, rather, by
anticipating the ontological understanding toward which the sciences
themselves are heading and reflecting that understanding back to them
in a perspicacious manner, thereby illuminating their developmental trajectory from within and so facilitating their continued progression.[75]

Indeed, Heidegger tried to do this himself for the positive science of
"historiography," through close readings of Nietzsche, Dilthey, and other
philosophers of history, a fact that reveals a heretofore unnoticed connection between his conception of "historicality" and his politics. For, if
we recall that *Being and Time*'s notion of authentic "historicality" seeks to
explain philosophically what it is that makes an entity (a term Heidegger
uses in the widest possible sense to designate anything that in any way "is,"
including persons, events, and processes) properly *historical*, and that this
understanding of the *being* of history is what enables historians to distinguish historical from nonhistorical entities, then we can see that, through
the notion of "authentic historicality," Heidegger was himself seeking to
provide a positive science – namely, history or "historiography" – with its
guiding ontological posit. As Charles Guignon shows, Heidegger sought
to derive an account of authentic "historiography" from his understanding of authentic historicality. Indeed, Heidegger was clear about this in
Being and Time, writing that, insofar as the existential analytic "works out
Dasein's historicality ontologically as the ontical condition for the possibility of historiography, it contains the roots of . . . the methodology of
those human sciences which are historiographical" (B&T 62/S&Z 38).
This makes the discussion of authentic historicality in *Being and Time* the
beginning of Heidegger's attempt actually to legislate philosophically the
ontological understanding that should guide the research of a positive
science. (It seems clear, moreover, that even when he restricted his focus to the ontological posit guiding the academic discipline of history,
Heidegger's project did not yield the kind of determinate, science-
guiding results for which he hoped. Unfortunately, rather than radically rethinking or else abandoning this project in 1927, Heidegger just

---

[75] Thus, Heidegger tells his students in 1930 that: "Although we should mistrust physics'
claims to authority [i.e., its pretensions to occupy the metaphysical throne neo-Kantian
philosophy vacated by resigning itself to epistemology], it is not permissible to dismiss
the content of its contemporary problems as so-called empirical material, for these *might point
toward new definitions of the essence of nature as such*" (EHF 104/GA31 147–8, emphasis
restored).

pushes it back to his even more ambitious quest for a fundamental ontology capable of guiding *all* of the positive sciences and, thus, the entire
university.)[76]

In sum, then, philosophy as Heidegger conceives it is no longer the
"train-bearer," following behind the sciences, retroactively straightening
out their methodological tangles. By clarifying the positive sciences' ontological posits, philosophy plays a guiding role with respect to the other
sciences, proactively clarifying their development, issuing "lucid directives for their inquiry" and so helping them "accomplish that for which
they are basically striving" (B&T 71/S&Z 45). In this way, Heidegger believes philosophy can reclaim its historic role as the "torch-bearer" of the
sciences. But toward what end will philosophy thus light the way? Does
Heidegger know the direction in which he seeks to guide the sciences,
the university, Germany?

§15. LESSONS LEARNED (AFTER 1934)

As such questioning reminds us, Heidegger's attempted restoration of
philosophy to her throne can easily sound, under a less flattering description, like a kind of philosophical imperialism. Such an impression would
seem to be reinforced by his idea that the positive sciences as such can neither account for nor supply their own guiding ontological posits, but must
rather take these over from philosophy. Recall, however, that Heidegger's

---

[76] *Geschichtlichkeit* is often translated as "historicity," but this is misleading when discussing
the views of the early Heidegger. The later Heidegger does indeed use *Geschichtlichkeit*
to convey his recognition that being has a history (his hard-won recognition of the fact
that humanity's fundamental sense of reality changes with time), and this is precisely
what most of us mean by the notoriously slippery term "historicity." Indeed, Heidegger's
increasingly radical "historicization of ontology" (to which he is driven by his deconstruction of metaphysics) is one of the definitive characteristics of his so-called turn, the
philosophical transformation that distinguishes the "early" (pre-1937) from the "later"
Heidegger. This means, however, that we cannot read the doctrine of "historicity" back
into 1927's *Being and Time*, in which Heidegger pursues a "fundamental ontology," which,
we will see, is ultimately incompatible with the results of this radical historicization of
ontology. We can, however, disambiguate *Geschichtlichkeit* by introducing a distinction
Heidegger's lifelong use of the term tends to elide, using *historicality* to refer to the being
of history (the early ontological issue about what history is), and reserving *historicity* for
the history of being (the later *Seinsgeschichte*, with its radical historicization of ontology).
Doing so helps us see that historicality and historicity are distinct but developmentally
related concepts, as Guignon shows in his insightful essay on "The History of Being."
More importantly, for our purposes, distinguishing historicality from historicity also helps
us recognize the connection between "authentic historicality" and Heidegger's politics
outlined here in the text.

view does not entail a subordination of scientists to philosophers, since, as we have seen, he does not conceive of the philosophizing that guides science as the exclusive provenance of any particular academic department. Scientists, too, can philosophize; indeed, Heidegger strongly urges that they should. It is just that when scientists philosophize they are no longer doing positive science; they are doing philosophy. Exchanging one hat for another, they have, in Kuhnian terms, left behind the background ontological presuppositions of their normal scientific paradigms in order to philosophize, entering, at least temporarily, into the uncharted waters of revolutionary science by throwing into question the basic ontological assumptions that normally guide their research.[77] In fact, Heidegger's Rectorial Address lays great stress on the need for scientists to philosophize, because he thinks that when "the faculties and disciplines get the essential and simple questions of their science underway," this will bring "down disciplinary barriers" and "transform the faculties and the disciplines from within" (Q&A 12/GA16 115). Still, the underlying worry remains. Given Heidegger's strong emphasis on the importance of cross-disciplinary philosophical questioning, and his assurance that such ontological questioning will transform the scientific disciplines from within by revitalizing and reunifying fragmented academic departments, how are we to understand the authoritarian character of some of the actual reforms he sought to impose during his brief tenure as the *Führer-Rektor* of Freiburg University – including, most notably, his proposal to abolish academic freedom and his seeming readiness to reorganize the departmental divisions of the university immediately, by philosophical fiat if necessary?[78]

To begin to answer this question, we need to understand several further aspects of Heidegger's view. At the time he wrote *Being and Time*, Heidegger believed that the various ontological presuppositions guiding the different positive sciences were not all distinct and irreducible. Instead, he held, first, that the positive sciences' guiding understandings of the being of life, history, the psyche, and so on, all stem from a small number of what he calls "regional ontologies," and, second, that these regional ontologies are all grounded in a single common foundation, what

---

[77] This comparison with Kuhn is intended only as a first approximation to Heidegger's views. (For a succinct explanation of some of their differences, see Dreyfus, *Being-in-the-World*, 279–80.)

[78] Heidegger's Rectorial Address audaciously declares that "this concept of science must intervene in and rearrange the basic forms in which teachers and students each act in a scientific community: In the *departmental faculties* and as *student bodies of specific departments*" (Q&A 11/GA16 115).

Being and Time calls a "fundamental ontology," that is, an understanding of "the meaning of being in general" (B&T 227/S&Z 183).[79] Taken together, these two claims entail that the different ontological posits implicitly guiding the various positive sciences all stem from a common ontological ground. An understanding of the meaning of being in general (a *fundamental ontology*) underlies the regional ontologies, which themselves underlie the positive sciences' various ontological posits. Thus, Heidegger writes (in 1927) that "it is integral to the positive character of a science that its prescientific comportment toward whatever is given (nature, history, economy, space, number) is . . . already illuminated and guided by an understanding of being, even if this understanding of being is not conceptualized" explicitly (PT 42/GA9 50). As *Being and Time* says:

> The question of being aims therefore at ascertaining the *a priori* conditions not only for the possibility of the sciences which examine entities as entities of such and such a type, and, in so doing, already operate with an understanding of being, but also for the possibility of those [regional] ontologies themselves which are prior to the ontical sciences and which provide their foundations.
>
> (B&T 31/S&Z 11)

What, then, is this fundamental ontology that ultimately underlies and implicitly guides all the positive sciences? It takes Heidegger most of the decade after *Being and Time* to answer unequivocally this difficult but crucial question.

Being and Time famously calls for a deconstruction of the history of ontology by which Heidegger believes he will be able to "recover" the fundamental understanding of being that has shaped every subsequent ontology in the history of the West (B&T 44/S&Z 22). This idea that a transhistorically binding ontology can be discovered "beneath" Western history helps explain the more authoritarian dimension of Heidegger's Rectorial Address. For, if a philosophical vision that recognized that and how all the different ontological posits fit together into a fundamental ontology could reunify the university (and, behind it, as we will see, the nation), then Heidegger, as the unique possessor of just such a vision, would be the natural ("fated") spiritual leader of the university, and, thus, the nation. In this sense, Heidegger's neo-Husserlian ambition to restore philosophy to her throne as the queen of the sciences clearly helped fuel

---

[79] For a clear account of Heidegger's slightly confused understanding of "fundamental ontology," see Guignon's important work, *Heidegger and the Problem of Knowledge*, 65–7. (Cf. Husserl, *Ideas: A General Introduction to Pure Phenomenology*, 59–62.)

his political vision for the revitalization of the German university. Such political defects in Heidegger's Rectorial Address now seem glaringly obvious. The main *philosophical* problem, however, is that Heidegger got ahead of himself here. For he had not yet actually worked out *how* the ontological posits fit into the regional ontologies, or how the regional ontologies fit into an underlying fundamental ontology, *before* he assumed this mantle of political leadership. It is in this sense that, despite Husserl's warning, Heidegger did indeed give "in to the force of the motive to influence practice more thoroughly than his theoretical vocation would permit." In 1933, Heidegger was still in the process of working out his view of the way in which an underlying ontology gave rise to the different ontological posits, and when he does, the details of the view undermine rather than support the authoritarian elements of his political project.

In his *History of the Concept of Time* (1925) and in *Being and Time*, Heidegger singles out the ontological classes of "nature" and "history" as "regional ontologies" (HCT 5/GA20 6–7; B&T 31/S&Z 10–11). By 1935, he has traced the regional ontologies of nature and history back to the pre-Socratic conceptions of *phusis* and *alêtheia*, respectively (IM 107/GA20 109). In 1941, he will explicitly characterize this "*phusis–alêtheia*" couple as "the inceptive essence of being," that is, as the first way Western thinkers conceptualized "being" (EP 10/NII 409). Already in 1937, however, he begins redescribing "being" as a never fully conceptualizable phenomenological "presencing" (*Anwesen*) which, because of its nonstatic and nonsubstantive nature, cannot fulfill the foundationalist role expected of the "meaning of being in general" (CP 173, 210/GA65 245, 295–6).[80] Between 1929 and 1937, that is, during the period of intense philosophical turmoil and transformation popularly known as Heidegger's "turn," one of his most significant realizations was that there was no substantive fundamental ontology waiting beneath history to be recovered. When Heidegger traces the regional ontologies of nature and history back to *phusis* and *alêtheia*, then traces this *phusis–alêtheia* couple back to a conceptually inexhaustible ontological "presencing," this is as close as he ever comes to actually "grounding" the regional ontologies in a fundamental ontology, and it is quite instructive. For it shows that the relations between the positive sciences, the regional ontologies, and fundamental ontology are too murky and indirect to allow for a top-down

---

[80] For more on Heidegger's important understanding of (what he calls) the "enowning" (*Ereignis*) of "being as such," see my "The Philosophical Fugue: Understanding the Structure and Goal of Heidegger's *Beiträge*."

hierarchical reorganization of the university in which the philosopher
who has learned to be receptive to phenomenological presencing will
be able first to carve the regional ontologies out of this fundamental
ontological presencing and then construct the new academic disciplines
around these regional ontologies.[81] In other words, had Heidegger succeeded in working out these views a few years earlier, in 1933 instead of
1937, they would have undermined some of the authoritarian policies
of his Rectorate, such as his apparent readiness immediately to legislate new academic disciplines from on high, instead of giving these new
disciplines "at least a generation" to develop. Ironically, Heidegger thus
starkly illustrates the real dangers he and Husserl had so presciently cautioned against; he allowed "external entanglements" to interfere with his
philosophical development and so gave in to the temptation to intercede
politically before having worked out the philosophical views that would
have legitimated – or, more to the point, *undermined* – such an engagement. What, then, did Heidegger learn from this mistake?

Heidegger drops the very notions of "fundamental ontology" and
"regional ontologies" from his later work, instead building his mature
understanding of university education around the insight that "ontotheologies," rather than regional ontologies, mediate between a basic ontological "presencing" and the guiding ontological presuppositions of the
positive sciences. Whatever its political motivations, this was, in the end, a
philosophical lesson. For, as we saw in Chapter 1, when Heidegger actually
carries out the deconstruction of the history of ontology called for in *Being
and Time*, he discovers that a series of metaphysical "ontotheologies" have
temporarily grounded and justified a succession of ontological "epochs"
or historical constellations of intelligibility; each historical age in the West
has been unified by such a basic metaphysical understanding of what and
how entities are. Heidegger will thus conclude that the ontological posits
that guide each of *our* positive sciences come not from some fundamental ontology beneath Western history, but rather from our contemporary
age's reigning ontotheology. Hence, the later Heidegger would hold that
present-day biology, for instance, takes over its implicit ontological understanding of what life *is* from the metaphysical understanding of the

[81] In his Rectorial Address, Heidegger adds "language" (a category meant to map onto his
understanding of the pre-Socratic *logos*) to the regional ontologies of nature and history
(which he traces back to *phusis* and *alêtheia*, respectively), suggesting that the university
should be reorganized into twelve academic disciplines, which would be unified as four
different ways of approaching and elucidating these three regional ontologies (Q&A
9/GA16 111).

being of entities that governs our own Nietzschean epoch of "enframing." And, indeed, one has to admit that when contemporary philosophers of biology proclaim that life *is* a self-replicating system, it certainly appears that they have unknowingly adopted the basic ontotheological presuppositions of Nietzsche's metaphysics, according to which life *is* ultimately the eternal recurrence of will-to-power, that is, sheer will-to-will, unlimited self-augmentation. (It is alarming – if predictable, given Heidegger's critique of our unnoticed reliance on this Nietzschean ontotheology – to thus find philosophers of biology extending the logic of this nihilistic metaphysics in such a way as to grant "life" to the computer virus, a cybernetic entity *par excellence*.) Because Heidegger comes to believe that all of the sciences' guiding ontological posits are implicitly taken over from the nihilistic Nietzschean ontotheology underlying our "atomic age," the first task of his mature understanding of *ontological education* involves making us reflective about the way in which our experience of what is commonly called "reality" has already been shaped by the fundamental conceptual parameters and ultimate standards of legitimacy provided by Nietzsche's metaphysics. As we will see in Chapter 4, when we become aware of the way our age's reigning ontotheology implicitly shapes our understanding of ourselves and our worlds, and thereby come to recognize the subtle but pervasive influence of this ontological understanding of entities as mere resources to be optimized, we begin to open up the possibility of understanding ourselves otherwise than in these nihilistic, Nietzschean terms.

In 1933, however, Heidegger was still "on the way" to clearly articulating these mature views, and so, not surprisingly, he had little success convincing audiences to follow a philosophical leadership they could barely understand. This lack of understanding was disastrous politically, for it allowed Heidegger to appear simply to be endorsing a regime he was in fact attempting philosophically to contest, redirect, and lead philosophically toward a "second, and more profound awakening."[82] So, if some of the

---

[82] For a convincing argument to this effect, see Frank Edler's "Philosophy, Language, Politics: Heidegger's Attempt to Steal the Language of Revolution in 1933–34." I would hasten to add, however, that because Heidegger did not succeed in his attempt to redefine Nazism, his own articulation of the "inner truth and greatness" of this movement proved to be a politically dangerous phantasm – a minor lure rather than a siren song, but no less awful for those few taken in by it. I already mentioned the main problem that follows from this (viz., that because Heidegger's alternative was not understood, its differences from mainstream ideology were not well appreciated, and so he could easily appear to be using his philosophy simply to endorse the existing regime). Yet, for an unlucky few, those distinctive Heidegger supporters who he thus led down the

most authoritarian aspects of Heidegger's Rectorial Address would have
been undermined by the views he worked out by 1937, how far does this
take us toward answering the Confucian question with which we began?[83]
To get to the crux of this question, we need to ask: Would Heidegger's
later claim that the sciences take their ontological preunderstandings
over from a subterranean ontotheology – one that they need to learn to
use the methods of Heideggerian phenomenology in order to recognize,
contest, and transcend – still have helped convince him both (1) to advance the research program driving the Rectorial Address, and (2) to seek
to enforce this research program by instituting a philosophical version
of the *Führer-Prinzip* at Freiburg University? This is a complex question,
and so it will help clarify matters to address its two strands separately.

In response to the first part of the question, I would suggest that
Heidegger's later views could indeed have justified the formal *structure* of
the politico-philosophical research program he advanced in the Rectorial
Address. For, if one examines "The Self-Assertion of the German University" carefully, the role of the Rector (as Heidegger presents it there) is to
unify the university around the various disciplines' shared commitment
to ontological questioning. I believe the later Heidegger would modify
this program primarily by *refining* it, focusing such potentially revolutionary ontological questioning more precisely on the nihilistic Nietzschean
ontotheology that, he came to realize, the various university disciplines
already implicitly shared. Thus, the goal would no longer be the Rectorial Address's neo-Nietzschean pursuit of ontological revolution simply
for the sake of revitalization.[84] By 1938, Heidegger will realize that this

primrose path, the real problem was that they did not get Heidegger's "private National
Socialism" (which had, as we will see, its own dangers and shortcomings), they got the
horrible real thing. If there is any silver lining to this dark cloud forever hanging over
Heidegger's thought, however, it is the one suggested by Gadamer: "There's no doubt
that Schadewaldt was influenced by Heidegger to become a Nazi, and likewise Berve,
who, as an old Silesian nationalist and conservative, became a Nazi. But it is thanks to
both of these people, especially Berve, that people like us were protected" (*Gadamer in
Conversation*, 124).

[83] Indeed, as Dreyfus points out ("Heidegger on the Connection between Nihilism, Art,
Technology, and Politics"), Heidegger understood his critique of technology *as* his philosophical repudiation of Nazism.

[84] In lectures given in 1931–1932, Heidegger gives his students the Nietzschean advice
that they should treat the present "just as every present deserves to be treated, namely
as something to be *overcome*" (ET 7/GA34 10). In 1934, his lectures on "The German
University" show him still entangled in this Nietzschean vision of education: "Knowing
and willing must be awakened, guided, strengthened, and constantly renewed. But that
is the meaning and the task of *education*" (GA16 292).

Nietzschean strategy of constant overcoming follows from Nietzsche's nihilistic metaphysics and so is part of the problem.[85] The basic strategy,
nevertheless, would likely remain the same: First, awaken the faculty to
the way in which their research is grounded in unquestioned ontological
presuppositions, then send these researchers – their philosophers' hats
at the ready – out to the ontological frontiers of knowledge, in order that
they might discover ways of understanding the being of the classes of entities they study otherwise than in terms of this underlying Nietzschean
ontotheology, the nihilistic effects of which Heidegger is just beginning
to recognize in 1933.[86] The basic structure of the Rectorial Address's
research program would be preserved in such an attempt to enlist the
entire academy in the philosophical struggle to transcend the nihilistic
ontotheology of the age. Indeed, such a project is deeply consistent with
Heidegger's lifelong philosophical goal, although it does not seem that
one would need the full authority of a *Führer-Rektor* – rather than, say, a
powerful university president, a committed academic senate, or even an
influential funding agency – in order to awaken the university community
to their possible role in fomenting such an ontohistorical revolution.[87]

If this is right, however, then what it shows is that it is not the structure of the research program advanced in the Rectorial Address that

---

[85] In 1937–1938, Heidegger will finally admit to himself that: "Any kind of theoretical-
scientific (transcendental) laying of the foundation [for the sciences] has become as
impossible as 'endowing a meaning,' which assigns to the existing...science and its
operation a national–political or some other anthropological purpose" (CP 99/GA65
142).

[86] Rather than ask when exactly Heidegger brought his critique of technology to bear on
the university, it is better to recognize that this critique of technology *grew out of* Heidegger's critique of the university. De Beistegui jumps the gun a bit when be writes that
the target in "The Self-Assertion of the German University" is already "the university
of the *Gestell*," but he is certainly right that "Heidegger's attacks on...technology, still
somewhat veiled in the Rectorial address, will become most explicit in the *Contributions
to Philosophy*" (*Heidegger and the Political*, 60, 50). When one reads the critique of the
university Heidegger elaborates in his 1929 Inaugural Address and his 1933 Rectorial
Address from the standpoint of his later work, one can indeed see that Heidegger is beginning to develop his critique of "enframing" there. Nevertheless, this critique of our
Nietzschean, "technological" understanding of the being of entities remained veiled
even to Heidegger himself in 1933. After the failure of his Rectorate, Heidegger sought to
understand the deeper ontohistorical etiology responsible for the crisis of the university
(see GA16 295–6), first fully sketching this underlying understanding of the history of
being in his 1936–1937 *Contributions to Philosophy: From Enowning*. On the "fugal argument" developed in this difficult but important text, see my "The Philosophical Fugue:
Understanding the Structure and Goal of Heidegger's *Beiträge*," esp. 62–4.

[87] Indeed, I will suggest, this is what Derrida has sought to do with the International College
of Philosophy he cofounded in Paris.

is objectionable but, rather, the philosophically misguided commitment to a substantive fundamental ontology underlying and informing that program in 1933, as well as the politically inept and, I shall argue, philosophically objectionable manner in which Heidegger sought to enact this insufficiently clarified research program by enthusiastically instituting the "leadership principle" at Freiburg University, thereby immediately alienating the very colleagues whose strong support his program would have needed simply to get off the ground, let alone to have had any chance of succeeding. Of course, the political challenges faced by anyone seeking to radically transform the structure and mission of a preexisting university – over the objections of well-entrenched countervailing interests – would be extremely formidable, perhaps almost insurmountable, and some recognition of this rather obvious fact may well have helped encourage the authoritarian strategy of top-down institutional change Heidegger so haplessly pursued. Still, such political problems would never have arisen in the first place, had it not been for the way Heidegger prematurely sought to put his insufficiently clarified philosophical project into action.

The main philosophical problem here, we saw, is that Heidegger will soon discover that the relations between a temporally dynamic ontological presencing, the regional ontologies, and the various ontological posits guiding the positive sciences are too murky and indirect to justify the immediate formation of new academic departments carved out around these regional ontologies. As his thought develops, this problem becomes simply intractable. For, when the basic task of his research program changes from the recovery of a fundamental ontology to the contestation of our own ontotheology, the substantive ontology Heidegger hoped to be able to apportion into the subject matter for new departments vanishes, and thus, I think, so does this whole confused version of his program. Ironically, Heidegger would probably have recognized this himself, had he not ignored his own earlier good advice about giving the new academic disciplines "at least a generation" of peace in which to mature and evolve on their own. Indeed, he seemed quickly to recall this lesson after the failure of his Rectorate; in 1934, a mere four months after stepping down, he returns to his earlier call for patience: "We know: All of this is a task that cannot be commanded, which cannot be realized today or tomorrow – perhaps in fifty years a new spiritual institution of higher education can be realized" (GA16 306). I thus think it likely that the flawed substantive philosophical commitment to fundamental ontology underlying this research program in 1933 would have been corrected if the program had been pursued and developed with the requisite patience Heidegger himself had originally called for, because in fact his own earlier belief in a fundamental ontology soon gave way to his recognition of a series of basic ontotheologies.[88] As we will see in Chapter 4, this crucial recognition that the different positive sciences take over their guiding ontological understandings of the being of the classes of entities they study, not from a fundamental ontology but, rather, from a series of different ontotheologies, radically transforms his mature vision for the university. That should not be too surprising, because, in effect, Heidegger abandons the most basic substantive commitment in the background of the research program advanced in the Rectorial Address when he changes its goal from the 1933 project of recovering a single, transhistorically binding fundamental ontology to the later project of recognizing and contesting our own epochal ontotheology.

Let us turn, then, to the second strand of the question posed above, namely: Would Heidegger's mature version of this research program still have encouraged him to institute a philosophical version of the *Führer-Prinzip* at Freiburg University? I have suggested that the authoritarian means Heidegger used to try to enact his earlier views were both politically inept and philosophically confused. If this is so, however, then why did he pursue such a disastrous course? I believe that the most troublingly authoritarian aspect of Heidegger's Rectorial Address – namely, his deservedly infamous discarding of academic freedom – can be much better understood, and so knowingly rejected rather than ignored or excused, if we remember that historically a great deal of the blame for the dissolution of the modern university of Fichte and Humboldt was placed on the new academic freedoms this university introduced. The new *Lehrfreiheit*, the professors' freedom to pursue an individual course of research and teaching, undoubtedly contributed the lion's share to this fragmentation, but, perhaps not surprisingly, most professors laid at least equal

---

[88] It is, of course, possible that Heidegger's political failure helped in some crucial way to make this philosophical recognition possible (e.g., by sending him back to the drawing board, or at least back to his own earlier advice about the importance of patience in the attempt to effect institutional change), or, conversely, that political success might have been stultifying philosophically (discouraging him from abandoning his early view of the role of fundamental ontology and developing his later insights into ontotheology). I will thus be less concerned to speculate about such "other possible worlds" than to reconstruct and develop what I take to be the most salutary aspects of Heidegger's mature vision for university education, because, I will argue, these latter are both of enduring philosophical merit and separable from much of what made the earlier program objectionable.

blame on the policy of *Lernfreiheit*; students' new freedom to develop individual courses of study was seen as having undermined the university's
attempt to unify itself around the shared goal of forming young minds.
This, in fact, is precisely the argument made by Nietzsche in his important but often overlooked early lectures *On the Future of Our Educational
Institutions.*

Here the twenty-seven-year-old Nietzsche, delivering his Inaugural Lectures at the University of Basel, takes aim at the university that has just
hired him (a bold gesture Heidegger will *repeat* in 1929). Nietzsche proposes that a sufficiently robust notion of *Bildung* could accomplish "a re-
juvenation, a reviviscence, and a refining of the spirit of Germany," and
that "as a result of this very process, our educational institutions may also
be indirectly remolded and born again." The young Nietzsche thinks he
can "see a time coming when serious men, working together in the service
of a completely rejuvenated and purified culture, may again become the
directors of a system of everyday instruction, calculated to promote that
culture." But this educational renaissance will require a revolution, Nietzsche proclaims: One must "dare to break with all that exists at present,"
because "the present system is a scandal and a disgrace." Complaining
that "philosophy itself has been banished from the universities" as a result
of the new academic freedoms, Nietzsche concludes by issuing a zealous
summons for the cultural *leadership* of a philosophical genius:

For I repeat it, my friends! All *Bildung* begins with the very opposite of that which
is now so highly esteemed as "academic freedom": *Bildung* begins with obedience,
subordination, discipline, and subjection. Just as great leaders need followers, so
those who are led need the leader [*der Führer*] – a certain reciprocal disposition
prevails here in the hierarchy of spirits: Yea, a kind of preestablished harmony.
This eternal order, toward which all things tend, is always threatened by that
pseudoculture which now sits on the throne of the present. It endeavors either
to bring the leaders down to the level of its own servitude, or else cast them
out altogether. It seduces the followers when they are seeking their predestined
leader, and overcomes them by the fumes of its narcotics. When, however, in spite
of all this, leader and followers have at last met, wounded and sore, there is an
impassioned feeling of rapture, like the echo of an ever-sounding lyre.[89]

89 *On the Future of Our Educational Institutions*, 10, 5, 45, 108, 41, 130, 140–1. Nietzsche's
   call for a return of "that earnest, manly, stern and daring German spirit; that spirit
   of the miner's son, Luther" (138) would have appealed to the young Heidegger,
   who strove to do for philosophy what Luther had done for religion. (See Derrida's insightful
   "Otobiographies: The Teaching of Nietzsche and the Politics of the Proper Name," in
   The Ear of the Other, 28.)

Nietzsche allows this ominous note to reverberate for another three paragraphs, then breaks off these early lectures. Nietzsche had the good sense to suppress their publication (citing his lack of a "clear conscience"), but Heidegger – who visited the Nietzsche archives several times even before joining, in 1935, the commission responsible for putting out a critical edition of Nietzsche's works (with a group of scholars that included Alfred Bäumler, a well-known Nietzschean Nazi who shared Heidegger's radical belief in the necessity of a revolutionary transformation of the university) – would surely have read these highly relevant pages eagerly (HJC 154). Indeed, it seems likely that Nietzsche's virulent critique of academic freedom and his call for a "great *Führer*" to lead the necessary revolution of the university exercised a strong and regrettable influence on the authoritarian program for university reform Heidegger set forth in the Rectorial Address. In my view, those seeking to understand Heidegger's oft-repeated later complaint that "Nietzsche ruined me! [*Nietzsche hat mich kaputt gemacht!*]" would do well to consider the political influence of these lectures carefully.[90]

We find some support for this hypothesis in Heidegger's two recently published talks from 1934 on "The German University."[91] For, if we focus

[90] See Nietzsche's "end of February, 1873" letter to Malvida von Meysenbug (*Sämtliche Briefe*, vol. 4, 127, quoted in Derrida, *The Ear of the Other*, 25). See also Walter Benjamin, "*Nietzsche und das Archiv seiner Schwester*" (1932), *Gesammelte Schriften*, vol. 3, 323–6. The young Nietzsche's influence seems unmistakable on the process whereby, for Heidegger, "the university radicalized by philosophizing became a fully politicized university," despite the truth behind John Caputo's observation that: "Instead of Nietzsche's flight from university philosophy, Heidegger puts his hope for renewal in a university which philosophizes" ("Heidegger's *Kampf*: The Difficulty of a Life," 66, 74). It was Nietzsche's declining health that forced him reluctantly to leave the university, however, and one of Nietzsche's final missives contained the famous statement that he would "rather be a Basel professor than God."

[91] Heidegger delivered these fascinating and troubling lectures to foreign students at Freiburg University on 15–16 August 1934, four months after resigning his failed Rectorship. The fact that these lectures are nowhere mentioned in the voluminous Heidegger controversy (cf. Safranski, *Martin Heidegger*, 252) – apparently escaping all the archives except Heidegger's own (from which they were published only in 2000, in GA16 285–307) – suggests that they had no lasting political impact, yet they remain significant philosophical documents from our perspective. The size and political importance of Heidegger's audience has diminished greatly since his Rectorial Address, but the self-certainty of his philosophical pronouncements remains. Nonetheless, the reader can detect a certain desperation beneath the surface, as Heidegger, on the verge of complete political irrelevance, tries even harder than he had in 1933 to put his vision of "the future German university" (GA16 297–302) in terms that resonate more directly with the National Socialist *Zeitgeist*. As a result, the historical narrative he advances to motivate his vision for this future university is a tangled mix of philosophical insight and Nazi rhetoric:

on the argument Heidegger sketches here in support of his notorious rejection of academic freedom, it seems clear that he is following in Nietzsche's footsteps, although Heidegger now invests more of his hopes for a revitalizing reunification of the German university in a neo-Idealist vision that would recognize and restore the systematic unity of knowledge than in the young Nietzsche's neo-Humboldtian and Wagnerian dream of a community of teachers led by a philosophical genius and jointly committed to a national renaissance. Thus, Heidegger celebrates the fact that philosophy was originally responsible for unifying the modern German university, which was to have been "guided by an all-encompassing philosophical orientation toward the internal connections of the essential domains of knowledge" (GA16 292), and contends that the academic freedoms ("*Lehr- und Lernfreiheit*") introduced at the founding of the modern university were justified solely "on the ground and within the frame of its great determination" (GA16 293). In other words, Heidegger believes these academic freedoms had a rightful place only within an institutional formation unified by a panoramic philosophical view of the essential, where the unifying guidance provided by the philosophical

The modern German university, inspired by the great poets and thinkers and instituted by statesmen, created academic freedoms that inadvertently facilitated the fragmentation and consequent decline of that university, but it can be reborn in the future through the National Socialist movement, which has united the people by spreading the genuine sense of community born on the front lines of World War I. Heidegger thus envisions a German University of the future, through which the essence of the Nazi movement can finally come to know itself ("*The education of the people through the state to the people*: That is the meaning of the National Socialist movement, that is the essence of the new formation of the state [*der neuen Staatsbildung*]"), and so recognize its future: "Through this education the people come to true self-responsibility. Self-responsible peoples are, however, the supreme and only guarantee of *peace*; for this self-responsibility binds itself to the courageous respect for others and demands for itself the unconditional respect of others" (GA16 307). In August 1934 (two months after the Röhm purge), Heidegger still vainly hopes that the future of Nazism will be peaceful ("The new spirit of the German people is not a Nationalism without reigns, addicted to dictating and warmongering, but rather a National *Socialism*" [GA16 304], a movement leading toward the "union and unity" of the German people [302]). He will nevertheless conclude these lectures with a Kantian-sounding argument (familiar from Heidegger's speeches of the time; cf. HC 47–9/GA16 188–9) against the very League of Nations Kant himself argued was necessary for establishing a perpetual international peace. Against Kant's cosmopolitan vision, Heidegger contends that: "Europe...will only preserve itself from decline and achieve a new ascent when each of its peoples act out of the spirit of responsibility and unconditional respect. The community of peoples then no longer needs to be established artificially through a League, rather, it is itself originally and enduringly already there" (GA16 307). (Cf. Kant, "To Perpetual Peace: A Philosophical Sketch," *Perpetual Peace*, 115–18, and Kant, "Idea for a Universal History with a Cosmopolitan Intent," *Perpetual Peace*, 34–6.) We will return to these troubling lectures in Chapter 4.

perspective was to have prevented the fragmentation of the university. Just like Nietzsche, moreover, Heidegger suggests that these academic freedoms undermined the unity of the very university that instituted them. The great German poets, thinkers, and statesmen who founded the modern German university, for all their foresight, had not recognized the "danger of disciplinary fragmentation concealed within the blossoming of academic disciplines" that these freedoms unleashed (GA16 295).[92]

To support and develop this claim, Heidegger sketches the specialization, fragmentation, technologization, and consequent degeneration of the university into vocationalization. As a particularly interesting – and problematic – anticipation of the critique of the university we will examine in Chapter 4, I take the liberty of quoting from Heidegger's heretofore unnoticed remarks at some length. Here is how he describes the dissolution of the university in 1934:

The domains of knowledge became ever broader and the objects of knowledge ever more manifold. The researcher became ever more bound to his *particular* domain. The connections with the other domains of knowledge were severed; *within* these particular domains themselves the whole was increasingly overlooked. The living philosophical *drive* was driven back out of the sciences. Even worse, the more the scientific disciplines came to stand on their own, the more explicit became their rejection of philosophy. The understanding was that science was more genuinely science the more it developed into a specialized discipline and severed itself from the philosophical ground in which it was rooted. This specialization and uprooting of the scientific disciplines was enforced through the emergence of technology and technical thinking. Procedure and method won, overwhelming *what* had been reached through the method. Technology promoted industrialization and the emergence of the proletariat, and thereby the tearing-asunder of the people into classes and parties. An original and unifying, binding spiritual power was lacking. The worldview became a matter of individual standpoints, groups, and parties. The original meaning of *freedom* as binding oneself to the law of the spirit of the people was perverted into its opposite: Arbitrariness of views and the expression of individual opinions. Now the state saw in the university more a practical-technical institution for the education of its bureaucrats. The disparate faculties became professional institutes and vocational schools.

(GA16 295–6)

[92] In 1915, even the young Benjamin joined the protest against a merely negative academic freedom, alleging (from a Marxian perspective) that "the true sign of decadence is . . . the theory and guarantee of academic freedom. . . . No tolerance of opinions and teachings, however free, can be beneficial, so long as there is no guarantee of a form of life that these ideas . . . imply." Like Nietzsche and Heidegger, moreover, Benjamin thought that: "In the universities, a huge problem lies buried, unresolved, and denied. It is a problem that is much larger than the countless causes of friction in society. It is this: How are we to unify spiritual life?" ("The Life of Students," *Selected Writings*, vol. 1, 44, 38).

However problematic, this passage is important for our purposes because it helps establish: (1) That Nietzsche is indeed in the background of Heidegger's thought as he develops his critique of academic freedom (notice that Heidegger's claim about the victory of "procedure and method" echoes Nietzsche's idea, to which Heidegger will later frequently refer, of "the victory of scientific method over science"; it is clear that this "still hardly understood admonisher, Nietzsche, the last great German philosopher" [GA16 297] haunts Heidegger's lecture).[93] (2) That Heidegger holds academic freedoms partly responsible for the disciplinary fragmentation and hyperspecialization by which he thinks the university lost sight of its original mission and degenerated into professionalism and vocationalism (as we will see in detail in Chapter 4). (3) That Heidegger's critique of technology grows out of this critique of the university (although here both critiques are twisted to serve political purposes that distort their aims and impede their development). And, finally, (4) that Heidegger did already understand the "inner truth and greatness" of Nazism as a countermovement to technology (cf. IM 213/GA40 208), however independently problematic such a view already was in 1934.[94]

Now, Nietzsche and Heidegger are surely correct that the proliferation of research domains, which the new academic freedoms made possible, contributed greatly to the disciplinary fragmentation of the modern university (which, let us recall, displaced a university structure with only four departments). Nevertheless, their proposals to eliminate these freedoms *several generations later* are like the proverbial call for the barn door to be closed *after* the animals have escaped – that is, an exacerbation of, not a viable treatment for, the real problems that do indeed accompany disciplinary fragmentation, as we will see in Chapter 4 (§18C). There I shall show (in §20), furthermore, that the authoritarian aspects of Heidegger's views in 1933–1934 are not only philosophically indefensible but also

93 *The Will to Power*, §466, 261: "It is not the victory of science that distinguishes our nineteenth century, but the victory of scientific method over science."
94 The romantic misconception of Nazism Heidegger advances here, in 1934, was definitively demolished by Marcuse in an article published that same year: In "The Struggle Against Liberalism in the Totalitarian View of the State," Marcuse shows National Socialism to be an extreme expression of, rather than a fundamental challenge to, the technological-industrial order. Marcuse persuasively argues that Nazism's propagandistic pretensions about overcoming class divisions by restoring the universal dignity to work, and its related celebration of "struggle" (*Kampf*) and the "people" (*Volk*), were merely ideological smokescreens enabling the Nazi state to rationalize its perpetuation of the harsh material and authoritarian political conditions its monopoly-capitalist system required. (I explore Marcuse's view in "The End of Ontotheology," 290–316.)

inimical to the radical educational research program suggested by his mature insights into ontotheology. I thus take such deeply problematic aspects of Heidegger's early views on the university to be, at best, Confucian "bad examples" (so to speak), that is, *dangers* to be understood, learned from, and so steered well clear of by those of us seeking to develop the more promising vision of education suggested by his later work.[95]

§16. CONCLUSIONS: PÖGGELER AND DERRIDA ON THE CONFUCIAN QUESTION

To clarify the conclusions we have reached in Chapter 3, let us turn now to examine the two other answers that have been given to the Confucian question with which we began: Did Heidegger learn from his failed excursion into university politics and transform the underlying philosophical views that motivated it accordingly? As I mentioned at the beginning (§12), Pöggeler and Derrida both think so. Now that we understand the basic development of Heidegger's views, we are ready to examine and evaluate their interpretations.

---

[95] Even as we examine and reject the anti-individualistic excesses of Heidegger's radical communitarianism (in §20), we might do well to remember, in the interests of political prudence as much as hermeneutic humility, that the elitist and authoritarian excesses found in the educational philosophies of the young Nietzsche and Heidegger (c. 1933–1934) were not entirely absent from those thinkers we honor as founders of our most cherished achievements in liberal-democratic individualism. To wit, Kant, confronting the "crooked timber of humanity," concluded that: "Man is *an animal that... has need of a master,... a master* who will break his self-will and force him to obey a universally valid will, whereby everyone can be free" ("Idea for a Universal History," 33–4). Even the leading liberal-individualist thinker of the nineteenth century, John Stuart Mill, thought that: "No government by a democracy or a numerous aristocracy, either in its political acts or in the opinions, qualities, and tone of mind which it fosters, ever did or could rise above mediocrity except insofar as the sovereign Many have let themselves be guided (which in the best times they have always done) by the counsels and influence of a more highly gifted and instructed *one* or *few*. The initiation of all wise or noble things comes and must come from individuals; generally at first from some one individual. The honor and glory of the average man is that he is capable of following that initiative; that he can respond internally to wise and noble things, and be led to them with his eyes open." Some may find such sentiments disconcerting, but, to his credit, Mill adds (showing a wisdom Heidegger learned rather too late): "I am not countenancing the sort of 'hero-worship' which applauds the strong man of genius for forcibly seizing on the government of the world and making it do his bidding in spite of itself. All he can claim is freedom to point out the way. The power of compelling others into it is not only inconsistent with the freedom and development of all the rest, but corrupting to the strong man himself" (*On Liberty*, 63–4).

According to Pöggeler, recently published notes from a reading group
Heidegger organized on the "threat" of politicized science in 1937–1938
show that "Heidegger finally sees the quest for university reform, set forth
in the questionable thoughts of 1933, to be an illusion." Pöggeler's contention that by 1938 Heidegger had seen through the "illusion" of his
quixotic "quest" for university reform is intriguing but difficult to sub-
stantiate, as both Pöggeler's interpretation and the notes it is based on
are problematically vague.[96] What exactly did Heidegger come to see
as an illusion? Apparently not the idea that the university needed to be
reformed, seeing as Pöggeler's sole clarificatory remark – namely, that
Heidegger "finds the threat of science to lie in the fact that mere specialists perform their work without conviction, and so are defenseless against
manipulation by the state and are enlisted in the struggle for world dom-
ination" – demonstrates that in 1938 Heidegger was still sharpening the
very critique of the university that motivated his quest to reform it, as
we have seen.[97] Some may be tempted to read Pöggeler's paraphrase
as Heidegger's admission that he himself had been "defenseless against
manipulation by the state and . . . enlisted in the struggle for world dom-
ination," but this would mean Heidegger counted himself among those
"mere specialists [who] perform their work without conviction," something no one familiar with Heidegger will find remotely plausible. In fact,
what Pöggeler inadvertently documents here is that Heidegger did not
reject the central features of his critique of the university's failure to live
up to its unifying and guiding ideals, hence its fragmentation and consequent vulnerability to forms of instrumentalization such as vocationalism
and politicization. So, perhaps what Heidegger retracts, then, are the
"questionable" proposals for reforming the university advanced in his
Rectorial Address? As it stands, this claim is still too general. Are we to
believe that Heidegger subsequently rejected the entire structure of the
research project for university reform outlined in the Rectorial Address?
Although Heidegger risks suggesting this in the private note Pöggeler
draws on, there is no evidence for it in his later work, and it is difficult
for those of us sympathetic to the formal structure of this program to believe that this could be the case.[98] If Heidegger does not simply reject his

---

[96] *The Paths of Heidegger's Life and Thought*, 50.

[97] Ibid.

[98] In full, the crucial "excerpt" from Heidegger's notes reads: "So, was that first approach to
      'Self-Assertion,' that is, the desire to return to *questioning* as the center of a new structural
      formation [*Gestaltung*], an illusion [or better, "error," *Irrtum*]? Indeed – an *error* in all pos-
      sible ways, and at the same time an ignorance about the actual drives and machinations

reform strategy *in toto*, however, then which are the dubious proposals? And why did he come to think them illusory?

On these crucial questions Pöggeler remains silent. Still, his way of framing the issue suggests that what Heidegger rejected in 1938 was the *politicization* of the university. Now, "politicization" standardly refers to the Nazi attempt to transform the university into a standing reserve of intellectual and material resources for the German war machine. The lesson Heidegger would have learned from the failure of his Rectorate, then, would be that he should not have subordinated the university to the war effort. If this were Pöggeler's interpretation, that would mean he accepts the view (currently championed by Wolin and others) which maintains, in effect, that Heidegger's Rectorial Address, "The Self-Assertion [*Selbstbehauptung*, literally Self-Heading] of the German University," actually represented "The Self-Beheading [*Selbstenthauptung*] of the German University," as detractors had quipped (to Heidegger's bitter chagrin) at the time. The problem with such a view, however, is that Heidegger directly opposed this Nazi politicization of science in his Rectorial Address, and so could not have come to reject a view he never held. In fact, Heidegger objects in the Rectorial Address that the Nazi demand for a "politicized science" would reduce the German university to an "arsenal of useful knowledge and values," merely another instrument in the war effort, a stockpile of potential weapons research and political propaganda (Q&A 9/GA16 112).

of those groups and interests vying [for political power]" (DBW 23). This seeming *mea culpa* is actually quite misleading. Notice that even as Heidegger appears to criticize his Rectorial Address in strong and general terms, his concrete explanations show he believed the real problem to be that he had misread the external political situation and so had been prevented (by the "machinations" of various "groups and interests") from putting his reforms into effect. Following this same pattern, Heidegger adds in another of these notes: "While I was Rector I truly made many and great mistakes [*Fehler*]," but when he enumerates "the two greatest mistakes," these turn out to be that, first, he did not reckon with the "mean-spiritedness" of his "so-called colleagues" or "the characterless betrayals of the student body," and second, he did not know that "one must not even approach a Ministry [i.e., the political Ministry of Education] with creative demands and far-reaching goals" (DBW 24). If, rather, the "error" was Heidegger's "first approach" (namely, the attempt to unify the university by focusing the disciplines on their shared commitment to ontological questioning), this both cuts against Derrida's interpretation (as we will see) and suggests Heidegger's desire for a *second* approach, one that, once it has been worked out, would focus such potentially revolutionary ontological questioning more precisely on the nihilistic metaphysical postulates that Heidegger comes to realize the various university disciplines already implicitly share. Indeed, Heidegger explicitly calls for a second approach in other notes, from 1937–1938, beginning to outline an "*other* way" that he contrasts to his "Self-Assertion of the German University" (CP 100/GA65 144).

Heidegger clearly meant the Rectorial Address's much-maligned title, "The Self-Assertion of the German University," to be heard as a refusal of the Nazi call for such a politicization of science. Of course, Heidegger's argument against reducing the university to a tool of the war effort bears only a superficial resemblance to Kant's argument in *The Conflict of the Faculties* that the pursuit of knowledge requires a neutrality the state infringes to its own long-term detriment. For Heidegger, the university cannot be a means in the National Socialist mobilization for war because only the university can provide National Socialism with its legitimate – and *legitimating* – end, the historico-philosophical mission in whose terms alone the "revolution" can be justified. What is needed, Heidegger provocatively implies in 1933, is not a politicization of *Wissenschaft* but, rather, a "scientization" of the *polis* (so to speak), a becoming-knowledgeable of Germany. The university will lead this charge, and Heidegger will lead the university.[99]

So, when Pöggeler somewhat misleadingly implies that Heidegger later rejected the *politicization* of the university, I suspect what he really means is that Heidegger finally gave up his belief that the university should play a fundamental political role in leading the Nazi movement. That this is the case is suggested by Pöggeler's assertion (in another essay from *The Paths of Heidegger's Life and Thought*) that *"for a short period* it really was Heidegger's intention to revolutionize the universities in order for the first time to give the National Socialist revolution an intellectual

---

99 Most careful readers of the Rectorial Address reach this same conclusion. Charles Scott writes that: "Heidegger is arguing that the German university...should mold and form the German state" ("Heidegger's Rector's Address: A Loss of the Question of Ethics," 243). As Young puts it, Heidegger sought "not the subordination of the university to the state, but precisely the reverse" (*Heidegger, Philosophy, Nazism*, 20). With such a move, as de Beistegui notes, "the political...is entirely subordinated to the philosophical" (*Heidegger and the Political*, 33). Hence I would also agree with the suggestions of Young (18–19) and de Beistegui (58) that Heidegger really meant what he was saying when, interpreting Plato's call for the philosopher-king, he tells students (in 1931–1932) that: "Plato maintains as his first principle that the authentic guardians of human association in the unity of the *polis* must be those who philosophize. He does not mean that philosophy professors are to becomes chancellors of the state, but that they are to become *phulakes*, guardians. *Control and organization of the state is to be undertaken by philosophers, who set standards and rules in accordance with their widest and deepest freely inquiring knowledge, thus determining the general course society should follow*" (ET 73/GA34 100, my emphasis). Kant himself thought political leaders should consult philosophers before going to war (albeit "secretly," so as to avoid embarrassment), yet also wisely held: "That kings should be philosophers, or philosophers kings, is neither to be expected nor to be desired, for the possession of power inevitably corrupts reason's free judgment" ("To Perpetual Peace," 126).

basis."[100] Pöggeler's idea, then, is that by 1938 Heidegger reversed himself, rejecting his earlier view that the university should shape the "revolution" by providing Nazism with a genuine "intellectual basis." Here we need to proceed carefully. It is certainly true that by 1937 Heidegger realized that those in power never took his "private National Socialism" seriously, and so he had given up his 1933 hope to guide the National Socialist "revolution" into "a second, deeper awakening" (HBC 571). By 1937, Heidegger knew that "the moment" had passed in which it might have been possible to redirect the political movement into the service of the ontohistorical revolution he never stopped pursuing. Nevertheless, for this very reason, Pöggeler is wrong if he thinks Heidegger learned any deep and lasting political lesson here. For Heidegger later clung to the idea that a philosophical redirection of the National Socialist movement had at one point been possible, and he never abandoned the philosophical project he had once hoped to use this political movement to advance. This we can see not only in the details of his often repeated exculpatory narrative, for instance, in his forlorn insistence that if only others had not been too high-minded to get their hands dirty, things could have turned out differently (Q&A 19/GA16 276; DDP 535–7). It is also made obvious by the notorious fact that, in 1953, he could still unabashedly refer to what in 1935 had seemed to him to be the "inner truth and greatness" of the National Socialist movement (IM 213/GA40 208). In this respect, Heidegger was never fully disabused of what Arendt recognized as his astounding political naïveté. Yet, before simply condemning the arrogance of Heidegger's dream of becoming the "spiritual leader standing next to the political leader" (as Hans Sluga puts it), hoping thereby "to lead the leader" (as Heidegger reportedly expressed his fateful ambition to Jaspers), let us also remember Martin Buber's prescient 1927 remark: "Certainly the people that has no leader is unfortunate, but thrice unfortunate is the people whose leader has no teacher."[101]

[100] *The Paths of Heidegger's Life and Thought*, 136 (my emphasis). Christopher Fynsk similarly claims that: "As early as 1934, Heidegger abandoned the idea that the sciences might play a leading role in shaping the course of the revolution" ("But Suppose We Were to Take the Rectorial Address Seriously...Gérard Granel's *De l'université*," 344). The problem with this reading is that Heidegger never believed the sciences, as sciences, could play such a leading role, as we have seen. The crucial question, then, is whether Heidegger ever gave up his idea that philosophy does and should lead the sciences, and, as we will see, he did not.

[101] See Arendt, "For Martin Heidegger's Eightieth Birthday"; Sluga, *Heidegger's Crisis*, 177 (Sluga points out that Hitler megalomaniacally took himself to be his own grand vizier, as it were, and so ignored the many philosophers clamoring for his attention); Pöggeler,

Heidegger realized by 1937 that it was too late to redirect the National Socialist movement into an ontological revolution, but did he also give up on his long-cherished dream of radically reforming the university, transforming higher education so that it would serve his philosophical cause? Pöggeler clearly thinks so, but one last bit of evidence is particularly telling against this interpretation. In the paper Heidegger delivered in 1937 to the natural science and medical faculties at Freiburg University on "The Threat of Science" (and in remarks he made publicly, not merely his private notes), he provocatively asserts that "the university is coming to an end." From these dramatic words it might sound as if Heidegger has simply given up on the university, but his point, heard in context, is nearly the opposite: The German university is self-destructing owing to its politicization by the Nazi regime, but this implosion of the politicized university now provides an opportunity to renew the university's true philosophical mission. Thus, Heidegger adds: "It is neither unfortunate nor fortunate that the university is coming to an end; rather it is only a necessity, and one long in the making. The fact that this day is coming is given to us now as an opportunity for reform" (DBW 25). As these words show, Heidegger was still agitating for his own distinctive variety of radical university reform in 1937, in the very text Pöggeler cites as evidence that Heidegger had given up his quest to transform the university.

The interpretation advanced by Derrida strikes closer to the mark, although he, too, exaggerates Heidegger's break with the university. Derrida's provocative "hypothesis" is that after Heidegger's Rectorial Address in 1933,

the enclosure of the university – as a common place and powerful contract with the state, with the public, with knowledge, with metaphysics and technology – will seem to him less and less capable of matching a more essential responsibility, one which, before having to answer for knowledge, power, or something or other determinate, or to respond as a being or determinate object in the face of a determinate subject, must first respond *to* Being, *from* the call of Being, and must ponder this coresponsibility.[102]

Up through 1933, in other words, Heidegger sought to make the university responsible for explicitly comprehending the dramatic historical transformations then taking place. Heidegger viewed the university as a privileged site for such an analysis, since he held that "questioning

---

"*Den Führer zu führen? Heidegger und kein Ende*"; and Buber, "People and Leader," *Pointing the Way*, 148.

[102] "Mochlos; or, The Conflict of the Faculties," 8.

must be posed...from the essential position of the existence [*Dasein*] that questions" (WIM 167/GA9 103), and the university is positioned at the intersection of the very forces whose history-transforming collision Heidegger thought it should seek to comprehend, namely, the state, the people (*Volk*), technology, metaphysics, and science or knowledge (*Wissenschaft*) itself. Because Heidegger adopts such an approach, he can be understood as extending the ambitious pedagogical agenda of the German Idealists and Humboldt (as we have seen). Derrida thus recognizes a certain tragic nobility in the Rectorial Address:

> Heidegger's discourse on the self-affirmation of the German university undoubtedly represents, in the tradition of [Kant's] *The Conflict of the Faculties* and the great philosophical texts concerning the University of Berlin (Schelling, Fichte, Schleiermacher, Humboldt, Hegel), the last great discourse in which the Western university tries to ponder its essence and its destination in terms of responsibility, with a stable reference to the one idea of knowledge, technology, the state and the nation, up to the very limit where a memorial gathering of thought makes a sudden sign toward the entirely-other of a terrifying future.[103]

As this "terrifying future" came to pass, Heidegger realized that such a "determinate" responsibility (the responsibility of *knowing*, as it were) must be preceded by a "more essential responsibility... *to* being," that is (on Derrida's interpretation), to ontological *questioning*, the "abyssal ground" of knowing, and this, Derrida maintains, is a responsibility to

---

[103] Ibid. What is this "sudden sign toward the entirely-other of a terrifying future" in the Rectorial Address? Derrida is most likely referring to Heidegger's definition of the "spiritual world of the people" as "the power that most deeply preserves the people's earth-and-blood-bound strengths [*erd- und bluthaften krafte*], as the power that most deeply arouses and most profoundly shakes the people's existence [*Dasein*]" (Q&A 9/GA16 112). Here, as Derrida elsewhere recognizes, Heidegger conditionally appropriates the racist, "biologistic" Nazi rhetoric of "blood," in order to substitute his own conception of the ineffable "earth" (*Erde*) for the trope of "soil" (*Boden*) in the Nazi's ideological rhetoric of "blood and soil" (*Blut und Boden*), thereby seeking (again, much too subtly) to ground German identity in his own philosophy (à la Fichte), rather than in the imperialistic ideology of a blood-drenched soil, an ideology that sought to constitute a "Germany" both in and beyond the existing German territory by imagining genetic connections to an ancient warrior people who spilled their blood defending this homeland from Roman invasions in mythic battles of the past (thus, ironically, using an anti-imperialistic mythology to rationalize imperialist aspirations). Derrida points out that Heidegger, by thus "spiritualizing" the biological rhetoric of the National Socialist ideology, inadvertently "biologizes" the *philosopheme* of spirit. For his view of the "fatal necessity" of this "contamination," according to which "one cannot demarcate oneself from biologism,... from racism in its genetic form, one cannot be *opposed* to them except by reinscribing spirit in an oppositional determination," see *Of Spirit: Heidegger and the Question*, 10, 35, 39.

which the university could not measure up. As an institution dedicated
to knowing, to providing determinate answers to pressing historical questions, the university can neither measure up to nor contain Heidegger's
question of being.[104]

If Derrida were right that the later Heidegger rejects the university
as a focal site for the transformation of human existence, this might be
edifying for politically beleaguered "left Heideggerians," that is, left-wing
philosophers deeply influenced by the later Heidegger who too often
stand accused of taking their inspiration from an "unrepentant fascist."
Indeed, it would perhaps be edifying for Derrida himself most of all,
not only because he has been the prime target of such dubious political attacks but also because, although his critics do not yet seem to have
recognized this, Derrida's interpretation of Heidegger's critique of the
university did much to inspire that institutional alternative to the university that Derrida cofounded in Paris (in 1983, but in the spirit of May
1968): the International College of Philosophy.[105] If there is thus a great

---

[104] Similarly, de Beistegui concludes that: "The failure of the Rectorate will also have
marked the failure of a nontechnical mode of organization of the university, of a university that would not entirely be submitted to the imperatives of the *Gestell* or the capital
state" (*Heidegger and the Political*, 36). This claim sits rather unhappily, however, with de
Beistegui's insightful observation (which I take to be an implicit correction to Derrida's
conclusion) that "Heidegger never attempted to turn away from the institution [of the
university] ... Heidegger always felt committed to the institution, as if at stake there
were a responsibility, perhaps responsibility itself, in the form of an ability to respond
to life by way of thought" (40).

[105] See *Who's Afraid of Philosophy? Right to Philosophy 1*, 1–66, 186–92. Derrida envisions the
International College of Philosophy as "a community of *thinking*" (13) whose "unity, the
unicity of its Idea, at least" (15), would come from thinking the "'unthought'" of other
university institutions, uncovering and interrogating what they repress but presuppose
(14–15). The later Heidegger's profound influence here is obvious, although Derrida
downplays it, asserting that "the line I am drawing here between thinking and philosophy, thinking and science, etc., has never taken the form and function Heidegger gives
it" (13). This is a telling denial (what Derrida, after Freud, calls a "denegation," that
is, a public attempt to exorcise a doubt, which, in fact, unconsciously reveals it), given
that Derrida's essay proceeds to extend the very logic of the Heideggerian strategy we
have been examining. Derrida writes, for example, that: "*Philosophy has no horizon*, if
the horizon is, as its name indicates, a limit, if 'horizon' means a line that encircles
or delimits a perspective. This is precisely not the case, by right, for other disciplines
or regions of knowledge. As such, and this is the very status of their identification or
delimitation, they can indeed think their object in an epistemology, transform it by
transforming the founding contract of their institution; but, at least in the institutional
act of their research or teaching, they cannot and must never doubt the pregiven and
preunderstood existence of an object or type of identifiable being" (16). What is this but
a "repetition" of Heidegger, one that, following the logic laid out in *Being and Time* (B&T
434–9/S&Z 382–7), seeks critically to appropriate, update, and so inherit the mission

deal riding on Derrida's interpretation of Heidegger's critique of the university, there are, nevertheless, also good philosophical reasons to be skeptical about Derrida's interpretation. Although Derrida's hermeneutic equation of "being" with "questioning" rehabilitates Heidegger's critique of the university, allowing Heidegger to serve as the prime philosophical inspiration for an international college dedicated to radical questioning, this equation rests heavily on Heidegger's famous claim that "questioning is the piety of thought," and so risks being toppled by important passages in which the later Heidegger stresses that there is something more basic than questioning, since questioning always takes place against the background of a previous answer or "prior claim" (*Zusage*).[106] What Derrida's equation thus misses is the specificity of Heidegger's later questioning; the "prior claim" Heidegger seeks to question is precisely that answer always already supplied by metaphysics – and that means, for our age, by Nietzsche's ontotheological preconception of all entities as eternally recurring will-to-power. My intention, of course, is not to advance some backdoor political attack on the philosophical inspirations of the International College of Philosophy, an admirable institution that has, in my view, more than vindicated its Heideggerian inspiration by successfully nurturing some of the most creative radical critique of our day (work associated with the likes of Derrida, Jean-François Lyotard, Philippe Lacoue-Labarthe, Giorgio Agamben, Luce Irigaray, Hélène Cixous, and

of a chosen "hero," thereby allowing this mission to speak to the changed demands of a contemporary world? (For more on this logic, see my "Deconstructing the Hero.") For Derrida, too, the "privilege" of philosophy is to question every "presupposition" ("to determine the implications of the implicit") taken for granted by the other "disciplines or regions of knowledge" in their "research or teaching" (*Who's Afraid of Philosophy*, 17). The differences between Heidegger and Derrida on these points are actually quite subtle (see 8–9, 60–1). (For other marks of this influence, see Derrida, "The Principle of Reason: The University in the Eyes of Its Pupils"; Geoffrey Bennington and Derrida, *Jacques Derrida*, 258–67; and Derrida, *Eyes of the University: Right to Philosophy 2*, 120–8, 162–8, 195–249.

[106] Derrida implicitly acknowledges the importance of this problem when he interrupts his interpretation of Heidegger's politics with a dense seven-page footnote (in response to an objection from the Heideggerian François Dastur), a note in which he struggles to square his reading of Heidegger's "questioning is the piety of thought" with Heidegger's later emphasis on the "prior claim" (*Zusage*), the preexisting answer already presupposed by every question, as the background understanding that makes the question meaningful (*Of Spirit: Heidegger and the Question*, 129–36, note 5; see also John Sallis, "Flight of Spirit," 127–32). Subsequently, Derrida will explicitly acknowledge the importance of this "preoriginary acquiescence" that undermines "the authority of the question" (*Without Alibi*, 301 note 2; and see also 210, in which Derrida professes his own continuing faith that historical progress will "come *through* the university").

Alain Badiou) but, rather, simply to examine Derrida's answer to the Confucian question with which we began, contrasting his answer with my own.

Derrida holds that after the Rectorial Address, Heidegger realized that the university could no longer serve as a catalytic site for ontohistorical transformation. I would say instead that although the later Heidegger no longer thinks the university *sufficient* to bring about the ontohistorical transformation he continued working philosophically to envision and achieve, he does not give up trying to transform education in general – and thus, by implication, university education as well.[107] It is true that after 1937 Heidegger discusses the university much less frequently, but these very discussions show that he remained true to his basic strategy for university reform. As we will see in detail in Chapter 4, the attempt philosophically to reconceive university education remains an underlying focus of important later texts such as "Plato's Doctrine of Truth" (1940) and *What Is Called Thinking?* (1951–1952), and the later Heidegger often reiterates the underlying philosophical views motivating this pedagogical project, even when he does not draw that connection explicitly. Indeed, the later Heidegger ceaselessly seeks to expand the parameters of the ontological education he sought to install at the heart of the university, thereby working to broaden the educational situation beyond the boundaries of the university. Hence, not only does he return to the university in 1951–1952 for a succinct presentation of his later thought, he also develops aspects of this thinking while communicating with businesspeople in Bremen, townspeople in Messkirch, psychiatrists in Switzerland, artists in Rome, and philosophers in Germany, France, Japan, and America – to name but a few of the groups the later Heidegger sought to *educate* philosophically. To the end, then, Heidegger never gives up the philosophical

---

[107] Derrida seems to concede and take this point aboard when, in 1990, he writes: "The philosopher authorizes himself to speak about the whole: And thus about everything. [The idea is that by conceptually delimiting the totality, philosophy necessarily relates this totality to that which exceeds it, that is, that which goes beyond our current capacities for conceptualization and so calls for the work of philosophy. Given these terms, Derrida is right to call even the later Heidegger a "philosopher."] Such is his mission, such is his power proper, what he bequeaths or delegates to himself in addressing it to himself, beyond every other instance. *To say of this self-authorization that it defines the autonomous power of the University as philosophy and [the] philosophical concept of philosophy does not mean that this discourse would be offered or implied only in the University, even less in chairs of philosophy. . . . We must correct our perception of it and recognize the university site outside the walls of the institution itself"* (*Who's Afraid of Philosophy?*, 61, my emphases).

project that led him to believe that the university might serve to help set off a history-transforming philosophical revolution, nor does he stop trying to reform higher education as an integral part of this revolutionary philosophical project.[108]

Let me, finally, try to forestall any unnecessary controversy by stating explicitly that the direct connection between Heidegger's philosophy and his politics uncovered and examined here will not enable philosophers simply to dismiss Heidegger's later thought, for at least two reasons. First, because, as we have seen, the excesses in his university politics rest in large part on an important philosophical mistake (the belief in a fundamental ontology), which he later corrected (as a philosophical "lesson learned"). Second, and admittedly more provocatively, because the underlying project that led Heidegger to National Socialism is motivated by a deeply insightful critique of the university he continued to develop and refine after the war, and, as I shall argue in the next chapter, this prescient critique has only become increasingly relevant in the meantime. Certainly, Heidegger realized by 1937 that it was too late to redirect the National Socialist movement into the ontological revolution he never

---

[108] For example, see Heidegger's 1951–1952 remarks on the relation between "thinking" and the "university" in *What Is Called Thinking?* (esp. WCT 12–18, 33–34, 134–7). In 1962, Heidegger tells students at his son's technical-vocational school that: "The university . . . is presumably the most ossified school, straggling behind in its structure. Its name 'University' trudges along only as an apparent title. . . . It can be doubted whether the talk about general education, about education as a whole, still meets the circumstances that are formed by the technological age" (TTL 130/USTS 6). As Parvis Emad correctly observes, "Heidegger maintained his relationship to the university up to the last years of his life" ("A Conversation on Heidegger's *Beiträge zur Philosophie* with Friedrich-Wilhelm von Herrmann," 145). Further support for this claim can be found in David Cooper's excellent essay, "Truth, Science, Thinking, and Distress," in Peters, ed., *Heidegger, Education, and Modernity*, esp. 59–61. (I cite this book for the first time here, and given our context, it would be irresponsible not to point out that its first chapter, an essay falsely presented by Valerie Allen and Ares D. Axiotis as an "abridged text of Martin Heidegger's deposition before the Committee on De-Nazification at Freiburg University, translated for the first time into English . . . from the official typewritten transcript of the record of the Committee's proceedings, preserved in the archives of the university" (and so on), is in fact a fanciful dialogue constructed by Allen and Axiotis of what they imagine Heidegger might have said to the de-Nazification hearings – a construction ignorant of what Heidegger *really* did say, indeed, ignorant *that* he did in fact formally submit such accounts himself (DDP 534–55) – and thus something of a hoax. Although the authors imply their ruse in the final paragraph of their (so-called) "Editors' Afterword," the entire piece intentionally blurs the hard-won line between truth and falsehood on the subject of Heidegger's politics and so, in my view, demonstrates an appalling lack of scholarly seriousness.)

stopped pursuing, but he did not give up on his long-developed program for radically reforming the university, nor did he abandon the positive project of transforming higher education so that it would serve his life-long philosophical cause. It is thus to this critique, and so to Heidegger's positive vision of the university, that I believe at least some of the discussion surrounding his politics should be shifted, and to which we will now turn, by way of a conclusion to our study.

4

Heidegger's Mature Vision of Ontological Education, or How We Become What We Are

§17. INTRODUCTION: DECONSTRUCTING EDUCATION

In his later work, Heidegger sought to deconstruct education. Rather than deny this, we should simply reject the polemical reduction of "deconstruction" (*Destruktion*) to "destruction" (*Zerstörung*), and instead be clear that the goal of Heidegger's deconstruction of education, like his deconstruction of the ontological tradition in general, is not to *destroy* our traditional Western educational institutions, but rather to "loosen up" this "hardened tradition and dissolve the concealments it has engendered," in order to "recover" from the beginning of the educational tradition those "primordial experiences" that have fundamentally shaped its subsequent historical development (B&T 44/S&Z 22). Heidegger's deconstructions are so far from being simple destructions that not only do they always include a positive as well as a negative moment, but this negative moment, in which the sedimented layers of distorting interpretations are cleared away, is invariably in the service of the positive moment, in which something long concealed is recovered (as we saw in the Chapter 1). To understand how this double deconstructive strategy operates in the case of education, then, we need simply clarify and develop these two moments: What distortions does Heidegger's deconstruction of education seek to cut through? And, more important, what does it seek to recover? Let us outline the answer to this second, more important question first.

Through a hermeneutic excavation of Plato's famous "allegory of the cave" in the *Republic* – the textual site where pedagogical theory emerged from the noonday shadows of Orphic mystery and Protagorean obscurity in order to institute, for the first time, the "Academy" as such – Heidegger seeks to place before our eyes the most influential understanding of "education" in Western history: Plato's conception of *paideia.* Heidegger maintains that aspects of Plato's founding pedagogical vision have exerted an unparalleled influence on our subsequent historical understandings of "education" (its nature, procedures, and goals), whereas other, even more profound aspects have been forgotten. These forgotten aspects of *paideia* are what his deconstruction of education seeks to recover. Back, then, to our first question: What hermeneutic misconceptions or distortions stand in the way of this recovery and so must first be cleared away? Heidegger's focus here, as we will see in Section 19, is on a troubling misconception about education that also forms part of the legacy of Plato's cave, a distortion embodied in and perpetuated by those institutions that reflect and transmit our historical understanding of education.

Now, many will expect Heidegger's assessment of the future prospects for our educational institutions to be unremittingly pessimistic, given that his later "ontohistorical" (*seinsgeschichtliche*) perspective – that is, his mature understanding of the ontotheological substructure of the history of being – allows him to both discern presciently and diagnose the ontological source of those interlocking historical trends whereby we have come increasingly to instrumentalize, professionalize, vocationalize, corporatize, and ultimately *technologize* education. I shall develop the later Heidegger's powerful critique of the way in which our educational institutions have come to express a nihilistic "technological understanding of being" in Section 18. Before assuming that the later Heidegger's diagnosis of higher education amounts to a death sentence, however, we need to recall the point with which we began: Heidegger's deconstructive strategies always have *two* moments. Thus, when he seeks to recover the ontological core of Platonic *paideia,* his intent is not only to trace the technologization of education back to an ontological ambiguity already inherent in Plato's founding pedagogical vision, thereby demonstrating the historical *contingency* of these disturbing educational trends and so loosening their grip on us. More importantly, he also means to show how forgotten aspects of the original Platonic notion of *paideia* remain capable of inspiring heretofore unthought possibilities for the *future* of education. Indeed, only Heidegger's hope for the future of our educational institutions can explain his otherwise entirely mysterious claim that his *paideia* "interpretation" is "made necessary from out of a future need [*aus einer künftigen Not notwendige*]" (PDT 167/GA9 218).

This oracular pronouncement might sound mysterious, but I believe Heidegger's deconstruction of education is motivated entirely by this "future need." I submit that this future need is double; like the deconstruction mobilized in its service, it entails a positive as well as a negative moment. These two moments are so important that much of Chapter 4 will be devoted to their explication. Negatively, we need a critical perspective that will allow us to grasp the underlying historical logic according to which our educational institutions have developed and will continue to develop if nothing is done to alter their course. As I shall show in Section 19, the later Heidegger was among the first to diagnose correctly what a growing number of incisive critics of contemporary education have subsequently confirmed: We now stand in the midst of an historical crisis in higher education. Heidegger's unique and profound understanding of the nature of this crisis – his insight that it can be understood as a near total eclipse of Plato's original educational ideal by the Nietzschean ontotheology underlying our own age – reveals the ontohistorical trajectory leading up to our current educational crisis and, more important, suggestively illuminates a pedagogical strategy meant to help lead us out of this crisis.

This is fortunate, because the gravity of the later Heidegger's diagnosis immediately suggests a complementary, positive need. We need an alternative to our contemporary understanding of education, one capable of favorably resolving our educational crisis by averting the technological dissolution of the historical essence of education. Put simply, but by way of anticipation, Heidegger's hope is this: Because an ambiguity at the heart of Plato's original understanding of education lent itself to an historical misunderstanding by which the essence of education has been obscured and is now in danger of being forgotten, the deconstructive recovery of this long-obscured essence of education can now help us begin to envision ways of restoring meaning to the increasingly formal and empty ideals guiding contemporary education. It thus makes perfect sense that this need for a positive alternative leads Heidegger back to Plato's cave. Retracing his steps in Section 19, we will reconstruct "the essence of education" Heidegger seeks to recover from the shadows of history, thereby fleshing out his positive vision. In Section 20, we will conclude by considering (1) how this reontologization of education might help us begin to envision a path leading beyond our contemporary educational crisis, and (2) whether this positive strategy suggested by Heidegger's later work can avoid the problems that, as we saw in Chapter 3, disastrously misdirected his own attempt to transform higher education circa 1933.

§18. HEIDEGGER'S ONTOHISTORICAL CRITIQUE OF THE TECHNOLOGIZATION OF EDUCATION

The first aspect of our "future need" is for a critical perspective that will allow us to discern the underlying logic that has long guided the historical development of our educational institutions, a perspective that will render visible the developmental trajectory these institutions continue to follow. As intimated earlier, Heidegger contends that his ontotheologically grounded "history of being" (*Seinsgeschichte*) provides precisely this perspective. As he puts it, "the essence of truth and the kinds of transformations it undergoes first make possible [the historical unfolding of] 'education' in its basic structures" (PDT 167/GA9 218). Heidegger means by this that the history of being *makes possible* the historical development of our educational institutions, although to see this we must carefully unpack his initially puzzling reference to "the essence of truth and the kinds of transformations it undergoes." In order to do so, we need first to remind ourselves of the main details of Heidegger's understanding of ontotheology as the substructure of this history of being, and then see how this understanding of ontotheology generates his profound critique of education.

A. From the Essence of Truth to the History of Being

Heidegger's pronouncement that the essence of truth undergoes historical transformations may initially sound paradoxical: How can an essence *change*? This will indeed seem impossible to someone like Kripke, who holds that an essence is a property an entity possesses necessarily, the referent of a "rigid designator" the extension of which is supposed to be fixed across "all possible worlds" (notions with much-debated problems of their own).[1] The paradox disappears for Heidegger's view, however, once we realize that he, too, uses "essence" (*Wesen*) as a technical term, albeit quite differently from Kripke. Recall that, in order to understand "essence" in phrases such as "the essence of truth" and "the essence of technology," we cannot conceive of "essence" the way we have been doing since Plato, as what "*permanently* endures," for that makes it seem as if by *essence* "we mean some mythological abstraction." As we saw in Section 8, we need instead to think of "essence" as a *verb*, as the way in which things "essence" or "remain in play" (QCT 30/GA7 31). In Heidegger's

---

[1] See, for example, Kripke's *Naming and Necessity* and David Lewis's *Counterfactuals* (Ch. 4) for competing construals of the ontological status of "possible worlds."

usage, "essence" picks out the extension of an entity unfolding itself in historical intelligibility. Otherwise put, Heidegger understands "essence" in terms of *being*, and since being is not a real predicate (as Kant showed), there is little likelihood that an entity's "essence" can be picked out by a single, fixed predicate or underlying property, as two thousand years of substance metaphysics leads us (and Kripke) to assume. Instead, for Heidegger "essence" simply denotes the historical way in which an entity comes to reveal itself ontologically and be understood by *Dasein*. Accordingly, "essence" must be understood in terms of the "ek-sistence" of *Dasein*, that is, in terms of "being set-out into the disclosedness of beings" (OET 145/GA9 189).

In "On the Essence of Truth" (1929), Heidegger applies this historical understanding of "essence" to *truth*, contending famously (if no longer terribly controversially) that the original historical "essence of truth" is not simply "unforgottenness" (*Unvergessenheit*), a literal translation of the original Greek word for "truth," *alêtheia* (composed of the *alpha*-privative "un-" plus *Lêthê*, the mythological "river of forgetting"), but phenomenological "un-concealedness" (*Un-verborgenheit*), a more general emergence from oblivion into intelligibility. Heidegger's point is that historically, "truth" first refers to *revealedness* or *phenomenological manifestation* rather than accurate representation; the "locus of truth" is not originally the correspondence of an assertion to a state of affairs, but the antecedent fact that there is something *there* to which the assertion might correspond. So conceived, the "essence of truth" is a "revealedness" fully coextensional with *Dasein*'s "existence," our "standing-out" (*ek-sistere*) historically into phenomenological intelligibility. "The essence of truth" thus refers to the basic way in which this "revealedness" takes shape historically, namely, as a series of different ontological *constellations of intelligibility*. It is not surprising, then, that Heidegger first began to elaborate his "history of being" in "On the Essence of Truth"; for him, "the essence of truth" *is* "the history of being."

Of course, such strong claims about the radically historical character of our concepts (especially cherished concepts such as *essence, truth, history, concept*, and *being*) tend to make philosophers nervous, and so suspicious: When Heidegger historicizes ontology by rerooting it in the historical existence of *Dasein*, how does he avoid simply dissolving intelligibility into the flux of time? Heidegger's answer is surprising. It is, as we saw in Chapter 1, the metaphysical tradition that prevents intelligibility from dissolving into an undifferentiated temporal flux. Unfortunately, Heidegger's complex and idiosyncratic understanding of Western metaphysics as *ontotheology*, coupled with his seemingly strong antipathy to metaphysics, has tended to obscure the unparalleled pride of place he in fact assigns to metaphysics in the historical construction, contestation, and maintenance of intelligibility. Still, careful readers will notice that when Heidegger writes that "ek-sistent, disclosive Da-sein possesses the human being so originarily that only *it* secures for humanity that distinctive relatedness to *the totality of entities as such* which first grounds all history" (OET 145–6/GA9 190, second emphasis mine), he is (with the phrase I have italicized) directly appealing to his account of the way in which metaphysics grounds intelligibility.

Remember that Heidegger defines ontotheology as "the truth concerning the totality of entities as such"; our metaphysicians' *ontological* understandings of what entities are "as such" ground intelligibility from the inside out, while their *theological* understandings of the way in which the "totality" of beings exist simultaneously secure the intelligible order from the outside in. Western history's successive constellations of intelligibility are thus "doubly grounded" in a series of ontotheologically structured understandings of "the being of entities" (*das Sein des Seienden*), "fundamental metaphysical positions" establishing both *what* and *how* entities *are*, or "the truth concerning the totality of entities as such." Heidegger's understanding of metaphysics as ontotheology thus answers our worry; for, although none of these double ontotheological grounds has served the history of intelligibility as an unshakeable "foundation" (*Grund*), nor have any of the major ontotheologies instantly given way like a groundless "abyss" (*Abgrund*). Rather, each ontotheology has served its historical constellation of intelligibility as an *Ungrund*, "a perhaps necessary appearance of ground," that is, as that point at which our deepest and broadest inquiries come temporarily to a rest (IM 3/GA40 5). Because each ontotheology serves for a time as the dual point where (to redeploy Wittgenstein's apt locution) our spades turn, the history of intelligibility has taken the form of a series of relatively durable, overlapping historical "epochs" rather than either a single monolithic understanding of what-is or a formless ontological flux.[2] In this way, metaphysics, by repeatedly supplying intelligibility with dual ontotheological anchors, is able "to hold back" (*epochê*) the floodwaters of historicity for a time – the time of an historical "epoch" – and it is this "overlapping" historical series of ontotheologically grounded epochs that Heidegger refers to as *the history of being.*

[2] *Philosophical Investigations*, ¶217, 85.

B. The History of Being as the Ground of Education

With this understanding of ontotheology serving as our philosophical background, we can now understand the reasoning behind Heidegger's claim that our changing historical understanding of "education" is grounded in the history of being.[3] Put simply, Heidegger defends what I have characterized as a kind of *ontological holism*: By giving shape to our historical understanding of "what *is*," metaphysics determines the most basic presuppositions of what *anything* is, including *education*. As he writes: "Western humanity, in all its comportment toward entities, and even toward itself, is in every respect sustained and guided by metaphysics" (N4 205/NII 343). The "great metaphysicians," we have seen, focus and disseminate an ontotheological understanding of what and how entities *are*, thereby establishing the most basic conceptual parameters and ultimate standards of legitimacy for their historical epochs. These ontotheologies function historically like self-fulfilling prophecies, focusing and reshaping intelligibility across the board. For, as a new ontotheological understanding of what and how entities *are* takes hold and spreads, it transforms our basic understanding of what *all* entities are. Our understanding of education is "made possible" by the history of being, then, since when our understanding of what entities *are* changes historically, our understanding of what "education" *is* transforms as well.

This conclusion is crucial; not only does it answer the question that has guided us thus far (namely, Why does Heidegger think that the history of education is grounded in the history of being?), it also positions us to understand what exactly Heidegger finds objectionable about our contemporary understanding of education and the educational institutions that embody this understanding. If our changing historical understanding of what "education" *is* has its place in an historical series of ontological "epochs," and if these holistic constellations of intelligibility are themselves grounded in a series of ontotheological understandings of *what* and *how* entities *are*, then the history of education is grounded in this historical succession of ontotheologies at the core of the history of being. Hence, in order fully to comprehend Heidegger's critique of contemporary education, we need to answer three interrelated questions: First, *what* exactly is the nature of our own epoch in this history of being? Second, in *which* ontotheology is our current constellation of intelligibility grounded? And, third, *how* has this underlying ontotheology shaped

---

[3] "The essence of 'education' is grounded in the essence of 'truth'" (PDT 170/GA9 222).

our present understanding of education? We will take these important questions in order.

Heidegger's name for our contemporary constellation of intelligibility is "enframing" (*das Gestell*). As we saw in Chapter 2, Heidegger chooses this polysemic term because, by etymologically connoting a *gathering together* ("*Ge-*") of the myriad forms of *stellen* ("to set, stand, regulate, secure, ready, establish," and so on), it succinctly conveys his understanding of the way in which our present "mode of revealing" – a "setting-upon that challenges forth" – forces the "presencing" (*Anwesen*) of entities into its metaphysical "stamp or mold" (*Prägung*) (QCT 16–21/GA7 16–22). This, let us recall, is not to substitute etymology for argument, as some detractors assume, because, although Heidegger uses etymology in order to come up with an appropriate name for our contemporary "mode of revealing," the argumentative work in his account is done by his understanding of metaphysics as ontotheology. This means that in order truly to understand why Heidegger characterizes our contemporary epoch as *das Gestell*, we must take the measure of his claim that this "enframing" is grounded in an ontotheology transmitted to us by Nietzsche. On Heidegger's reductive and thus controversial – but in my view deeply insightful – interpretation, Nietzsche's staunch antimetaphysical stance merely conceals the fact that he actually philosophized on the basis of an "unthought" metaphysics. Although this is evident in his published works as well, Nietzsche's *Nachlaß* clearly demonstrates that he conceptualized "the totality of entities as such" *ontotheologically*, as "eternally recurring will-to-power," that is, as an unending disaggregation and reaggregation of forces without purpose or goal.[4] This Nietzschean ontotheology not only inaugurates the "metaphysics of the atomic age," *it grounds enframing*: Our unthinking reliance on Nietzsche's ontotheology is leading us to transform all beings, ourselves included, into mere "resources" (*Bestand*), entities lacking intrinsic meaning that are thus relentlessly optimized and ordered with maximal efficiency so as to serve the purely instrumental interests of flexible use (N4 199–250/NII 335–98).

---

[4] See especially the last note preserved in *The Will to Power* (549–50), in which Nietzsche clearly conceives of entities *as such* as will-to-power and also of the way that the *totality* exists as eternal recurrence. Nor can Heidegger's controversial reading be rejected simply by excluding this unpublished work on the basis of its politically compromised ancestry (as some Nietzscheans allege), because the core doctrines of Nietzsche's metaphysics also can be found in his published works – most prominently, in *Thus Spoke Zarathustra*. For convincing arguments to this effect from two leading Nietzsche scholars, see John Richardson's *Nietzsche's System* and Laurence Lampert's *Nietzsche's Teaching*.

Heidegger, for reasons we examined at the end of Section 9, characterizes this "enframing" as a *technological* understanding of being. As an
historical "mode of revealing" in which entities increasingly show up only
as resources to be optimized, enframing generates a "calculative thinking"
that, like the mythic touch of King Midas, quantifies all qualitative relations. This "limitless 'quantification,'" which absorbs all qualitative relations – until we come to treat "quantity *as* quality" (CP 94/GA65 135) –
is rooted in enframing's ontologically reductive mode of revealing, which
requires that: "Only what is calculable in advance counts as being" (CP
95/GA65 137). Enframing thus tends to reduce all entities to bivalent,
programmable "information" (TTL 136/USTS 17), digitized data, which
increasingly enters into "a state of pure circulation" (as Baudrillard aptly
expresses our paradoxical, endless destination).[5] Heidegger, however, is
not criticizing digitization *per se*, but rather the way such universal quantification facilitates the empty optimization imperative that presses itself upon our lives, increasingly shaping our understanding of self and
world down to its most minute details.[6] As Heidegger's phenomenological meditation on a highway interchange revealed to him in the
1950s – and as our "information superhighway," the Internet, now makes
plain – we exhibit a growing tendency to relate to our world and ourselves merely as a "network of long distance traffic, paced as calculated for
maximum yield" (PLT 152/GA7 155). Reading quotidian historical de-
velopments in terms of this ontohistorical logic, Heidegger believed our
passage from Cartesian modernity to Nietzschean late modernity was already visible in the transformation of employment agencies into "human

[5] *The Transparency of Evil*, 4. Baudrillard envisions a dystopian fulfillment of this dream,
a "grand delete" in which computers succeed in exhaustively representing meaning,
then delete human life so as not to allow us to upset the perfectly completed equation. Baudrillard's ominous vision of this technological "final solution," although vividly
brought to life in films such as the *Terminator* and *Matrix* series, seems to stem from a
faulty premise, because intelligibility can never be exhaustively represented. (See Dreyfus,
What Computers Still Can't Do, and below.) Unfortunately, more defensible versions of
Baudrillard's nightmare scenario are not difficult to imagine.

[6] David Brooks nicely describes the way our "ideology of potentiality" encourages "object-
less striving" from our youth: "There exists in this country a massive organic apparatus for
the production of children, a mighty Achievatron. Nobody planned it. There is no central
control deck. But all the anxious parents, child psychologists, teachers, tutors, coaches,
counselors, therapists, family-centered activist groups, and social critics organically cohere
into an omnipresent network of encouragement, improvement, advice, talent maximization, and capacity fulfillment. This system is frightening, when you step back and grasp
its awesome power, its ability to mold little ones for frictionless ascent and smooth their
eccentricities to maximize social aerodynamics. . . . [T]he Achievatron micromanages the
tiniest issues in young people's lives" (*On Paradise Drive*, 136, 142, 175, 183).

resource" departments. The technological move afoot to reduce teachers and scholars to "online content providers" merely extends, and so clarifies, the logic whereby modern subjects transform themselves into late-modern "resources" (*Bestand*) by turning techniques developed for controlling nature back onto themselves (QCT 18/GA7 18). Unfortunately, as this historical transformation of subjects into resources becomes more pervasive, it further eludes our critical gaze. Indeed, we blithely risk the "total thoughtlessness" of merely instrumental "calculative thinking" (QCT 27/GA7 28; DT 46/G 13) by coming to treat ourselves in the very terms that underlie our technological refashioning of the world: no longer as conscious Cartesian subjects taking control of an objective world, but, rather, as one more resource to be optimized, ordered, and enhanced with maximal efficiency – whether cosmetically, psychopharmacologically, genetically, or even *educationally*.

It is precisely here, then, that Heidegger uncovers the subterranean ontohistorical logic guiding the development of our educational institutions. This brings us to our third and final question: *How* does contemporary education reflect this nihilistic logic of enframing? In what sense are today's educational institutions caught up in an unlimited quantification of qualitative relations, one that strips entities of their intrinsic meanings, distinctive traits, and unique capacities, transforming them into mere resources to be optimized, ordered, and enhanced with maximal efficiency?

C. Education as Enframing

Heidegger began developing his critique of higher education in 1911 and continued elaborating it well into the 1960s (as we saw in Chapter 3), but he provides perhaps his most direct answer to our question in 1929. Having just been awarded a philosophical chair (on the basis of *Being and Time*), the thirty-nine-year-old Heidegger gives his official "Inaugural Lecture" at Freiburg University, the famous "What Is Metaphysics?" Heidegger begins boldly, emphasizing philosophy's concrete "existential" foundations and so directing his critical attention to the university itself, a move he justifies by appealing to the principle that "metaphysical questioning must be posed...from the essential position of the existence [*Dasein*] that questions." Within this lifeworld of the university, he observes, "existence" (*Dasein*) is determined by *Wissenschaft*, the knowledge embodied in the humanities and natural sciences. "Our *Dasein* – in the community of researchers, teachers, and students – is

determined by science or knowledge [*durch die Wissenschaft bestimmt*]"
(WIM 82/GA9 103).[7] Our very "being-in-the-world" is shaped by the
knowledge we pursue, uncover, and embody. When Heidegger claims
that existence is fundamentally shaped by knowledge, he is not thinking
of a professoriate shifting in the winds of academic trends, nor simply arguing for a kind of pedagogical or performative consistency, according to
which we should practice what we know. His point, rather, is to emphasize
a troubling sense in which it seems that we cannot help practicing what
we know, since we are "always-already" implicitly shaped by our guiding
metaphysical presuppositions. Heidegger's question thus becomes: What
is the *ontological impact* of our unquestioned reliance on the particular
metaphysical presuppositions that tacitly dominate the Academy? "What
happens to us essentially, in the ground of our existence," when the *Wissenschaft* pursued in the contemporary university becomes our guiding
"passion," fundamentally shaping our view of the world and of ourselves?

Heidegger's answer famously presents his radical critique of the hyperspecialization and consequent fragmentation of the modern university:

The fields of science are widely separated. Their ways of handling the objects
of their inquiries differ fundamentally. Today only the technical organization of
universities and faculties consolidates this multiplicity of dispersed disciplines,
only through practical and instrumental goals do they maintain any meaning.
The rootedness of the sciences in their essential ground has dried up and died.

(WIM 82–3/GA9 103–4)

Here in 1929 Heidegger accurately describes the predicament of that
institution which, almost half a century later, Clark Kerr would satirically
label the "multiversity," an internally fragmented *uni*-versity-in-name-only,
where the sole communal unity seems to stem from a common grievance
over the lack of parking spaces.[8] Historically, as the modern university
loses sight of the shared goals that originally justified the endeavors of
the academic community as a whole – at first, with the German Idealists,
the collective pursuit of the unified "system" of knowledge, and then,
with Humboldt, the mutual dedication to the formation of cultivated
individuals – its members begin to look outside the university for some

---

[7] Heidegger's insistence on existentially situated questioning – and thus on the university
as the "life context" or "situation" within which his ontological questioning must begin –
goes back to his work from the early 1920s (see GA61 63).
[8] We cannot even add "and faculty salaries," as Kerr did, because the diminishing funding
of public education has turned students against increases in faculty and staff salaries,
which they perceive as directly linked to tuition increases.

purpose to give meaning to lives of research. Since only those disciplines (or, more often today, subdisciplines) able to produce instrumentally useful results regularly find such external support, all disciplines increasingly try to present themselves in terms of their use-value. Without a countervailing ideal, students, too, will tend to adopt this purely instrumental mentality, coming to see education merely as a means to an increased salary down the road. In this way, fragmentation leads to the professionalization of the university and, eventually, its deterioration into vocationalism. At the same time, moreover, the different disciplines, lacking any shared, substantive sense of a unifying purpose or common subject matter, tend by the logic of specialization to develop internal standards appropriate to their particular object-domains. As these domains become increasingly specialized, these internal standards become ever more disparate, if not simply incommensurable. In this way, disciplinary fragmentation leaves the university without common standards, other than the now ubiquitous but entirely empty and formal ideal of *excellence.*

Following in Heidegger's footsteps, important critics of higher education such as Bill Readings and Timothy Clark show how our contemporary "university of excellence," owing to "the very emptiness of the idea of excellence," is "becoming an excellent bureaucratic corporation," "geared to no higher idea than its own maximized self-perpetuation according to optimal input/output ratios."[9] Such diagnoses support Heidegger's argument that the development of our educational institutions continues to follow the underlying metaphysical logic of enframing, the progressive

---

9 See Readings, *The University in Ruins,* 152, 125; and Clark, "Literary Force: Institutional Values." In his keynote address to the National Association of Scholars (31 May 2002), Bruce Cole, the chairman of the National Endowment for the Humanities, observes that: "Too many colleges and universities are turning their focus away from liberal education and toward professional training....As a result [of a market with many more qualified applicants than desirable jobs], humanities scholars have been called upon to justify their existence and measure their success against inappropriate standards. When a university begins to set its priorities and determine its class offerings according to the return on the dollar, it is not long before accounting will force out philosophy" ("Shoring Up the Humanities," 11). I would add that the growing ethical challenges Cole criticizes (cheating, plagiarism, and the like) also need to be understood as symptoms of the ontotheological problem Heidegger uncovers. For, when all entities are understood only as resources to be optimized, students and education included, any sense of the intrinsic meaning, purpose, or value of education is lost or forsaken, and instrumental justifications rush into the breach. The burgeoning culture of cheating needs to be viewed in this light, as the result of an instrumentally rational calculation performed by those who understand "education" merely as a means to external ends (such as career advancement and monetary gain). I will thus conclude by suggesting how we might begin to remedy these problems at their roots by restoring our shared sense of the intrinsic meaning of education.

transformation of all entities into intrinsically meaningless resources to be optimized. Unfortunately, these critics fail to recognize the underlying ontotheology ultimately responsible for this empty optimization imperative, and so offer diagnoses without cures. Thus, although Readings calls for a recognizably left-Heideggerian refusal "to submit Thought to the exclusive rule of exchange-value," this is not a call he can justify in the materialist terms he adopts. Indeed, Readings's materialist explanation for the historical obsolescence of *Bildung* as the unifying ideal of the modern university (the result of an "implacable . . . bourgeois economic revolution") leads him to succumb to a cynicism in which future denizens of the university can hope for nothing more than "pragmatic" situational responses in an environment increasingly transformed by "the logic of consumerism."[10] Although these important critics of the university convincingly extend and update aspects of Heidegger's analysis, they do not recognize these disturbing trends as interlocking symptoms of an underlying ontotheological problem, and, as a result, they are unable to provide a positive vision for the future of higher education. By understanding our educational crisis in terms of its ontotheological roots, Heidegger, in contrast, is able to suggest an alternative, ontological

---

[10] *The University in Ruins*, 132, 178, 222 note 10. Readings distinguishes three historical phases in the development of the modern university, characterizing each by reference to its guiding idea, namely, "the university of reason," "the university of culture," and "the university of excellence." These distinctions are elegant but a bit simplistic; for example, the university of reason existed for only a few fabled years at the end of the eighteenth century at the University of Jena, where the greatest pedagogical and philosophical thinkers of the time (Fichte, Goethe, Schiller, Schelling, Schleiermacher, the Schlegel brothers, and others) developed the implications of German Idealism for education. Ironically, when representatives of this assemblage sought to formalize the principles underlying their commitment to the system of knowledge in order to inaugurate the University of Berlin, they inadvertently helped create the model of the university that succeeded their own: Humboldt's university of "culture" (or better, *Bildung*, the cultivation and development of fully formed individuals). According to Readings's materialist account, the industrial revolution's push toward globalization undermined this university of culture's unifying idea of serving a *national* culture (cf. Gerald Graff, *Beyond the Culture Wars*), eventually generating its institutional successor, the contemporary "university of excellence," a university defined by its *lack* of any substantive, unifying self-conception. Readings's work is insightful, but this account of the historical transition from "the university of culture" to "the university of excellence" is overly dependent on a dubious reduction of *Bildung* – the educational cultivation of fully formed individuals – with *national culture*. The later Heidegger's account of the development of education – as reflecting an ontohistorical *dissolution* of its guiding idea – is, I will suggest, more satisfactory. Although Heidegger is critical of aspects of what Readings calls "the university of culture" and "the university of excellence," we will see that Heidegger's vision for the reinstauration of the university nevertheless combines his ontological reconceptions of *Bildung* and excellence.

conception of education meant to help us bring about a renaissance of the university.

To see that Heidegger himself was not relinquishing his hope for the future of higher education when he developed this prescient critique in 1929, we need only carefully attend to the performative dimension of his "Inaugural Lecture." On the surface, it may seem as if Heidegger, fully welcomed at last into the arms of the university, rather perversely uses his celebratory lecture to pronounce the death of the institution that has just made him a full professor, proclaiming that: "The rootedness of the sciences in their essential ground has dried up and died." With this deliberate provocation, however, Heidegger is not beating a dead horse; his pronouncement that the university is dead at its roots implies that it is fated to wither and decay *unless it is revivified*, reinvigorated from the root. He thus uses this organic metaphor of "rootedness" (*Verwurzelung*) to put into effect what Derrida (who has self-consciously repeated this scene himself) recognizes as "a phoenix motif": "One burns or buries what is *already dead* so that life . . . will be reborn and regenerated from these ashes."[11] Indeed, Heidegger begins to outline his program for a renaissance of the university in the lecture's conclusion: Existence is determined by science, but science itself remains rooted in metaphysics, whether it realizes it or not. Because the roots of the university are metaphysical, a reinstauration of the scientific lifeworld requires a renewed attention to this underlying metaphysical dimension. "Only if science exists on the basis of metaphysics can it achieve anew its essential task, which is not to amass and classify bits of knowledge, but to disclose in ever-renewed fashion the entire expanse of truth in nature and history" (WIM 95/GA9 121).

What exactly is Heidegger proposing here? We have seen where this project took him in 1933, when he yoked it to a political movement before it was sufficiently developed and clarified. To understand the details of his mature vision for a rebirth of the university, however, we need to turn to a pedagogically crucial text Heidegger began writing the next year, in 1930, but continued to develop, distill, and refine up until its

---

[11] *The Ear of the Other*, 26. Derrida deliberately restages this scene in "The Principle of Reason: The University Through the Eyes of Its Pupils," in which he gives "something like an inaugural address" (5), and again in the lecture published as the "Appendix" to his "Philosophy of the Estates General" (*Who's Afraid of Philosophy*, 186–92), a "repetition" whereby Derrida again seeks to *inherit* Heidegger (just as Heidegger himself had done with Nietzsche).

publication in 1940 as the essay "Plato's Doctrine of Truth."[12] In this important work, Heidegger offers a highly suggestive sketch for the future of higher education, a sketch we can develop on the basis of his mature insights into ontotheology, thereby seeking to avoid the problems that, we have seen, plagued his work on the university *circa* 1933. Here, in 1941, by tracing the ontohistorical roots of our educational crisis back to Plato's cave, Heidegger begins to *excavate* (as it were) an alternative.

§19. HEIDEGGER'S RETURN TO PLATO'S CAVE: ONTOLOGICAL EDUCATION AS THE ESSENCE OF *PAIDEIA*

Plato seeks to . . . show that the essence of *paideia* does not consist in merely pouring knowledge into the unprepared soul as if it were a container held out empty and waiting. On the contrary, real education lays hold of the soul itself and transforms it in its entirety by first of all leading us to the place of our essential being and accustoming us to it.

(PDT 167/GA9 217)

Our contemporary educational crisis can be traced back to and understood as an ontohistorical dissolution of Plato's original conception of education, Heidegger contends, so the deconstructive recovery of this "essence of *paideia*" is crucial to successfully resolving the crisis. A deeply resonant Greek word, *paideia* can mean "civilization, culture, development, tradition, literature, or education"; thus it encompasses what to our ears seems to be a rather wide range of semantic frequencies.[13]

---

[12] Published in 1940, Heidegger's essay *Platons Lehre von der Wahrheit* summarizes, refines, and develops themes from a 1930 lecture of the same title as well as from lecture courses he gave on Plato in 1931–1932 and 1933–1934 (see ET 237/GA34 333–4). Were this important essay not already known by the title "Plato's Doctrine of Truth," I would translate *Platons Lehre von der Wahrheit* as "Plato's Teaching on Truth" in order both to preserve Heidegger's reference to *teaching* and to emphasize his title's dual implication (1) that education is grounded in (the history of) truth, as we have seen; and (2) that Plato's own influential views on truth cover over and so obscure truth's historically earlier and ontologically more basic meaning, as we will see. The second implication underwrites the standard translation, but the first is not often recognized.

[13] Contending that "*paideia*, the shaping of the Greek character," best explains "the unique educational genius which is the secret of the undying influence of Greece on all subsequent ages," Jaeger pitched his work in terms that harmonized only too well with the dominant Nazi concerns (vitalism, the breeding of the Nietzschean "higher man," race, eugenics, people, community, leader, state, and so on), writing, for example, that: "Every nation which has reached a certain stage of development is instinctively impelled to practice education. Education is the process by which a community preserves and transmits its physical character. For the individual passes away, but the type remains. . . . Education, as practiced by man, is inspired by the same creative and directive vital force which impels

Heidegger was deeply drawn to the word, not only because, thanks largely to Werner Jaeger, it served as a key term in that intersection of German academic and political life that Heidegger sought in vain to occupy during the 1930s, but also because he had an undeniable fondness for what we could call (with a wink to Freud) the *polysemic perversity* of language, that is, the fortuitous ambiguities and unpredictable interconnections that form the warp and weave of its semantic web. Recognizing that such rich language tends to resist the analyst's pursuit of an unambiguous exactness, Heidegger argued that "rigorous" philosophical precision calls instead for an attempt to do justice to this semantic richness.[14]

As both Gadamer and Derrida have frequently shown, however, this demand for us to do justice to language is *aporetic* (a "necessary impossibility"), because the holism of meaning renders the attempt ultimately impossible, not only practically (for finite beings like ourselves, who cannot follow all the strands in the semantic web at once) but also in principle (despite our Borgesian dreams of a complete hypertext capable of capturing the entire semantic web in its links, a dream even the celebrated "World Wide Web" barely inches toward realizing). This unfulfillable call for the philosopher *to do justice to language* is, nevertheless, *ethical* in the Kantian sense; it constitutes a regulative ideal, orienting our progress while remaining unreachable, like a guiding star. It is also, and for Heidegger more primordially, "*ethos*-ical" (so to speak), because such a call can be answered "authentically" only if it is taken up existentially and embodied in an *ethos*, a way of being. In *Being and Time*, Heidegger describes the called-for comportment as *Ent-schlossenheit*, "disclosedness or re-solve"; later he will teach it as *Gelassenheit*, "releasement or letting-be." *Ent-schlossenheit* and *Gelassenheit* are not, of course, simply equivalent terms; releasement evolves out of resolve through a series of intermediary formulations and notably lacks resolve's voluntarism.[15] Yet,

---

every natural species to maintain and preserve its own type" (*Paideia: The Ideals of Greek Culture*, xiii).

14 On Heidegger's view, "Polysemy is no objection against the rigorousness of what is thought thereby. For all genuine thinking remains in its essence thoughtfully...polysemic [*mehrdeutig*].... Polysemy is the element in which all thinking must itself be underway in order to be rigorous" (WCT 71/WHD 68).

15 Heidegger writes "*Entschlossenheit*" ("resoluteness" or "decisiveness") as "*Ent-schlossenheit*" ("un-closedness") in order to emphasize that the existential "resoluteness" whereby Dasein finds a way to repossess itself by authentically choosing the commitments that define it (and is thus reborn, in effect, after having been radically individualized in being-toward-death) does not entail deciding on a particular course of action ahead of time and obstinately sticking to one's guns come what may but, rather, requires an

both entail a responsive hermeneutic receptivity (whether existential or phenomenological), and both designate comportments whereby we embody, reflexively, an understanding of what we *are*, ontologically, namely, *Da-sein*, "being here," a making intelligible of the place in which we find ourselves.

Such considerations allow us to see that we *are* the place to which Heidegger is referring (in the epigraph above) when he writes that "real education lays hold of the soul itself and transforms it in its entirety by first of all leading us to the place of our essential being [*Wesensort*] and accustoming us to it." As this epigraph shows, Heidegger believes he has fulfilled the ethical dictate to do justice to language by recovering "the essence of *paideia*," the ontological carrier wave underlying *paideia*'s multiple semantic frequencies. Ventriloquizing Plato, Heidegger deploys this notion of the essence of *paideia* in order to contrast two different conceptions of education. He warns first against a "false interpretation": We cannot understand education as merely the transmission of "information," filling the *psyche* with knowledge as if inscribing a *tabula rasa* or, in more contemporary parlance, "training-up" a neural net. This understanding of education is false not only because (in the terms of *Being and Time*) we are "thrown" beings, "always already" shaped by a tradition we can never "get behind," and so we cannot be blank slates or "empty containers" waiting to be filled, but also, and more tellingly, because (as we will see) education itself cannot be reduced to the mere transmission of information.[16] Such a "reductive and atrophied" misconception

---

"openness" whereby one continues to be responsive to the emerging solicitations of the particular existential "situation." The existential situation is thus not unlike a living puzzle we need to repeatedly "re-solve" (a pun not available in German, and so an example of the perverse polysemy of language mentioned earlier). The later notion of *Gelassenheit* (or, more precisely, *Gelassenheit zu den Dingen*) names a comportment in which we maintain our sensitivity to some of the interconnected ways in which *things* show themselves to us – viz., as grounded, as mattering, as taking place within a horizon of possibilities, and as showing themselves to finite beings who disclose a world through language – four phenomenological modalities of "presencing" that Heidegger, in a *détournement* of Hölderlin, calls "earth," "heavens," "divinities," and "mortals" (see QCT 149–51/GA7 179–82). On this "fourfold," see also my "Ethics and Ontology at the Intersection of Phenomenology and Environmental Philosophy" and Wrathall's "Between the Earth and the Sky: Heidegger on Life after the Death of God."

[16] The increasingly dominant *metaphor*, too often literalized, of the brain as a computer forgets (to paraphrase a line from Heidegger's 1942–1943 lecture course, *Parmenides*) that we do not only think *because* we have a brain; we also *have* a brain because we can think (PAR 145–6/GA54 217). Of course, one need not commit oneself to an understanding of human beings as either blank slates or neural nets in order to conceive of education

of education reflects the nihilistic logic of enframing, that ontohistorical trend by which intelligibility is "leveled out into the uniform storage of information" (P xiii/GA9 x). This ontohistorical development explains the increasingly ubiquitous quantification of education, which preconceives of students as *Bestand*, not as human beings with intrinsic talents and capacities to be identified and cultivated, but rather as educational "outcomes" to be "optimized" in uniformly quantifiable terms, shackling educators to systems of standardized testing to which they must conform or else be deprived further of their already severely limited material resources. Students, moreover, blithely adopt this empty optimization imperative, seeking continually to "keep their options open" (as they often express the logic that guides them), and so failing to recognize that such a strategy is not only impossible (because, as ontologically finite beings, we necessarily develop some existential possibilities at the expense of others) but also incompatible with the difficult decisions we in fact should make, insofar as real *fulfillment* (Heidegger, like other perfectionists, would argue) follows from *narrowing* our preexisting array of options by learning to recognize and develop our own unique and significantly *distinctive* talents and capacities.[17] Assisting in the endeavor to identify and develop such inherent talents and capacities will thus be an essential part of the task of any teacher. Yet, here again we face a situation in which as the problem spreads we become less likely to recognize it; the "impact" of this underlying ontological drift toward meaninglessness can "barely be noticed by contemporary humanity because we are continually covered over with the latest information" (TTL 142/USTS 27), inundated by the newest and latest theoretical and technological innovations for this endless pursuit of maximal self-optimization.

It is against this self-insulating but false interpretation of education that Heidegger advances his conception of "real or genuine education" (*echte Bildung*), the "essence of *paideia*." Drawing on the allegory of the cave, an allegory that – as Plato himself claims at the beginning of Book VII of the *Republic* – "illustrates the essence of 'education' [*paideia*]" (PDT 167/GA9 217–18), Heidegger seeks to effect nothing less than a reontologizing revolution in our understanding of education. Recall Heidegger's succinct and powerful formulation: "Real education lays hold of the soul

---

as information transfer, so I take Heidegger's broader critique of this latter conception to be the more telling one.

[17] For an admirably clear reconstruction of Dasein's "constant closing down of possibilities," see Carman, *Heidegger's Analytic*, 276–84.

itself and transforms it in its entirety by first of all leading us to the place of our essential being and accustoming [*eingewöhnt*] us to it." This, for Heidegger, is how we "become what we are."[18] Genuine education leads us back to ourselves, to the place we *are* (the *Da* of our *Sein*), teaches us "to dwell" (*wohnen*) "there" and transforms us in the process. This transformative journey back to ourselves is not a flight away from the world into thought, but a reflexive return to the fundamental "realm of the human sojourn [*Aufenthaltsbezirk des Menschen*]" (PDT 168/GA9 219).[19] The goal of this educational odyssey is simple but literally revolutionary: to bring us full circle back to ourselves, first by turning us away from the world in which we are most immediately immersed, then by turning us back to this world in a more reflexive way. As Heidegger explains, "*Paideia* means the turning around of the whole human being in the sense of displacing us out of the region of immediate encountering and accustoming us to another realm in which beings appear" (PDT 167/GA9 218).

How, then, does Heidegger propose that we accomplish such an *ontological revolution* in education? What are the pedagogical methods of this alternative conception of education? And how, finally, does he think this ontological conception of education can help us overturn the *enframing* of education?

---

[18] Heidegger already appropriates this famous exhortation (with which Nietzsche echoes the second of Pindar's *Pythian Odes*) in *Being and Time*: Dasein can exhort itself to: "'Become what you are'... only because it *is* what it becomes" (B&T 186/S&Z 145); that is, we can meaningfully develop our distinctive capacities only because our future goals, roles, and life-projects constitutively inform our present, implicitly organizing our experience. Moreover, when Dasein makes the world discovered in the light of its self-understanding explicit, and so "works out" the possibilities implicitly disclosed in its self-understanding, Dasein "does not become something different. *It becomes itself*" (B&T 188–9, my emphasis/S&Z 148).

[19] *Aufenthalte* ("abidance, sojourn, stay, or stop-over") is an important term of art for the later Heidegger; it nicely connotes the *finitude* of our existential journey through intelligibility. Because *Aufenthalte* is also the title Heidegger gave to the journal in which he recorded his thoughts during his first trip to Greece in the spring of 1962 (see A), it is tempting to render it as "odyssey" in order to emphasize Heidegger's engagement with the Homeric heritage and the crucial sense of coming full circle back to oneself. The idea of a journey between nothingnesses adds a more poetic – and tragic – dimension to Heidegger's etymological emphasis on "existence" as the "standing-out" (*ek-sistere*) into intelligibility. Yet, like the Hebrew *gêr*, the "sojourn" of the non-Israelite in Israel (see, e.g., Exodus 12:19), *Aufenthalte* clearly also connotes the "homecoming through alterity" Heidegger powerfully elaborates in his 1942 lecture course on *Hölderlin's Hymn "The Ister"* (HHI), and is thus properly polysemic (and "jewgreek," as Lyotard puts it in *Heidegger and "the Jews,"* borrowing James Joyce's provocative expression). See also John Taber, *Transformative Philosophy: A Study of Sankara, Fichte, and Heidegger,* 104–15.

A. Ontological Education Against Enframing

In "Plato's Doctrine of [or "Teaching on," *Lehre von*] Truth," Heidegger's exposition is complicated by the fact that he is simultaneously explicating his own positive understanding of "education" and critiquing an important transformation in the history of "truth" inaugurated by Plato, namely, the transition from truth understood as *alêtheia*, phenomenological "unhiddenness," to *orthotês*, the "correctness" of an assertion. From this "ambiguity in Plato's doctrine," in which "truth still is, at one and the same time, unhiddenness and correctness" (PDT 177–8/GA9 230–1), the subsequent tradition will develop only the *orthotic* understanding of truth at the expense of the *alêtheiac*. In so doing, we lose sight of "the original essence of truth," the manifestation of entities themselves, and come to understand truth solely as a feature of our own representational capacities. In this way truth becomes the subject of epistemology rather than ontology, that is, a matter of the way in which we secure our knowledge of entities, rather than of the way entities disclose themselves to us. According to Heidegger, this displacement of the locus of truth from being to human subjectivity paves the way for a *metaphysical humanism* (or *subjectivism*) in which the "essence of *paideia*" will be eclipsed, allowing "education" to be absorbed by enframing and so become merely a means for "bringing 'human beings' ... to the liberation of their possibilities, the certitude of their destination, and the securing of their 'living'" (PDT 181/GA9 236).

Despite such dramatic rhetorical flourishes, however, Heidegger has not entirely given up on "genuine education" (or *Bildung*). He dismisses the understanding of *Bildung* as a belle-lettrist cultivation of taste and other "subjective qualities" as a "misinterpretation to which the notion fell victim in the nineteenth century," but maintains that once *Bildung* is "given back its original naming power," it is the word that "comes closest to capturing the [meaning of the] word *paideia*." For, *Bildung* is literally ambiguous, Heidegger tells us; its "naming force" drives in two directions:

What "*Bildung*" expresses is twofold: First, *Bildung* means forming [*Bilden*] in the sense of impressing a character that unfolds. But at the same time this "forming" [*"Bilden"*] "forms" [*"bildet"*] (or impresses a character) by antecedently taking its measure from some measure-giving vision, which for that reason is called the pre-conception [*Vor-bild*].

"Thus," Heidegger concludes, "'education' [*"Bildung"*] means impressing a character, especially as guiding by a preconception" (PDT 166–7/GA9

217). (The English *education* harbors an analogous ambiguity: "Education" comes from the Latin *educare*, "to rear or bring up," which is closely related to *educere*, "to lead forth." Indeed, our "education" seems to have absorbed the Latin *educere*, for "education" means not only "bringing up" in the sense of *training* but also "bringing forth" in the sense of *developing*, meanings that come together in the perfectionist conception of education as a training that identifies and develops our intrinsic and relevantly distinctive aptitudes and abilities.)[20]

Few would quibble with Heidegger's first claim: Education stamps us with a character that unfolds within us. But what forms the "stamp" that forms us? *Who educates the educators?* According to Heidegger, the answer to this question is built into the very meaning of *paideia*; it is the second sense he seeks to "restore" to *Bildung*. To further unfold these two senses of "education," Heidegger immediately introduces the term's contrast-class: "the contrary of *paideia* is *apaideusia*, lack of education [*Bildunglosigkeit*], where no fundamental comportment is awakened, no measure-giving preconception established" (PDT 167/GA9 217). This helpfully clarifies Heidegger's first claim: It is by awakening a "fundamental comportment" that education stamps us with a character that unfolds within us. In the educational situation – a situation without predelimitable boundaries, indeed, a situation the boundaries of which Heidegger ceaselessly sought to expand (in accordance with his view that "*paideia* is essentially a movement of passage, from *apaideusia* to *paideia*," so that education is not something that can ever be *completed*) – the "fundamental comportment" perhaps most frequently called for is not the heroic *Entschlossenheit*, or even the gentler *Gelassenheit*, but rather a more basic form of receptive spontaneity Heidegger will simply call *hearing* or *hearkening* (*hören*), that is, an attentive and responsive way of dwelling in one's environment (OWL 75–6/GA12 169–70).[21] Yet, whether the comportment implicitly guiding education is "resoluteness," "releasement," "hearing," or that anxiety tranquilizing *hurry* that generally characterizes contemporary life

---

[20] Similarly, as Geuss emphasizes, "*Bildung* can be used to refer to a process of formation or to the form imparted in such a process" (*Morality, Culture, and History*, 32). See also Cavell, *Conditions Handsome and Unhandsome: The Constitution of Emersonian Perfectionism*.

[21] There is thus a notion of *being poised* at work here throughout, a shared call for a kind of vigilance amid repose. As Heidegger put it in 1931–1932, "the soul is as such striving for being... it is what it genuinely is only insofar as it maintains itself in this striving. What it means for the human being to be *himself*, or to be a *self*, can be understood only from this phenomenon of striving for being" (ET 166/GA34 232–3).

(B&T 222/S&Z 177) depends on the second sense of *Bildung*, which remains puzzling: From where do we derive the measure-giving vision that implicitly informs all genuine education?

Heidegger's answer is complicated, let us recall, by the fact that he is both elaborating his mature *philosophy of education*, on the one hand, and performing a critical exegesis of Plato's decisive metaphysical contribution to "the history that we *are*," the history of metaphysics, on the other. These two aims are in tension with one another because the education Heidegger seeks to impart – the fundamental attunement he seeks to awaken in his students – is itself an attempt to awaken us *from* the ontological education that we have "always already" received from the metaphysical tradition. For, this generally unnoticed antecedent measure comes to us from metaphysics, that is, from the ontotheologically structured understanding of the being of entities. In other words, Heidegger seeks to educate his students *against* their preexisting ontotheological education. He will later call this educating-against-education simply "teaching." The crucial question, then, is: *How* can Heidegger's ontological education combat the metaphysical education we have always already received?

B. The Pedagogy of Ontological Freedom

Heidegger's suggestions about how the ontological education he advocates can transcend enframing are surprisingly specific, and so constitute a decisive rejoinder to the common criticism (mentioned in §9 earlier) that Heidegger offers us no concrete suggestions about *how* we might transcend enframing. To fully develop his suggestions, we need to recall the four stages that make up Plato's famous allegory: The prisoner (1) begins in captivity within the cave; (2) escapes the chains and turns around to discover the fire and objects responsible for the shadows on the wall previously taken as reality; then (3) ascends from the cave into the light of the outside world, coming to understand what is seen there as made possible by the light of the sun; and, finally (4) returns to the cave, taking up the struggle to free the other prisoners, who violently resist their would-be liberator. What I will now show is that, for Heidegger, this well-known scenario suggests the precise pedagogy of ontological education. On his interpretation, the prisoner's "four different dwelling places" suggest the four successive stages whereby ontological education breaks students' bondage to the technological mode of revealing, freeing them to understand the being of what-is differently. Let us thus flesh out this view.

When students' ontological educations begin, they "are engrossed in what they immediately encounter," taking the shadows cast by the fire on the wall to be the ultimate reality of things. Yet, this "fire" is only "man-made"; the "confusing" light it casts represents enframing's ontologically reductive mode of revealing. Here in this first stage, all entities show up to students merely as resources to be optimized, including the students *themselves*. Thus, if pressed, students will ultimately "justify" even their education itself merely as a means to making more money, getting the most out of their potentials, or some other equally empty form of enframing's optimization imperative. Stage 2 is only reached when a student's "gaze is freed from its captivity to shadows"; this happens when a student recognizes "the fire" (enframing) as the source of "the shadows" (entities understood as mere resources). In stage 2, the *metaphysical* chains of enframing are recognized and thereby broken. Yet, *how* does this liberation occur? Despite the importance of this question, Heidegger answers it only in an aside, writing that "to turn one's gaze from the shadows to entities as they show themselves within the glow of the firelight is difficult and fails" (PDT 170/GA9 222). His point, I take it, is that entities do not show themselves *as they are* when forced into the metaphysical mold of enframing, because its underlying ontotheology reduces them to mere resources to be optimized. Students can be lead to this realization through a guided investigation of the being of any entity, which they will tend to understand only as eternally recurring will-to-power, that is, as forces endlessly coming together and breaking apart with no goal beyond their own self-augmenting increase. Because this metaphysical understanding dissolves being into becoming, the attempt to see entities as they *are* in its light is doomed to failure; put simply, resources ultimately have no *being*, they are merely "constantly becoming" (as Nietzsche realized). With this recognition – and the anxiety it tends to induce – students can attain a negative *freedom from* enframing.

Still, Heidegger insists that "real freedom," "effective freedom" (*wirk-liche Freiheit*) – the positive freedom in which students realize that entities are more than mere resources and so become *free for* understanding their being otherwise – "is attained only in stage 3, in which someone who has been unchained is . . . conveyed outside the cave 'into the open.'" (Notice the implicit reference to someone doing the unchaining and conveying here; for Heidegger, the educator plays a crucial role facilitating students' passages between each of the stages.) Here the open is one of Heidegger's names for "being as such"; that is, for "what appears antecedently in everything that appears and . . . makes whatever appears be accessible"

(PDT 170/GA9 222).[22] The attainment of – or better, comportmental *attunement to* – this "open" is what Heidegger famously calls "dwelling."[23] When such positive *ontological freedom* is achieved, "what things are ... no longer appear merely in the man-made and confusing glow of the fire within the cave. The things themselves stand there in the binding force and validity of their own visible form" (PDT 169/GA9 221). Ontological freedom is achieved, in other words, when entities show themselves in their full phenomenological richness and complexity, overflowing and so exceeding the conceptual boundaries our normally unnoticed on-totheological enframing places on them. The goal of the third stage of ontological education, then, is to teach students to "dwell," to help attune them to the *being* of entities, and thus to teach them to see that the being of an entity – be it a book, cup, rose, or, to use a particularly salient example, *they themselves* – cannot be fully understood in the ontologically reductive terms of enframing.[24] For, when we learn to *dwell* – and so become attuned to the phenomenological "presencing" whereby "being as such" manifests itself – we come to understand and experience entities as being richer in meaning than we are capable of doing justice to conceptually, rather than taking them as intrinsically meaningless resources awaiting optimization, and so learn to approach them with care, humility, patience, gratitude, even awe. Such experiences can become microcosms of, as well as inspiration for, the revolution beyond our underlying ontotheology that Heidegger argues we need in order to transcend enframing and begin to set our world aright.

---

[22] When being careful (as he is here), the later Heidegger often employs a subtle distinction between two different senses of "clearing" (nominal and verbal), namely, the *open* and the *lighting*, the "open" referring to being as such, the "lighting" to a particular understanding of the being of entities. His ontological *plural realism* thus comes through in his view that the open *informs* the lighting without being exhausted by it, a view implicit in his explanation that: "The open into which the freed prisoner has now been placed does not mean the unboundedness of some wide-open space; rather, the open sets boundaries to things and is the binding power characteristic of the brightness [i.e., the *lighting*, in this case, Plato's doctrine of *ideas*] radiating from the light of the sun [i.e., the *open*, being as such]" (PDT 169/GA9 221).

[23] See also PLT 145–61/GA7 147–64.

[24] Metaphysics forgets that the condition of its own possibility – namely, the temporally dynamic "presencing" (*Anwesen*) of entities – is also the condition of its impossibility. For, as we saw in Chapter 1, the phenomenological presencing that elicits conceptualization can never be entirely captured by the yoke of our concepts, metaphysical or otherwise; it always partially defies conceptualization, lingering behind as an extraconceptual phenomenological excess.

With the attainment of this crucial third stage, then, Heidegger's "genuine" ontological education may seem to have reached its completion, since "the very essence of *paideia* consists in making the human being strong for the clarity and constancy of insight into essence" (PDT 176/GA9 229). Heidegger's oft-repeated claim that genuine education teaches students to recognize "essences" is not merely a Platonic conceit but plays an absolutely crucial role in his program for a reunification of the university (as we will see in §20). Nevertheless, ontological education reaches its true culmination only in the fourth stage: *the return to the cave.* Heidegger clearly understood his own role as a teacher in terms of just such a return, that is, as a struggle to free technologically anaesthetized enframers from their bondage to a self-reifying mode of ontological revealing.²⁵ Nevertheless, his ranking of the return to the cave as the highest stage of ontological education is not simply an evangelistic call for others to adopt his vision of education as a revolution in "consciousness" or, better (because the very concept of an interior consciousness stems from the dualistic metaphysical tradition Heidegger seeks to undercut and transcend), in our very Dasein, that is, our *being here* – our making intelligible of the place in which we find ourselves (and so can repossess ourselves and come genuinely into our own).²⁶ The great emphasis Heidegger places on the return to the cave reflects his recognition that in ontological education, *learning culminates in teaching.* We must thus ask: What is called "teaching"?

C. What Is Called Teaching?

The English "teach" comes from the same linguistic family as the German verb *zeigen,* "to point or show."²⁷ Indeed, as its etymology suggests, *to teach*

---

²⁵ Heidegger knew from personal experience that this is no easy task. Someone who has "escaped the cave" by learning to develop a comportment receptive to modes of phenomenological revealing other than enframing "no longer knows his or her way around the cave and risks the danger of succumbing to the overwhelming power of the kind of truth that is normative there, the danger of being overcome by the claim of the common reality to be the only reality" (PDT 171/GA9 222–3).

²⁶ I discuss Heidegger's philosophical efforts to undercut and transcend the metaphysics of mentalism in "Ontology and Ethics"; on his radical challenge to Cartesian dualism more generally, see the influential works by Dreyfus, *Being-in-the-World*; Guignon, *Heidegger and the Problem of Knowledge*; and John Richardson, *Existential Epistemology: A Heideggerian Critique of the Cartesian Project.*

²⁷ As the *Oxford English Dictionary* recounts, the etymology of "teach" goes back through the Old English *tæcan* or *tæcean.* One of the first recorded uses of the word in English

is to reveal, to point out or make manifest through words. To reveal *what,* however? What does the teacher, who "points out" or reveals with words, point to or indicate?[28] *What* do teachers teach? The question seems to presuppose that all teaching shares a common "subject matter," not simply a shared method or goal (the inculcation of critical thinking, persuasive writing, and the like), but something more substantive: a common subject matter that would implicitly unify the University. Now, of course all teachers use words to disclose, but to disclose a common subject matter? How could such a supposition not sound absurd to us professional denizens of a postmodern polyversity, where relentless hyperspecialization continues to fragment our subjects, and even reunifying forces like interdisciplinarity seem to thrive only insofar they open new subspecialties for our relentless vascular-to-capillary colonization of the scientific lifeworld? For those of us used to this situation, it is not surprising that the Heideggerian idea of all teachers ultimately sharing a unified subject should sound absurd, or at best like an outdated myth – albeit the myth that founded the modern university. So, *is* the idea of such a shared subject matter a myth? What *do* teachers teach? Let us approach this question from what might at first seem to be another direction, attempting to *learn* its answer.

If teaching is revealing through words, then conversely, learning is experiencing what a teacher's words reveal. That is, to learn is actively to allow oneself to share in what the teacher's words disclose. Again, however, *what* do the teacher's words reveal? We will notice, if we read closely

can be found in *The Blickling Homilies,* A.D. 971 *"Him tæcean lifes weg."* Heidegger would have appreciated the fortuitous ambiguity of *weg* or "way" here, which, like the Greek *hodos,* means both *path* and *manner.* For Heidegger too, the teacher teaches two different "ways," both *what* and *how,* subject and method. The Old English *tæcean* has near cognates in Old Teutonic (*taikjan*), Gothic (*taikans*), Old Spanish (*tekan*), and Old High German (*zeihhan*), and this family can itself be traced back to the pre-Teutonic *deik-,* the Sanskrit *diç-,* and the Greek *deik-nunai, deigma. Deik,* the Greek root, means to bring to light, display, or exhibit, hence to *show* by words.

[28] Agamben traces this important ambiguity between *demonstration* and *indication* back to Aristotle's distinction between "primary and secondary substance" (*Language and Death: The Place of Negativity,* 16–8). We saw in Chapter 1 that Aristotle's formalization of this distinction constitutes the inaugural *unification* of metaphysics as ontotheology but that the two elements Aristotle unified can be traced back even further, to Thales and Anaximander's two different ways of conceiving of the *archê* they were searching for, and thus to the very birth of Western philosophy. Aristotle then, in effect, performs a strange, retroactive *Siamese twinning* of what began as separate but related conceptual children (the two different kinds of *archê*). Thus Aristotle incorporates a fracture into the very core of metaphysics, a fracture that, unified as ontotheology, will subsequently function to unify each of our epochal understandings of the being of entities.

enough, that Heidegger answers this question in 1951, when he writes: "To learn means to make everything we do answer to whatever essentials address us at a given time [*Lernen heißt: das Tun und Lassen zu dem in die Entsprechung bringen, was sich jeweils an Wesenhaftem uns zuspricht*]" (WCT 14/WHD 49).[29] Here it might sound at first as if Heidegger is simply claiming that learning, as the complement of teaching, means actively allowing oneself to share in that which the teacher's words disclose. Yet, remember Wittgenstein's saying that philosophy should be like a bicycle race the point of which is to go as slowly as possible without falling off; if we slow down (and balance ourselves carefully over Heidegger's words), we will notice that these words – the words of a teacher who would teach what learning means (in fact, the performative situation is even more complex) – say more: *Learning means actively allowing ourselves to respond to what is essential in that which always addresses us*, that which has always already claimed us.[30]

In a basic sense, then, learning means responding appropriately to the solicitations of the environment. Of course, Heidegger is thinking of the *ontological* environment (the way in which what-is discloses itself to us), but even common ontic analogs show that this capacity to respond appropriately to the environment is quite difficult to learn.[31] We learn to respond appropriately to environmental solicitations through a long (and often painful) process of trial and error. We must, in other words, learn how to learn. Here problems would seem to abound, however, for it is not clear how learning to learn can be taught. Indeed, to the overly analytically minded, this demand may even seem to generate a vicious regress (for if we need to learn to learn, then we need to learn to learn to learn, and so on). Logic misleads phenomenology here, however; as Heidegger realized, it is simply a question of jumping into this pedagogical circle in the right way. Such a train of thought leads Heidegger to claim that

---

[29] See also James Ward, *Heidegger's Political Thinking*, 177.

[30] Apropos this performative situation, remember that Heidegger had been banned from teaching by the University of Freiburg's "de-Nazification" hearings in 1946 (a decision based in large part on Jasper's damning judgment, as we saw in Chapter 3, note 21), and that these lectures marked his official return to university teaching. Here Heidegger treads a tightrope over this political abyss, seeking quite *unapologetically* to articulate and defend his earlier pedagogical method (although, with Jaspers's charges ringing in his ears, it is hard not read his text as a kind of *apology*). See also Safranski, *Martin Heidegger*, 332–52.

[31] Heidegger believes that learning the appropriate approach to the environment requires "awakening" a phenomenological comportment sensitive to phenomenological presencing (a view I develop in "Ontology and Ethics").

if "teaching is even more difficult than learning," this is only because the teacher must be an *exemplary learner*, capable of teaching his or her students to learn, through a kind of exemplary learning-in-public, by actively responding to the emerging demands of each unique educational situation. Hence the famous passage:

> Why is teaching more difficult than learning? Not because the teacher must have a larger store of information, and have it always at the ready. Teaching is more difficult than learning because what teaching calls for is this: To let learn. The real teacher, in fact, lets nothing else be learned than learning. ... The teacher is ahead of his apprentices in this alone, that he has still far more to learn than they – he has to learn to let them learn. The teacher must be capable of being more teachable than his apprentices.
>
> (WCT 15/WHD 50)

The teacher teaches students to learn – to respond appropriately to the solicitations of the ontological environment – *by* responding appropriately to the solicitations of his or her environment, which is, after all, the students' environment, too. Learning culminates in teaching, then, because teaching is the highest form *of learning*; unlike "instructing" (*belehren*) – Heidegger's derogatory term for the mere conveying of information – "teaching" (*lehren*) is ultimately a "letting learn" (*lernen lassen*). Michael Oakeshott nicely expresses something of Heidegger's point when he says: "Teaching is a practical activity in which a 'learned' person (to us an archaism) 'learns' his pupils."[32] Although Heidegger's famous words (quoted above) are from 1951 to 1952, he clearly maintained this view since at least 1934, when he told students:

> Teaching means: *Letting-learn*. Teaching means: Bringing everything essential and simple into knowing nearness. Teaching means: Letting be known what possesses importance and necessity and what does not. Teaching means: Becoming vigilant [*sichermachen*] for an insight into the essential. Teaching means: Allowing the *in*essential to pass by. Teaching means: Bringing students to that point where they no longer remain students. / Only from out of such teaching does genuine

---

[32] Some philosophically unfortunate word-choice aside, Heidegger would also find much to agree with in Oakeshott's views (derived from a similar reading of Plato) that: "The business of the teacher ... is to release his pupils from their servitude to the current dominant feelings, emotions, images, ideas, beliefs and even skills, not by inventing alternatives to them which seem to him more desirable, but by making available to him [the student] something which approximates more closely to the whole of his inheritance," and that "to enter it ["our common inheritance"] is the only way of becoming a human being, and to inhabit it is to be a human being" (*The Voice of Liberal Learning*, 36, 42, 38).

research spring forth again, that is, research which is conscious of its limits and its obligation.

(GA16 306)

Heidegger's last sentence here anticipates, without yet elaborating, his later vision of the way in which ontological education unifies teaching with research, and we will return to this important aspect of his view in Section 20.[33] The preceding, penultimate sentence echoes *Zarathustra's* adage: "One repays a teacher badly if one always remains nothing but a pupil." This suggests that Heidegger may well have developed his view of teaching as exemplary learning in response to Nietzsche (whose *Zarathustra* had also proclaimed, "And you shall first *learn* from me how to learn"), and thus, appropriately, by going well beyond Nietzsche (by anticipating that which was most essential not only in what he said, but also in what he thereby left unsaid).[34] Still, even after Heidegger decisively distances himself from Nietzsche (in response to the ruinous political errors he sees Nietzsche as having encouraged), Heidegger's guiding understanding of teaching as exemplary learning remains intact. As late as the 1960s, he will continue to tell students that: "The true teacher is ahead of the students only in that he has more to learn than they, namely, the letting learn. (Learning [means]: To bring what we do and allow into a correspondence [or suitable response, *Entsprechung*] with that which in each case grants itself to us as the essential)" (TTL 129–30/USTS 5).

Heidegger's repeated, essentialist-sounding assertions should remind us of his aforementioned claim that "the very essence of *paideia* consists in making the human being strong for the clarity and constancy of insight into essence" (PDT 176/GA9 229). I said previously that this Platonic claim plays a crucial role in Heidegger's program for a reunification of the university. Let us now conclude our study by developing this idea, recapitulating some crucial points from Chapter 3 in order to critically appropriate, develop, and defend some of the later Heidegger's most important positive suggestions for the future of higher education.

---

[33] Heidegger introduces his call for the reunification of teaching and research with these words: "Up until now the opinion was held that teaching had to spring from research – but the horizonlessness of research has made teaching aimless. Not research and thereby also teaching, but rather teaching and in teaching researching. That teaching is the *primordial* task" (GA16 305–6). Michael Bonnett suggests that "there are resonances here with Dewey's attempt to give intrinsic direction to education" ("Education as a Form of the Poetic: A Heideggerian Approach to Learning and the Teacher–Pupil Relationship," 239).

[34] *Thus Spoke Zarathustra*, 190, 318.

§20. CONCLUSIONS: ENVISIONING A COMMUNITY
OF LEARNERS

How can Heidegger's understanding of ontological education help us restore substance to our currently empty guiding ideal of educational "excellence" and, in so doing, provide the contemporary university with a renewed sense of *unity*, not only restoring substance to our shared commitment to forming *excellent* students, but also helping us recognize the sense in which we are in fact all working on the same project? The answer is surprisingly simple: by *reessentializing* the notion of *excellence*. As mentioned earlier, Heidegger, like Aristotle, is a *perfectionist*; that is, he argues both that there is an importantly distinctive human essence and that the *good life*, the life of "excellence" (*aretê*), is the life spent cultivating this distinctively human essence. For Heidegger, as Michael Bonnett observes, "education is conceived as initiation into what it is to be human in some founding sense."[35] Yet, in *what*sense? For Heidegger, as we have seen, the human "essence" is *Dasein*, "being-here," that is, the making-intelligible of the place in which we find ourselves, or, even more simply, *world disclosing*. For such a world-disclosing being to cultivate its essence, then, means for us to recognize and develop this essence, not only acknowledging our participation in the creation and maintenance of an intelligible world but actively embracing our ontological role in such world disclosure. The full ramifications of this seemingly simple insight are profound and revolutionary, as Charles Spinosa, Fernando Flores, and Hubert L. Dreyfus show in their groundbreaking work, *Disclosing New Worlds: Entrepreneurship, Democratic Action, and the Cultivation of Solidarity*. Dreyfus describes the work as "a revolutionary manifesto for business and politics," but the central Heideggerian insight it elaborates has revolutionary implications for higher education as well.[36] In this final section, we will develop

---

[35] "Education as a Form of the Poetic," 239.

[36] See Spinosa, Flores, and Dreyfus, *Disclosing New Worlds*; and Dreyfus, "Responses," 347. Although *Disclosing New Worlds* concludes by touching on the topic of education (151–61), suggesting ways educators might teach historicity and so encourage world disclosing (159–61), this is not one of its three main themes. Perhaps the basic difference between our views can be found in the fact that Spinosa, Flores, and Dreyfus do not take into account the insights into ontotheology that I have argued are central to Heidegger's later thought. Thus, although they rightly recognize that in "the current state of our culture, . . . history-making skills are being displaced in the name of practices for constant transformation" (175), they do not trace this displacement back to its source in the Nietzschean ontotheology underlying our culture (and, increasingly, the entire world). As a result, they underestimate the dangers and obstacles posed by "crude partisans of one or another epoch's or culture's ordering of concerns and dominant mode of inquiry"

the two most important aspects of Heidegger's reontologization of education – namely, his perfectionism (his reessentialization of excellence) and his vision of philosophical thinking as revolutionary science – drawing out the main implications of these linked views for the future of the university.

These two main aspects of Heidegger's mature ontological conception of education are meant to work in tandem, transforming the existing relations between teaching and research, on the one hand, and between the now fragmented departments, on the other. In effect, Heidegger thus dedicates himself to finally redeeming the two central ideals that guided the formation of the modern university, namely, (1) that teaching and research should be harmoniously integrated, and (2) that the university community should be meaningfully reunified around its shared commitment to a common task. How does Heidegger think he can help us achieve such ambitions without falling back into the errors and excesses that derailed his own earlier attempt circa 1933? In this respect, the first goal is less problematic, because (as we saw in detail in §15) the later Heidegger would refine his strategy for reuniting teaching with research precisely so as to eliminate the main philosophical error (the belief in a fundamental ontology) behind his earlier political mistake. When students are taught to develop the aforementioned "insight into essence" – learning "to disclose the essential in all things" – they are still being taught to disclose and investigate the ontological presuppositions that underlie all research. In other words, the later Heidegger still thinks that today's academic departments are "positive sciences," disciplines that rest on ontological "posits" or fundamental assumptions about what the class of entities they study *are*, which implicitly guide their actual research (CP 101/GA65 145). The crucial difference, we have seen, is that Heidegger gives up his earlier belief that these guiding presuppositions derive from some "fundamental ontology" that the philosopher need only recover from beneath history in order to obtain a panoramic overview of the shared "meaning of being in general" that substantively informs and implicitly unites the investigations of all the different academic disciplines. The later Heidegger's deconstruction of metaphysics teaches him that there is no such fundamental ontology waiting to be recovered from beneath history, and that the various disciplines' guiding ontological

(160). Their important positive suggestions thus lack what I, like Heidegger, take to be a necessary propaedeutic, namely, the prior labor of first recognizing and breaking the hold of enframing in order to clear the conceptual space for, and help to motivate, the development of alternatives.

posits instead stem from the particular historical ontotheology that implicitly guides our own age, an ontotheology that, owing to its destructive implications, we need to learn to *recognize, contest, and transcend,* rather than simply *recover.*

For instance, as we have seen (in §14), Heidegger's later views predict that biology, the academic discipline that allows us to understand the order and structure of living organisms, would take over its guiding ontological understanding of what life *is* from the ontotheological understanding of the being of entities that implicitly governs our Nietzschean epoch of enframing. And, indeed, when contemporary philosophers of biology claim that life *is* "a self-replicating system," a view they extend so far as (in a seeming *reductio*) to inadvertently grant "life" to the computer virus, it certainly looks as if they have unknowingly adopted the basic ontotheological presupposition of Nietzsche's metaphysics, according to which life *is* ultimately the eternal recurrence of will-to-power, that is, sheer will-to-will, unlimited self-augmentation. This is only one telling example, but Heidegger's mature view predicts that all our positive sciences will tacitly appropriate their guiding presupposition of the being of the classes of entities they study from the reigning ontotheology of the age, such that our sciences will themselves increasingly come to reflect and reinforce enframing's empty optimization imperative. The later Heidegger's ontologically reconceived notion of education is inextricably entwined with research, then, because his reontologization of education teaches students to question the ontological presuppositions that guide research in all of the positive sciences. Here the goal is precisely to identify and contest the reifying entrenchment of this ontotheology throughout the academic disciplines, and so work to open the conceptual space within which these disciplines can seek to understand the being of the classes of entities they study otherwise than in enframing's ontologically reductive terms. In sum, then, by teaching students to focus on, explicitly investigate, and thereby work toward overturning the ontotheological presuppositions implicitly guiding research in each of the academic disciplines' domains of knowledge, the later Heidegger's reconceptualization of education reunites teaching with research in an attempt to encourage *revolutionary* transformations in the sciences and humanities.

What about Heidegger's second, more politically problematic goal, namely, the attempt to meaningfully reunify the university community around its shared commitment to a common task? Recall that, since its founding, one of the modern university's major concerns has been how it could maintain the unity of structure and purpose taken to be definitive of the *uni*versity as such. German Idealists such as Fichte and

Schelling believed that this unity would follow naturally from the underlying unity of the *system* of knowledge, but their faith in this system proved less influential on posterity than Humboldt's alternative "humanist" ideal, according to which the university's unity would come from a shared commitment to the educational formation of character: The university would be responsible for forming fully cultivated individuals, a requirement Humboldt hoped would serve to guide and unify the new freedom of research. Of course, historically, as we have seen, neither the German Idealists' reliance on the unity of knowledge nor Humboldt's emphasis on a shared commitment to the educational formation of students succeeded in unifying the university community. In his Rectorial Address, Heidegger maintained that the university community's shared commitment to the recovery of a fundamental ontology could reunify this community; if this community could learn "to engage in [this "reflection on the essential foundations"] as reflection and to think and belong to the university *from the base of this engagement*" (Q&A 16/GA16 373-4), it could finally succeed in "shattering the encapsulation of the sciences in their different disciplines and bringing them back from their boundless and aimless dispersal in individual fields and corners" (Q&A 9/ GA16 111).

Because we have already uncovered the intractable philosophical problem that renders this earlier version of Heidegger's program untenable (namely, his precritical belief that he could discover a *fundamental ontology*), the crucial question for us here is this: Can the later Heidegger's refined research program – in which the goal of recognizing, contesting, and transcending our guiding ontotheology replaces the Rectorial Address's misguided attempt to recover a fundamental ontology – still generate a meaningful sense of common purpose for the university community, a real sense of solidarity for those individuals who choose to dedicate themselves to such a collective task? I will now suggest, by way of conclusion, that the answer is "yes." Indeed, although Heidegger would not have thought so circa 1933, the sense of communal solidarity generated by such a shared commitment to uncovering and overturning the nihilistic ontotheology of the age may well be as robust and meaningful as any for which we post-Heideggerian liberal individualists can reasonably hope. In order to recognize this, however, we need first to appropriately calibrate our expectations concerning communal solidarity by explicitly criticizing and rejecting the totalitarian ideal of such unity that Heidegger adopted in 1934. For, the communal ideal Heidegger himself then advocated betrays the uncritical residue of a romantic longing for communal fusion, an infantile desire for an ecstatic union in which all individual differences (which the early Nietzsche, following Schopenhauer, under-stood as the source of ordinary human suffering) are submerged and dissolved.[37]

We observed at the end of Section 15 that Nietzsche and Heidegger may well have been correct to hold the academic freedoms introduced by the modern university responsible for its subsequent disciplinary frag-mentation, but that this is nevertheless a poor excuse for abolishing these academic freedoms long after this fragmentation has been institutional-ized. Indeed, I will now go further and suggest that Heidegger's own total-itarian ideal of the kind of *unity* appropriate to the university community, and the authoritarian means he seems ready to use to enforce this ideal circa 1933, represent, at best, an historically retrogressive movement back toward the premodern university (known for its static and unchanging disciplines, which it maintained only by excluding research from the uni-versity), if not all the way back to the medieval university (a community of itinerant monks), rather than a feasible or desirable model for restoring a meaningful sense of communal unity and solidarity to the contemporary university.[38] The basic philosophical problem here, in my view, is that Heidegger took his vision of the university community jointly advanc-ing toward the frontlines of knowledge much too literally, modeling his understanding of this academic community's "*proper, primordially spiritual unity*" (GA16 301) on the widely romanticized ideal of *Frontgemeinschaft*, that is, the intense communal bonding experienced by soldiers who faced death together on the front lines during World War I (GA16 298–301). The powerful bonds of camaraderie formed under such terrible condi-tions do in fact seem capable of undermining many entrenched social divisions (such as class and race, if not sex and gender), and so have often been romanticized by socialists.[39] In 1934, Heidegger valorized

---

[37] See Nietzsche, *The Birth of Tragedy*, 17–18.

[38] In 1934, Heidegger celebrates the fact that the philosophical faculty was originally made responsible for unifying the modern university, which was to have been "guided by an all-encompassing philosophical orientation toward the internal connections of the essential domains of knowledge" (GA16 292). He even seems nostalgic for this modern university when he objects to the "fundamental principle" of "research for research's sake, regardless of what is explored," because this emphasis on pure research led the sciences to develop by making "discovery after discovery, until it became impossible [for philosophy] to oversee what had been discovered" (GA16 296). In the medieval university, Haskins tells us, "the word university had no connection with the universe or the universality of learning; it denotes only the totality of a group…an association of masters and scholars living the common life of learning" (*The Rise of Universities*, 14, 34).

[39] Cf. Billy Bragg's powerful acappella ballad, "Tender Comrade," on his *Worker's Playtime* (Elektra, 1988). As Ted Kisiel reminded me, moreover, Steven Spielberg romanticized

this "completely new idea of community" (GA16 298–99) as the genuine "spirit" of "National *Socialism*" (GA16 302), thereby simply ignoring the way the real Nazis were already artificially creating and viciously persecuting all manner of innocent "enemies" in order to enforce their totalitarian ideal of lock-step social unity. Heidegger's terribly absurd desire to transpose such intense communal bonds from the military to the university community is clearly motivated extraphilosophically, however, and so is not difficult to criticize and reject.

Serving with the weather service during World War I, Heidegger never fought on the front lines himself, but he had long been impressed by Ernst Jünger's grim yet romantic semiphenomenological depictions of life in the trenches.[40] (Indeed, the heroic image of "charging forward [*vorlaufen*] toward death" – drawn from Jünger's description of German soldiers charging blindly from the trenches through clouds of poisonous

this same communal bond, from the American perspective, in his aptly titled "Band of Brothers" mini-series.

[40] Among a dozen similar refrains which would have appealed to Heidegger, Jünger writes that "the front is a great freemasonry whose members are cemented together with blood more closely than any other bond could cement them. The spirit that is set only on endurance will wilt and fail, but the spirit in which a hundred thousand volunteers fell in front of Ypres will stand because it was bent on doing, not on living. Systems may perish, the empire change, but what was planted here will bear fruit. The survivors must take on the heritage of the dead. They must always be hard and never weak. They must have nothing but contempt for him who cannot stake his life on future greatness." Intriguingly, as an example of such a perishable system, Jünger refers to "a delightful but quite forgotten novel called *Spitzbart*, by Schummel, in which a rector of that name was undone as soon as he was compelled to put into practice his highly theoretic system of education" (See *Copse 125* [published in 1925], 105–6, 101, 101, and cf. 181–4, where Jünger links this unity of the people with the total mobilization Heidegger would soon criticize. See also Jünger's famous *The Storm of Steel* [first published in 1920]; GA39 72–5; Zimmerman, *Heidegger's Confrontation with Modernity*, 50–54; Losurdo, *Heidegger and the Ideology of War*, 27, 55–61; Young, *Heidegger, Philosophy, Nazism*, 30–3; and Bambach, *Heidegger's Roots*, 27 note 24.) In his romantic infatuation with Jünger's heroic martial ideal, Heidegger reportedly even embellished his own service record so that it would include "combat in the trenches at Verdun" (Sheehan, "'Everyone Has to Tell the Truth,'" 31). For his part, Foucault goes so far as to suggest that: "Risking one's life, being exposed to total destruction, was one of the principles inscribed in the basic duties of the obedient Nazi, and it was one of the essential objectives of Nazism's policies. It has to reach the point at which the entire population was exposed to death. Exposing the entire population to universal death was the only way it could truly constitute itself as a superior race and bring about its definitive regeneration once other races had been exterminated or enslaved forever.... We have [here] an absolutely racist state, an absolutely murderous state, and an absolutely suicidal state.... This is where the mechanism inscribed in the workings of the modern state leads" (*"Society Must Be Defended,"* 259–60). Nancy reiterates Foucault's point, writing that: "The suicide of the German nation itself might have represented a plausible extrapolation of the process" (*The Inoperative Community*, 12).

gas meant to cover and aid their *Blitzkrieg*, gas attacks Heidegger's own
"weather service" unit would have helped plan – already plays a crucial
role in Heidegger's famous phenomenological depiction of authenticity
in *Being and Time* [B&T 306/S&Z 262].) Perhaps the most important
disanalogy between the frontiers of knowledge and the front lines of war
is that only in the case of war does the community confront a mortal
enemy. Because it is precisely this shared confrontation of mortal danger
that generates the unity of the *Frontgemeinschaft*, the university community, in order actually to inculcate such powerful martial bonds, would
have to create its own "mortal enemies," enemies its members would have
to band together and confront in order to survive.[41] However appropriate it might be on the battlefield, this martial ideal of a community of
comrades-in-arms would thus foist an extremely polarizing friend/enemy
"attitude or bearing" (*Haltung*) on the university community (GA16 298),
a siege mentality that inevitably would be extremely divisive for any free
community, and so would ultimately exacerbate rather than address the
university community's lack of a meaningful sense of communal solidarity. Unfortunately, it is not difficult for us to imagine how an insular community united by such a siege mentality would react toward members who
break ranks with the struggle against this community's imagined mortal
enemies, for we have all witnessed such dramas played out in miniature
within the divided groups that currently compose the university's communal patchwork – a "community" in which, as Heidegger saw clearly
enough seventy years ago, we have at most an "empty consciousness" of
belonging to the same institution, in which the different "faculties are
held together barely, and only externally, through a common adminis-
tration" (GA16 296).

   Still, if Heidegger could enthusiastically adopt a martial ideal of communal unity in 1934 that can only seem repressive and misguided to
the mostly liberal-democratic denizens of the contemporary university,
we must thus ask: Can the research program suggested by his later work
help us envision ways to foster a meaningfully unified academic community without sacrificing the academic freedoms of individual research
and study we now cherish and consider indispensable? I think it can, insofar as Heidegger's mature suggestions for a response to the problems

---

[41] Here one perhaps begins to glimpse the rationale behind the Nazi's *Gemeinschaftlager*, the
"community camps" required for the political reeducation of university professors. See
Gadamer, *Gadamer in Conversation*, 123–4, 164 note 19; and Safranski, *Martin Heidegger*,
280.

of disciplinary fragmentation follow from his deepest philosophical insights into ontotheology, rather than merely borrowing from the totalitarian *Zeitgeist* and so adopting its radical communitarian aversion to our cherished liberal-democratic freedoms.[42] For, as I have reconstructed it, Heidegger's mature reontologization of education would *combine* his own versions of the two strategies for reunifying the university advocated by Fichte and Humboldt. That is, the university community would be unified *both* by its shared commitment to forming excellent individuals (where excellence is understood in terms of the ontological perfectionism outlined earlier) *and* by the shared recognition on the part of this community that its members are all committed to the same important pursuit, namely, the ultimately revolutionary task not simply of understanding what *is*, but of recognizing, contesting, and seeking to transcend the underlying ontotheology that generates the ontological presuppositions implicitly guiding the various fields of knowledge. Pursuing this project in ways appropriate to their particular areas of expertise, the individual members of such an academic community would draw a sense of communal solidarity from their shared participation in the struggle against the nihilistic undercurrents of the age.

Now, in reconstructing the later Heidegger's views on higher education, I have sought to steer well clear of the totalitarian excesses evident in his misguided desire to transpose an inappropriate ideal of comrades-in-arms to the university community. Interestingly, however, Paul Standish suggests, in effect, that I may have moved too far in the other direction. After sympathetically presenting my reconstruction of Heidegger's mature ideal of an academic community whose members are united by a shared commitment to discerning, confronting, and supplanting the nihilistic ontotheology of the age, Standish raises the worry that: "Welcome though such commitments in education in many respects are, these are

---

[42] Heidegger's 1934 lectures confirm Young's valuable insights into the great influence on Heidegger's political views (c. 1933) of the radically communitarian, anti-individualistic "Ideas of 1914." (See *Heidegger, Philosophy, Nazism*, 13–27.) Heidegger even says here that "the essence of the National Socialist revolution consists in the fact that Adolph Hitler has elevated that new [1914] spirit of community into a new formation of the people and made it victorious" (GA16 302). By the end of the war, however, Heidegger will reject these conceptions of "the people" (PAR 137/GA54 204) and "the leader" (EP 105/GA7 92) as unthinking extensions of the modern metaphysics of subjectivity and the technological understanding of being, and he will drop the particular positive conception of freedom – as "responsibility for the destiny of the people" (GA16 291) – with which he had sought to replace the (in his view) merely negative academic freedoms in 1933–1934.

somewhat abstract and formal outcomes from Thomson's enquiry."[43] Let us thus conclude by asking: Is the kind of unity suggested by Heidegger's mature ontologization of education too abstract and formal to provide the academic communities inspired by and formed around this ideal with a meaningful sense of communal solidarity?

For his part, Heidegger always insisted that the question of being is no "mere matter for soaring speculation about the most general of generalities," but is, "*rather, of all questions, the most basic and the most concrete*" (B&T 28/S&Z 9). Because our age's reigning ontotheology now supplies its reductive and nihilistic answer to this question of being, this suggests that our various struggles against the nihilistic symptoms of this ontotheology will need to be just as concrete. Indeed, thinking globally but acting locally (so to speak), rather than following the philosophical mainstream in denigrating "applied philosophy," post-Heideggerian thinkers have sought to respond to the full range of specific problems that confront thinkers in fields as diverse as education, science and technology studies, cognitive science, psychology, nursing, environmentalism, cultural studies, and even politics – a fact borne ironic witness to in Wolin's complaint that "the realm of public philosophy has been abandoned to the so-called left Heideggerians."[44]

Such concrete struggles, because of the expertise they require, usually emerge locally, but their developing self-understanding tends to pull broader communities into the struggle, generating a sense of common purpose and shared commitments with these other communities. The

---

[43] "Essential Heidegger: Poetics of the Unsaid," 165. Although I am in broad agreement with Standish's insightful essay, I am not convinced by his conclusion that we need to go beyond Heidegger to Levinas in order to find the ethical perspective Heidegger is supposedly missing. As I argue in "Ontology and Ethics," that popular move is motivated by a hermeneutically unjustified refusal to recognize the notion of *being as such* at work in Heidegger's later thought. This is ironic, given that Levinas's ethics is grounded in alterity ("ethics is the other; the other is ethics," as Levinas told Derrida), and Levinas's notion of alterity (as a radical other who issues aporetic commands both necessary and impossible to obey) is closer to the later Heidegger's understanding of being as such (as a temporally dynamic presencing that simultaneously elicits and defies conceptual circumscription) than most Levinas scholars acknowledge. Of course, these Levinasians are simply following Levinas himself, whose notorious animosity toward Heidegger (an extreme instance of Bloom's "anxiety of influence") distorted his own understanding of the profound conceptual debts he owed to Heidegger's thinking. Still, as David Wood pointedly observes: "If you're going to be a Levinasian" (i.e., someone who strives to practice a Levinasian hermeneutic ethics), then "you couldn't possibly read Heidegger in the way Levinas reads Heidegger" (Wood and John Dalton, "The Art of Time: An Interview with David Wood," 12).

[44] "Kant at Ground Zero," 26.

communal solidarity generated by this network of commitments – commitments which both shape and give purchase to the broader struggle against the nihilistic undercurrents of the age – is certainly more robust than the "empty consciousness" of institutional unity formally unifying the contemporary university community, although it may still appear somewhat abstract or formal when compared, for example, to the community of the front Heidegger himself foolishly romanticized in 1934. We have seen that the siege mentality typical of such a martial community locked into survival mode makes it a fundamentally inappropriate ideal for a university or broader academic community, so I should be clear that Heidegger's mature ontologization of education, as I have developed it, would abjure such a repressive us-against-them approach. Indeed, insofar as there is such a "them," *they* are merely the prisoners remaining in the cave, the "happy enframers" whom it is the teacher's highest calling to help set free from the chains of an underlying ontotheology they do not yet recognize as binding them, although its nihilistic effects permeate not only their own self-understanding but that of the university – and many of the other institutions that shape them. Not surprisingly, the very pervasiveness of the damage already done by this endless optimization to "what is essential to the 'university'" did occasionally lead Heidegger to despair over its future (CP 108/GA65 155), but such despair, we have seen, was not his final word on the matter.[45] Indeed, the later Heidegger's persistent dedication to the educational ideal he elaborated is a clear testament to his faith in the future generations who he recognized were needed to carry this project further, a faith already amply justified, in my view, by the work being done by such post-Heideggerian thinkers as Derrida, Kadowaki, and Dreyfus and Wrathall, thinkers who have helped create and inspire diverse communities of post-Heideggerian teachers dedicated to the exemplary art of learning-in-public, as well as the institutions capable of supporting the important work that continues to emerge from these communities.[46]

---

[45] See also Cooper, "Truth, Science, Thinking, and Distress," 47–61.

[46] I am thinking here of the International College of Philosophy, the University of Tokyo Center for Philosophy in the 21st Century, and the International Society for Phenomenological Studies, respectively, communities in which those engaged in local struggles come together to learn from one another and so expand their common commitments as well as advance their different aims. I do not, however, mean to devalue the importance of other similar institutions (with which I am unfortunately less familiar), nor do I want to appear overly optimistic about the real challenges – institutional, political, and financial, as well as philosophical – that these communities continue to face.

Once we have drawn the complex but important philosophical lessons of Heidegger's own grave political mistakes, moreover, do we not find ourselves increasingly averse to the continued creation of artificial enemies and endless academic infighting while the underlying ontotheological roots of our problems go undiagnosed and so untreated? If so, then we will not be quick to dismiss the important philosophical insights emerging from the different post-Heideggerian communities dedicated to "opening up the possibility of saying 'we' and enunciating and announcing by this 'we' the historicity of existence" (as Jean-Luc Nancy puts it), that is, communities dedicated to radically criticizing and thoughtfully responding to the deepest and most pressing problems of the age.[47] These communities may not always resemble traditional universities, but a sympathetic and informed gaze will not fail to register their international proliferation, or the fact that their members and ideas already circulate across, beneath, and between the boundaries of more traditional academic disciplines and institutions, as well as within them. Here I believe we can begin to discern the outlines of a broader post-Heideggerian community, one whose significant internal differences we need neither overlook nor downplay. For, as Heidegger saw in *Being and Time*, communities are "authentically bound together" not by "doing the same thing" (which often breeds "mistrust") but, rather, when they freely "devote themselves to the same matter together" (B&T 159/S&Z 122). In other words, a communal solidarity that genuinely enables rather than undermines the "freedom" of each of its members (or "frees the other in his freedom for himself," as Heidegger puts it) comes from sharing a common goal, not from approaching that goal in a uniform way.[48]

What, then, is this common goal? I have suggested throughout that, insofar as this community remains dedicated, in a word, to the *future*, it will be formed and informed by a shared commitment to uncovering, contesting, and transcending the nihilistic ontotheology of the age. For members of such a *community of the future*, our sense of communal solidarity will be reinforced even by our different attempts to understand ourselves and the meaning of our worlds in terms other than those

---

[47] *The Birth to Presence*, 163–4.

[48] As even Young now acknowledges, Heidegger's "thinking did, for a brief period [viz., "the mid-1930s"], fall into a perilous proximity to fascist totalitarianism" (*Heidegger's Philosophy of Art*, 82). Still, it seems that, even circa 1934, Heidegger did leave room for the alternative I am envisioning, for he held that "genuine comradeship only arises under the pressure of a great common danger *or* from the ever-growing commitment to a clearly perceived common task" (HC 53, my emphasis/GA16 238).

prescribed by our nihilistic ontotheology. For, in Nancy's terms, "We share what divides us: the freedom of an incalculable and improbable *coming* to presence of being, . . . the exposure in which the community is founded."[49] After tracing the important historical and conceptual connections between this post-Heideggerian community of the future and the *radical democracy* movement (both share a strategic vision of situated local struggles progressively coming together to form new counterhegemonic movements), Fred Dallmayr concludes that: "The absence of communitarian substance does not mean a lack of bonding." Indeed, I would go further and affirm that – although this post-Heideggerian community of the future remains dispersed, decentralized, and, as Heidegger put it, very much still "to come" (*Zu-kunft*) – the real sense of solidarity generated by this community's shared commitment to uncovering, contesting, and transcending the deepest metaphysical presuppositions of the age is likely to be as meaningful as any for which we are currently entitled to hope.[50]

---

49 *The Experience of Freedom*, 95 (cf. Heidegger: "[T]hinking . . . is content with awakening a readiness in humanity for a possibility whose contour remains obscure, whose coming remains uncertain. Thinking must first *learn* what remains reserved and in store for thinking to get involved in, a *learning* in which thinking prepares its own transformation" [T&B 60, my emphasis/ZSD 66–7]). Nancy argues that the later Heidegger's insights give rise to an "inoperative community," that is, a critical community of resistance which is itself resistant to top-down managerial control, and which experiences its lack of substantive communality *as* the key to understanding the happening of a future community, just as Heidegger holds that we need to understand "the nothing" at the heart of nihilism *as* the way "being as such" happens for us today (see Chapter 1, note 16). Thus, for Nancy, "being 'itself' comes to be defined . . . *as community*." Nancy does well to make Penelope the emblem of such a community, constantly reweaving "the fabric of intimacy without ever managing to complete it." Given my criticisms of Heidegger's romantic infatuation with the frontline community in 1934, however, I remain suspicious of Nancy's own faith in: "The genuine community of mortal beings, or death as community," since the criticisms we have advanced here seem to undermine Nancy's strangely confident claim (his "denegation," Derrida would say) that Heidegger's political fiasco "proves no doubt that Dasein's 'being-toward-death' was never radically implicated in its being-with – in *Mitsein* – and that it is this implication which remains to be thought" (*The Inoperative Community*, 6, 10, 14–15).

50 See Dallmayr, "An Inoperative Global Community?" 191, and his valuable *The Other Heidegger*, esp. 77–105. I develop the later Heidegger's vision of a future human community ("those to-come") – whose members attempt to understand being otherwise than in the nihilistic terms prescribed by Nietzsche's ontotheology, working thereby to foster a new historical sense of what matters – in "The Philosophical Fugue: Understanding the Structure and Goal of Heidegger's *Beiträge*."

References

Agamben, Giorgio, *Language and Death: The Place of Negativity.* K. Pinkus and M. Hardt, trans. Minneapolis: University of Minnesota Press, 1991.
———, *Remnants of Auschwitz: The Witness and the Archive.* D. Heller-Roazen, trans. New York: Zone Books, 1999.
Alcalay, Rubin, *The Complete Hebrew–English Dictionary.* Tel Aviv: Massadah Publishing Co., 1965.
Allison, Henry E., *Kant's Transcendental Idealism: An Interpretation and Defense.* New Haven, CT: Yale University Press, 1983.
Arendt, Hannah, "For Martin Heidegger's Eightieth Birthday." (In Q&A.)
Arendt, Hannah, and Karl Jaspers, *Hannah Arendt / Karl Jaspers: Correspondence, 1926–1969.* Lotte Kohler and Hans Saner, eds., R. Kimber and R. Kimber, trans. San Diego: Harcourt, Brace, 1993.
Aristotle, *Categories.* H. P. Cooke, trans. Cambridge, MA: Harvard University Press, 1938.
———, *Metaphysics.* H. Tredennick, trans. Cambridge, MA: Harvard University Press, 1935 (Vol. I), 1935 (Vol. II).
———, *Physics,* Vols. I–IV. P. H. Wicksteed and F. M. Cornford, trans. Cambridge, MA: Harvard University Press, 1986.
———, *Politics.* H. Rackham, trans. Cambridge, MA: Harvard University Press, 1932.
———, *Posterior Analytics.* H. Tredennick, trans. Cambridge, MA: Harvard University Press, 1960.
Bambach, Charles R., *Heidegger, Dilthey, and the Crisis of Historicism.* Ithaca, NY, and London: Cornell University Press, 1995.
———, *Heidegger's Roots: Nietzsche, National Socialism, and the Greeks.* Ithaca, NY, and London: Cornell University Press, 2003.
Baudrillard, Jean, *The Transparency of Evil: Essays on Extreme Phenomena.* J. Benedict, trans. London: Verso, 1993.
Benjamin, Walter, *Gesammelte Schriften,* Vol. 3. Hella Tiedmann-Bartels, ed. Frankfurt: Suhrkamp, 1972.

————, *Selected Writings*. Vol. 1: 1913–1926. Marcus Bullock and Michael W. Jennings, eds. Cambridge, MA: Harvard University Press, 1996.

Bennington, Geoffrey, and Jacques Derrida, *Jacques Derrida*. G. Bennington, trans. Chicago: University of Chicago Press, 1993.

Blattner, William D., *Heidegger's Temporal Idealism*. Cambridge: Cambridge University Press, 1999.

Boden, Margaret A., ed., *The Philosophy of Artificial Life*. Oxford: Oxford University Press, 1996.

Bonnett, Michael, "Education as a Form of the Poetic: A Heideggerian Approach to Learning and the Teacher–Pupil Relationship." In Michael Peters, ed., *Heidegger, Education, and Modernity*. Lanham, MD: Rowman & Littlefield, 2002.

Borges, Jorge, *Collected Fictions*. A. Hurley, trans. New York: Viking, 1998.

Bourdieu, Pierre, "Back to History: An Interview." (In HC.)

————, *The Political Ontology of Martin Heidegger*. P. Collier, trans. Stanford: Stanford University Press, 1991.

Brodsly, David, *L.A. Freeway: An Appreciative Essay*. Berkeley: University of California Press, 1981.

Brooks, David. *On Paradise Drive: How We Live Now (and Always Have) in the Future Tense*. New York: Simon & Schuster, 2004.

Buber, Martin, *Pointing the Way*. M. Friedman, trans. Atlantic Highlands, NJ: Humanities Press International, 1990.

Caputo, John D., "Heidegger's *Kampf*: The Difficulty of a Life." *Graduate Faculty Philosophy Journal* 14–15 (1991): 61–83.

Carman, Taylor, *Heidegger's Analytic*. Cambridge: Cambridge University Press, 2003.

Cavell, Stanley, *Conditions Handsome and Unhandsome: The Constitution of Emersonian Perfectionism*. Chicago: University of Chicago Press, 1990.

————, *This New Yet Unapproachable America: Lectures After Emerson After Wittgenstein*. Albuquerque, NM: Living Batch Press, 1989.

Celan, Paul, *Poems of Paul Celan*. M. Hamburger, trans. New York: Persea Books, 1988.

Cerbone, David, "World, World-Entry, and Realism in Early Heidegger." *Inquiry* 38 (1995): 401–21.

Clark, Timothy, "Literary Force: Institutional Values." *Culture Machine* 1 (1998). Available from http://www.culturemachine.tees.ac.uk/Cmach/Backissues/j001/articles/art_clar_html. Accessed 21 August 2000.

Cole, Bruce, "Shoring Up the Humanities." *Academic Questions* 15 (2002): 8–12.

Collins, Jeff, *Heidegger and the Nazis*. New York: Totem Books, 2000.

Collins, Randall, *The Sociology of Philosophies: A Global Theory of Intellectual Change*. Cambridge, MA: Harvard University Press, 1998.

Confucius, *The Analects of Confucius*. A. Waley, trans. New York: Vintage Books, 1989.

Connolly, William E., *The Ethos of Pluralization*. Minneapolis: University of Minnesota Press, 1995.

Cooper, David E., "Truth, Science, Thinking, and Distress." In Michael Peters, ed., *Heidegger, Education, and Modernity*. Lanham, MD: Rowman & Littlefield, 2002.

Crowell, Steve, *Husserl, Heidegger, and the Space of Meaning: Paths toward Transcendental Phenomenology*. Evanston, IL: Northwestern University Press, 2001.

———, "Philosophy as a Vocation: Heidegger and University Reform in the Early Interwar Years." *History of Philosophy Quarterly* 14 (1997): 255–76.

Dallmayr, Fred, "An Inoperative Global Community? Reflections on Nancy." In Darren Sheppard, Simon Sparks, and Colin Thomas, eds., *On Jean-Luc Nancy: The Sense of Philosophy*. London and New York: Routledge, 1997.

———, *The Other Heidegger*. Ithaca, NY, and London: Cornell University Press, 1993.

De Beistegui, Miguel, *Heidegger and the Political: Dystopias*. London and New York: Routledge, 1998.

———, *Thinking with Heidegger: Displacements*. Bloomington and Indianapolis: Indiana University Press, 2003.

De Fonteney, Elisabeth, "'In Its Essence the Same Thing.'" In Alan Milchman and Alan Rosenberg, eds., *Heidegger and the Holocaust*. Atlantic Highlands, NJ: Humanities Press, 1996.

Derrida, Jacques, *Eyes of the University: Right to Philosophy 2*. J. Plug, trans. Stanford: Stanford University Press, 2004.

———, "Interpreting Signatures (*Nietzsche/Heidegger*): Two Questions." In Diane P. Michelfelder and Richard E. Palmer, eds. and trans., *Dialogue and Deconstruction: The Gadamer–Derrida Encounter*. Albany: State University of New York Press, 1989.

———, *Margins of Philosophy*. A. Bass, trans. Chicago: University of Chicago Press, 1982.

———, "Mochlos; or, The Conflict of the Faculties." R. Rand and A. Wygant, trans. In Richard Rand, ed., *Logomachia: The Conflict of the Faculties*. Lincoln: University of Nebraska Press, 1992.

———, *Of Grammatology*. G. Spivak, trans. Baltimore, MD: Johns Hopkins University Press, 1974.

———, *Of Spirit: Heidegger and the Question*. G. Bennington and R. Bowlby, trans. Chicago: University of Chicago Press, 1989.

———, *The Ear of the Other: Otobiography, Transference, Translation*. Christie V. McDonald, ed., P. Kamuf and A. Ronell, trans. New York: Schocken Books, 1985.

———, "The Principle of Reason: The University in the Eyes of Its Pupils." *Diacritics* 14 (1983): 3–20.

———, *Who's Afraid of Philosophy? Right to Philosophy 1*. J. Plug, trans. Stanford: Stanford University Press, 2002.

———, *Without Alibi*. Peggy Kamuf, ed. and trans. Stanford: Stanford University Press, 2002.

———, *Writing and Difference*. A. Bass, trans. Chicago: University of Chicago Press, 1978.

Dreyfus, Hubert L., "Being and Power: Heidegger and Foucault." *International Journal of Philosophical Studies* 4 (1996): 1–16.

———, "Being and Power: Revisited." In Alan Milchman and Alan Rosenberg, eds., *Foucault and Heidegger*. Minneapolis: University of Minnesota Press, 2003.

———, *Being-in-the-World: A Commentary on Heidegger's* Being and Time, *Division I.* Cambridge, MA: MIT Press, 1991.

———, "Could Anything Be More Intelligible Than Everyday Intelligibility? Re-interpreting Division I of *Being and Time* in the Light of Division II." In J. E. Faulconer and M. Wrathall, eds., *Appropriating Heidegger.* Cambridge: Cambridge University Press, 2000.

———, "Heidegger on Gaining a Free Relationship to Technology." In Andrew Feenberg and Alastair Hannay, eds., *Technology and the Politics of Knowledge.* Bloomington: Indiana University Press, 1995.

———, "Heidegger on the Connection between Nihilism, Art, Technology, and Politics." In Charles Guignon, ed., *The Cambridge Companion to Heidegger.* Cambridge: Cambridge University Press, 1993.

———, "Heidegger's Hermeneutic Realism." In David R. Hiley, James F. Bohman, and Richard Schusterman, eds., *The Interpretive Turn: Philosophy, Science, Culture.* Ithaca, NY: Cornell University Press, 1991.

———, "Mixing Interpretation, Religion, and Politics: Heidegger's High-Risk Thinking." In Christopher Ocker, ed., *Protocol of the Sixty-first Colloquy of the Center for Hermeneutical Studies.* San Anselmo, CA: Center for Hermeneutical Studies, 1992.

———, "Responses." In Mark Wrathall and Jeff Malpas, eds., *Heidegger, Coping, and Cognitive Science.* Cambridge, MA: MIT Press, 2000.

———, *Thinking in Action: On the Internet.* London and New York: Routledge, 2003.

———, *What Computers* Still *Can't Do: A Critique of Artificial Reason.* Cambridge, MA: MIT Press, 1992.

Dreyfus, Hubert L., and Paul Rabinow, "Can There Be a Science of Existential Structure and Social Meaning?" In Craig Calhoun, Edward LiPuma, and Moishe Postone, eds., *Bourdieu: Critical Perspectives.* Chicago: University of Chicago Press, 1993.

———, *Michel Foucault: Beyond Structuralism and Hermeneutics.* Second edition. Chicago: University of Chicago Press, 1982.

Dreyfus, Hubert L., and Charles Spinosa, "Highway Bridges and Feasts: Heidegger and Borgmann on How to Affirm Technology." *Man and World* 30 (1997): 159–77.

Dreyfus, Hubert L., and Mark Wrathall, eds., *A Companion to Heidegger.* Oxford: Blackwell Publishing, 2005.

———, *Heidegger Reexamined.* Volume II: *Truth, Realism, and the History of Being.* New York and London: Routledge, 2002.

Edler, Frank, "Philosophy, Language, Politics: Heidegger's Attempt to Steal the Language of Revolution in 1933–34." *Social Research* 57 (1990): 197–238.

Emad, Parvis, "A Conversation on Heidegger's *Beiträge zur Philosophie* with Friedrich-Wilhelm von Herrmann." In Burt C. Hopkins, ed., *Phenomenology: Japanese and American.* Dordrecht: Kluwer Academic Publishers, 1997.

Feenberg, Andrew, *Alternative Modernity: The Technical Turn in Philosophy and Social Theory.* Berkeley: University of California Press, 1995.

———, "Constructivism and Technology Critique: Response to Critics." *Inquiry* 43 (2000): 225–38.

——, *Critical Theory of Technology*. New York and Oxford: Oxford University Press, 1991.

——, *Heidegger and Marcuse: The Catastrophe and Redemption of History*. London and New York: Routledge, 2005.

——, "Modernity Theory and Technology Studies: Reflections on Bridging the Gap." In Tom Misa, Philip Brey, and Andrew Feenberg, eds., *Modernity and Technology*. Cambridge, MA: MIT Press, 2003.

——, *Questioning Technology*. London and New York: Routledge, 1999.

——, "The Ontic and the Ontological in Heidegger's Philosophy of Technology: Response to Thomson." *Inquiry* 43 (2000): 445–50.

Feenberg, Andrew, and Jim Freedman, *When Poetry Ruled the Streets: The French May Events of 1968*. Albany: State University of New York Press, 2001.

Foucault, Michel, *"Society Must Be Defended": Lectures at the Collège de France, 1975–76*. Mauro Bertani and Alessandro Fontana, eds., D. Macey, trans. New York: Picador, 2003.

——, *The Order of Things: An Archeology of the Human Sciences*. New York: Vintage Books, 1970.

Freeman, Kathleen, trans., *Ancilla to the Presocratic Philosophers*. Cambridge, MA: Harvard University Press, 1948.

Friedman, Michael, *A Parting of the Ways: Carnap, Cassirer, and Heidegger*. Chicago and La Salle, IL: Open Court, 2000.

Fritsche, Johannes, *Historical Destiny and National Socialism in Heidegger's* Being and Time. Berkeley: University of California Press, 1999.

Fynsk, Christopher, "But Suppose We Were to Take the Rectorial Address Seriously... Gérard Granel's *De l'université.*" *Graduate Faculty Philosophy Journal* 14–15 (1992): 335–62.

——, *Heidegger: Thought and Historicity*. Ithaca, NY: Cornell University Press, 1993.

Gadamer, Hans-Georg, "Back from Syracuse?" John McCumber, trans. *Critical Inquiry* 15 (1989): 427–30.

——, *Gadamer in Conversation: Reflections and Commentary*. Richard E. Palmer, ed. and trans. New Haven, CT, and London: Yale University Press, 2001.

——, *On Education, Poetry, and History: Applied Hermeneutics*. Dieter Misgeld and Graeme Nicholson, eds., L. Schmidt and M. Reuss, trans. Albany: State University of New York Press, 1992.

Glazebrook, Trish, "From *Phusis* to Nature, *Technê* to Technology: Heidegger on Aristotle, Galileo, and Newton." *The Southern Journal of Philosophy* 38 (2000): 95–118.

——, "Heidegger on the Experiment." *Philosophy Today* 42 (1998): 250–61.

Geuss, Raymond, *Morality, Culture, and History: Essays on German Philosophy*. Cambridge: Cambridge University Press, 1999.

——, *The Idea of a Critical Theory: Habermas and the Frankfurt School*. Cambridge: Cambridge University Press, 1981.

Graff, Gerald. *Beyond the Culture Wars*. New York: Norton, 1992.

Guignon, Charles B., *Heidegger and the Problem of Knowledge*. Indianapolis: Hackett Publishing Company, 1983.

——, "History and Commitment in the Early Heidegger." In Hubert L. Dreyfus and Harrison Hall, eds., *Heidegger: A Critical Reader.* Cambridge, MA: Blackwell, 1992.

——, ed., *The Cambridge Companion to Heidegger.* Cambridge: Cambridge University Press, 1993.

——, "The History of Being." In Hubert L. Dreyfus and Mark Wrathall, eds., *A Companion to Heidegger.* Oxford: Blackwell Publishing, 2005.

Habermas, Jürgen, *The Philosophical Discourses of Modernity: Twelve Lectures.* F. G. Lawrence, trans. Cambridge, MA: MIT Presss, 1987.

Hannay, Alastair, *Kierkegaard: A Biography.* Cambridge: Cambridge University Press, 2001.

Harries, Karsten, and Christoph Jamme, eds., *Martin Heidegger: Politics, Art, and Technology.* New York: Holmes and Meier Publishers, 1994.

Haskins, Charles, *The Rise of Universities.* New York: Henry Holt and Company, 1923.

Hegel, Georg Wilhelm Friedrich, *Phänomenologie des Geistes.* Hans-Friedrich Wessels and Heinrich Clairmont, eds. Hamburg: G. Meiner, 1988.

——, *Phenomenology of Spirit.* A. V. Miller, trans. Oxford: Oxford University Press, 1977.

Heidegger, Martin. See "Abbreviations Used for Works by Heidegger."

Heim, Michael, "Heidegger Online: An Interview with Michael Heim." In Geert Lovink, ed., *Uncanny Networks: Dialogues with the Virtual Intelligentsia.* Cambridge, MA: MIT Press, 2002.

Hill, R. Kevin, *Nietzsche's Critiques: The Kantian Foundations of His Thought.* Oxford: Oxford University Press, 2003.

Honderich, Ted, ed., *The Oxford Companion to Philosophy.* Oxford: Oxford University Press, 1995.

Horace, *Satires, Epistles, Ars Poetica.* H. R. Fairclough, trans. Cambridge, MA: Harvard University Press, 1926.

Hsiao, Paul, "Heidegger and Our Translation of the *Tao Te Ching.*" In Graham Parkes, ed., *Heidegger and Asian Thought.* Honolulu: University of Hawaii Press, 1990.

Humboldt, Wilhelm von, *Die Idee der deutschen Universität.* Darmstadt: Hermann Gentner Verlag, 1956.

Husserl, *Ideas: A General Introduction to Pure Phenomenology.* W.R.B. Gibson, trans. New York: Collier, 1962.

——, *Ideas Pertaining to a Pure Phenomenology and to a Phenomenological Philosophy, Third Book: Phenomenology and the Foundations of the Sciences.* T. E. Klein and W. E. Pohl, trans. *Collected Works* (Vol. 1). The Hague: Nijhoff, 1980.

——, *Phenomenology and the Crisis of Philosophy.* Quentin Lauer, ed. and trans. New York: Harper & Row, 1965.

Ihde, Don, *Bodies in Technology.* Minneapolis: University of Minnesota Press, 2002.

——, *Technology and the Lifeworld: From Garden to Earth.* Bloomington: Indiana University Press, 1990.

Jabès, Edmond, *The Little Book of Unsuspected Subversion.* R. Waldrop, trans. Stanford: Stanford University Press, 1996.

Jaeger, Werner, *Paideia: The Ideals of Greek Culture.* Vol. 1. G. Highet, trans. New York: Oxford University Press, 1965.

Jaspers, Karl, *Man in the Modern Age.* E. Paul and C. Paul, trans. New York: Anchor Books, 1957.

Jünger, Ernst, *Copse 125: A Chronicle from the Trench Warfare of 1918.* Basil Creighton, trans. New York: Howard Fertig, 1988.

————, *The Storm of Steel: From the Diary of a German Storm-Troop Officer on the Western Front.* Basil Creighton, trans. New York: Howard Fertig, 1996.

Kant, Immanuel, *Critique of Pure Reason.* Paul Guyer and Allen W. Wood, eds. and trans. Cambridge: Cambridge University Press, 1998.

————, *Kritik der reinen Vernunft.* Raymund Schmidt, ed. Hamburg: F. Meiner, 1926.

————, *Lectures on Metaphysics.* Karl Ameriks and Steve Naragon, eds. and trans. Cambridge: Cambridge University Press, 1997.

————, *Perpetual Peace and Other Essays.* T. Humphries, trans. Indianapolis and Cambridge: Hackett, 1983.

————, *The Conflict of the Faculties.* M. J. Gregor, trans. Lincoln: University of Nebraska Press, 1992.

Kirk, G. S., J. E. Raven, and M. Schofield, eds., *The Presocratic Philosophers.* Second edition. Cambridge: Cambridge University Press, 1983.

Kisiel, Theodore, *The Genesis of Heidegger's* Being and Time. Berkeley: University of California Press, 1993.

Kripke, Saul, *Naming and Necessity.* Cambridge, MA: Harvard University Press, 1980.

Kuhn, Thomas, *The Structure of Scientific Revolutions.* Second edition. Chicago: University of Chicago, 1970.

Laclau, Ernesto and Chantal Mouffe, *Hegemony and Socialist Strategy: Towards a Radical Democratic Politics.* W. Moore and P. Cammack, trans. London: Verso, 1985.

Lacoue-Labarthe, Philippe, *Heidegger, Art, and Politics: The Fiction of the Political.* C. Turner, trans. Oxford: Basil Blackwell, 1990.

Lacoue-Labarthe, Philippe, and Jean-Luc Nancy, *Retreating the Political.* Simon Sparks, ed. London and New York: Routledge, 1997.

Lampert, Laurence. *Nietzsche's Teaching: An Interpretation of* Thus Spoke Zarathustra. New Haven, CT: Yale University Press, 1986.

Lang, Berel, *Heidegger's Silence.* Ithaca, NY: Cornell University Press, 1996.

Lefort, Claude, *Democracy and Political Theory.* David Macey, trans. Minneapolis: University of Minnesota Press, 1988.

Levinas, Emmanuel, *Humanism of the Other.* N. Poller, trans. Urbana and Chicago: University of Illinois Press, 2003.

Lewis, David, *Counterfactuals.* Oxford: Blackwell, 1973.

Losurdo, Domenico, *Heidegger and the Ideology of War: Community, Death, and the West.* M. Norris and J. Norris, trans. Amherst, NY: Humanity Books, 2001.

Löwith, Karl, *Martin Heidegger and European Nihilism.* Richard Wolin, ed. G. Steiner, trans. New York: Columbia University Press, 1995.

————, *My Life in Germany Before and After 1933.* E. King, trans. London: The Athlone Press, 1994.

Lyotard, Jean-François, *Heidegger and "the Jews."* A. Michel and M. Roberts, trans. Minneapolis: University of Minnesota Press, 1990.

Marcuse, Herbert, *Negations: Essays in Critical Theory.* J. J. Shapiro, trans. London: Free Association Books, 1988.

———, *Technology, War, Fascism. Collected Papers of Herbert Marcuse.* Vol. 1. Douglas Kellner, ed. London: Routledge, 1998.

Marx, Karl, *The Marx–Engels Reader.* Second edition. R. Tucker, ed. New York: Norton, 1978.

Mendieta, Eduardo, "Bodies of Technology." *Journal of Applied Philosophy* 20 (2003): 95–101.

Milchman, Alan, and Alan Rosenberg, "Martin Heidegger and the University as a Site for the Transformation of Human Existence." *The Review of Politics* 59 (1997): 75–96.

Moran, Dermot, *Introduction to Phenomenology.* London and New York: Routledge, 2000.

———, "The Destruction of the Destruction: Heidegger's Versions of the History of Philosophy." In Karsten Harries and Christoph Jamme, eds., *Martin Heidegger: Politics, Art, and Technology.* New York: Holmes and Meier Publishers, 1994.

Murray, James, Henry Bradley, W. A. Craigie, and C. T. Onions, eds., *The Compact Oxford English Dictionary.* Second edition. Oxford: Clarendon Press, 1991.

Nancy, Jean-Luc, *The Birth to Presence.* B. Holmes and others, trans. Stanford: Stanford University Press, 1993.

———, *The Experience of Freedom.* B. McDonald, trans. Stanford: Stanford University Press, 1993.

———, *The Inoperative Community.* P. Connor, trans. Minneapolis: University of Minnesota Press, 1991.

Nietzsche, Friedrich, *On the Advantage and Disadvantage of History for Life.* P. Preuss, trans. Indianapolis: Hackett, 1980.

———, *On the Future of Our Educational Institutions.* J. M. Kennedy, trans. *The Complete Works of Friedrich Nietzsche,* Oscar Levy, ed. Vol. 6. Edinburgh: T. N. Foulis, 1909.

———, *Sämtliche Briefe.* Giorgio Colli and Mazzimo Montinari, eds. *Kritische Studienausgabe.* Vol. 4. Berlin: Walter de Gruyter, 1986.

———, *The Birth of Tragedy and Other Writings.* Raymond Geuss and Ronald Speirs, eds. R. Speirs, trans. Cambridge: Cambridge University Press, 1999.

———, *The Gay Science.* W. Kaufmann, trans. New York: Vintage Books, 1974.

———, *The Pre-Platonic Philosophers.* Greg Whitlock, ed. and trans. Urbana and Chicago: University of Illinois Press, 2001.

———, *The Twilight of the Idols.* Tracy Strong, ed., R. Polt, trans. Indianapolis: Hackett Publishing, 1997.

———, *The Will to Power.* Walter Kaufmann, ed. and trans. New York: Random House, 1967.

———, *Thus Spoke Zarathustra.* In Walter Kaufmann, ed. and trans., *The Portable Nietzsche.* New York: Viking, 1982.

Norris, Christopher, *What's Wrong with Postmodernism: Critical Theory and the Ends of Philosophy.* Baltimore, MD: Johns Hopkins University Press, 1990.

Oakeshott, Michael, *The Voice of Liberal Learning*. Indianapolis: Liberty Fund, 2001.

Okrent, Mark, *Heidegger's Pragmatism: Understanding, Being, and the Critique of Metaphysics*. Ithaca, NY: Cornell University Press, 1988.

Olafson, Frederick A., *Heidegger and the Ground of Ethics: A Study of Mitsein*. Cambridge: Cambridge University Press, 1998.

———, *Heidegger and the Philosophy of Mind*. New Haven, CT: Yale University Press, 1987.

———, "Heidegger's Politics: An Interview with Herbert Marcuse." In Robert Pippin, Andrew Feenberg, and Charles P. Webel, eds., *Marcuse: Critical Theory and the Promise of Utopia*. South Hadley, MA: Bergin & Garvey, 1988.

———, "Heidegger's Thought and Nazism." *Inquiry* 43 (2000): 271–88.

Ott, Hugo, *Martin Heidegger: A Political Life*. A. Blunden, trans. London: Basic Books, 1993.

Parkes, Graham, ed., *Heidegger and Asian Thought*. Honolulu: University of Hawaii Press, 1990.

Peters, Michael, ed., *Heidegger, Education, and Modernity*. Lanham, MD: Rowman & Littlefield, 2002.

Petzet, Heinrich Wiegand, *Encounters and Dialogues with Martin Heidegger, 1929–1976*. P. Emad and K. Maly, trans. Chicago: University of Chicago Press, 1993.

Pinkard, Terry, *Hegel: A Biography*. Cambridge: Cambridge University Press, 2000.

Pippin, Robert B., "Heideggerian Postmodernism and Metaphysical Politics." *European Journal of Philosophy* 4 (1996): 17–37.

———, *Modernity as a Philosophical Problem*. Cambridge, MA: Basil Blackwell, 1991.

Plato, *Laches, Protagoras, Meno, Euthydemus*. W. R. M. Lamb, trans. Cambridge, MA: Harvard University Press, 1924.

———, *Lysis, Symposium, Gorgias*. W. R. M. Lamb, trans. Cambridge, MA: Harvard University Press, 1925.

———, *Phaedo*. H. N. Fowler, trans. Cambridge, MA: Harvard University Press, 1914.

———, *Republic*. P. Shorey, trans. Cambridge, MA: Harvard University Press, 1937 (Vol. I), 1935 (Vol. II).

Pöggeler, Otto, "*Den Führer zu führen? Heidegger und kein Ende.*" *Philosophische Rundschau* 32 (1985): 26–67.

———, *The Paths of Heidegger's Life and Thought*. J. Bailiff, trans. Amherst, NY: Humanity Books, 1998.

———, "West–East Dialogue: Heidegger and Lao Tzu." In Graham Parkes, ed., *Heidegger and Asian Thought*. Honolulu: University of Hawaii Press, 1990.

Readings, Bill, *The University in Ruins*. Cambridge, MA: Harvard University Press, 1996.

Richardson, John, *Existential Epistemology: A Heideggerian Critique of the Cartesian Project*. Oxford: Clarendon Press, 1986.

———, "Nietzsche Contra Darwin." *Philosophy and Phenomenological Research* 65 (2002): 537–75.

———, *Nietzsche's System*. Oxford: Oxford University Press, 1996.

Rickey, Christopher, *Revolutionary Saints: Heidegger, National Socialism, and Antinomian Politics*. University Park: Pennsylvania State University Press, 2002.

Ringer, Fritz, *The Decline of the German Mandarins: The German Academic Community, 1890–1933*. Cambridge, MA: Harvard University Press, 1969.

Rorty, Richard, *Achieving Our Country: Leftist Thought in Twentieth-Century America*. Cambridge, MA: Harvard University Press, 1998.

——, "A Master from Germany." *New York Times Book Review*, 3 May 1998.

——, *Philosophy and Social Hope*. New York: Penguin Books, 1999.

——, "Philosophy as Science, as Metaphor, and as Politics." In Avner Cohen and Marcelo Dascal, eds., *The Institution of Philosophy: A Discipline in Crisis?* La Salle, IL: Open Court, 1989.

——, "Taking Philosophy Seriously." *The New Republic* 198 (1988): 31–4.

Safranski, Rüdiger, *Ein Meister aus Deutschland: Heidegger und seine Zeit*. München: C. Hansen Wien, 1994.

——, *Martin Heidegger: Between Good and Evil*. E. Oslers, trans. Cambridge, MA: Harvard University Press, 1998.

Sallis, John, "Flight of Spirit." In David Wood, ed., *Of Derrida, Heidegger, and Spirit*. Evanston, IL: Northwestern University Press, 1993.

Schürmann, Reiner, *Broken Hegemonies*. Bloomington: Indiana University Press, 2003.

——, *Heidegger on Being and Acting: From Principles to Anarchy*. C.-M. Gros and R. Schürmann, trans. Bloomington: Indiana University Press, 1990.

——, "How to Read Heidegger." *Graduate Faculty Philosophy Journal* 19–20 (1997): 3–8.

Scott, Charles E., "Heidegger's Rector's Address: A Loss of the Question of Ethics." *Graduate Faculty Philosophy Journal* 14–15 (1991): 237–64.

Sheehan, Thomas, "'Everyone Has to Tell the Truth': Heidegger and the Jews." *Continuum* I (1990): 30–44.

Shenk, David, "Watching You." *National Geographic* 204 (2003): 2–29.

Shirer, William L., *The Rise and Fall of the Third Reich: A History of Nazi Germany*. New York: Simon & Schuster, 1960.

Sluga, Hans, *Heidegger's Crisis: Philosophy and Politics in Nazi Germany*. Cambridge, MA: Harvard University Press, 1993.

Sokal, Alan, and Jean Bricmont, *Fashionable Nonsense: Postmodern Intellectuals' Abuse of Science*. New York: Picador, 1998.

Spengler, Oswald, *The Decline of the West*. Helmut Werner, ed., C. F. Atkinson, trans. New York and Oxford: Oxford University Press, 1991.

Spinosa, Charles, Fernando Flores, and Hubert L. Dreyfus, *Disclosing New Worlds: Entrepreneurship, Democratic Action, and the Cultivation of Solidarity*. Cambridge, MA: MIT Press, 1997.

——, "Skills, Historical Disclosing, and the End of History: A Response to Our Critics." *Inquiry* 38 (1995): 157–97.

Standish, Paul, "Essential Heidegger: Poetics of the Unsaid." In Michael Peters, ed., *Heidegger, Education, and Modernity*. Lanham, MD: Rowman & Littlefield, 2002.

Stenstad, Gail, "The Turning in *Ereignis* and Transformation of Thinking." *Heidegger Studies* 12 (1996): 83–94.

Sternhall, Zeev, *Neither Left Nor Right: Fascist Ideology in France*. D. Maisel, trans. Berkeley: University of California Press, 1986.

Strawson, Peter S., *The Bounds of Sense: An Essay on Kant's Critique of Pure Reason.* London: Metheun, 1966.

Taber, John A., *Transformative Philosophy: A Study of Sankara, Fichte, and Heidegger.* Honolulu: University of Hawaii Press, 1983.

Terrell, Peter, Horst Kopleck, Hega Holtkamp, and John Whitlam, eds., *HarperCollins German Dictionary.* Unabridged second edition. New York: HarperCollins, 1993.

Thomson, Iain, "Deconstructing the Hero." In Jeff McLaughlin, ed., *Comics as Philosophy.* Jackson: University Press of Mississippi, in press.

———, "From the Question Concerning Technology to the Quest for a Democratic Technology: Heidegger, Marcuse, Feenberg." *Inquiry* 43 (2000): 203–16.

———, "Heidegger and National Socialism." In Hubert L. Dreyfus and Mark Wrathall, eds., *A Companion to Heidegger.* Oxford: Blackwell Publishing, 2005.

———, "Heidegger and the Politics of the University." *Journal of the History of Philosophy* 41 (2003): 515–42.

———, "Heidegger on Ontological Education, or: How We Become What We Are." *Inquiry* 44 (2001): 243–68.

———, "Interpretation as Self-Creation: Nietzsche on the Pre-Platonics." *Ancient Philosophy* 23 (2003): 195–213.

———, "Ontology and Ethics at the Intersection of Phenomenology and Environmental Philosophy." *Inquiry* 47 (2004): 380–412.

———, "Ontotheology? Understanding Heidegger's *Destruktion* of Metaphysics." *International Journal of Philosophical Studies* 8 (2000): 297–327.

———, "The End of Ontotheology: Understanding Heidegger's Turn, Method, and Politics." Ph.D. diss., University of California, San Diego, 1999.

———, "The Philosophical Fugue: Understanding the Structure and Goal of Heidegger's *Beiträge.*" *The Journal of the British Society for Phenomenology* 34 (2003): 57–73.

———, "What's Wrong with Being a Technological Essentialist? A Response to Feenberg." *Inquiry* 43:4 (2000): 429–44.

Van Buren, John, *The Young Heidegger: Rumor of the Hidden King.* Bloomington: Indiana University Press, 1994.

Vigliotti, Robert, "The Young Heidegger's Ambitions for the Chair of Catholic Philosophy and Hugo Ott's Charge of Opportunism." *Studia Phaenomenologica* 1 (2001): 323–50.

Wahrig, Gerhard, ed., *Deutsches Wörterbuch.* Gütersloh: Bertelsmann Lexikon, 1994.

Ward, James F., *Heidegger's Political Thinking.* Amherst: University of Massachusetts Press, 1995.

Weber, Max, *From Max Weber: Essays in Sociology.* H. H. Gerth and C. Wright Mills, eds. New York: Oxford University Press, 1946.

Wiggershaus, Rolf, *The Frankfurt School: Its History, Theories, and Political Significance.* M. Robertson, trans. Cambridge, MA: MIT Press, 1995.

Wittgenstein, Ludwig, *Philosophical Investigations.* Third edition. G. E. M. Anscombe, trans. New York: Macmillan, 1968.

Wolin, Richard, *Heidegger's Children: Hannah Arendt, Karl Löwith, Hans Jonas, and Herbert Marcuse.* Princeton, NJ and Oxford: Princeton University Press, 2001.

———, "Kant at Ground Zero." *The New Republic* 230 (2004): 25–32.

———, "Review of *Martin Heidegger: Between Good and Evil*, by Rüdiger Safranski." *Los Angeles Times Book Review*, 12 April 1998.

———, *The Politics of Being: The Political Thought of Martin Heidegger.* New York: Columbia University Press, 1990.

Wood, David, and John Dalton, "The Art of Time: An Interview with David Wood." *Contretemps* 3 (2002): 2–23.

Wrathall, Mark A., "Between the Earth and the Sky: Heidegger on Life after the Death of God." In Mark Wrathall, ed., *Religion after Metaphysics.* Cambridge: Cambridge University Press, 2003.

———, ed., *Religion after Metaphysics.* Cambridge: Cambridge University Press, 2003.

Wyschogrod, Edith, *Spirit in Ashes: Hegel, Heidegger, and Man-Made Mass Death.* New Haven, CT: Yale University Press, 1985.

Young, Julian, *Heidegger, Philosophy, Nazism.* Cambridge: Cambridge University Press, 1997.

———, *Heidegger's Later Philosophy.* Cambridge: Cambridge University Press, 2002.

———, *Heidegger's Philosophy of Art.* Cambridge: Cambridge University Press, 2000.

Zimmerman, Michael, *Heidegger's Confrontation with Modernity: Technology, Politics, and Art.* Bloomington: Indiana University Press, 1990.

Ziolkowski, Theodore, *German Romanticism and Its Institutions.* Princeton, NJ: Princeton University Press, 1990.

Index

abyss, 19
Agamben, Giorgio, 79, 83, 137, 166
agribusiness, 83, 84
airport, 75
alêtheia (disclosure), 40–42, 118, 145,
   160
Allen, Valerie, 139
Allison, Henry, 54
Anaximander, 31–32, 37, 40, 42, 166
Anselm, Saint, 7
anti-essentialism, 45, 48, 58
aporia, 62
Arendt, Hannah, 1, 83, 133
Aristotle, 12, 14, 25, 32–33, 34–35, 36,
   85, 86, 166, 170
army, Heidegger's service in, 92,
   175–176
art, work of, 71
atheism, Heidegger's alleged, 15, *see
   also* polytheism
Auden, W. H., 75
Auschwitz, 78, 83, *see also* Shoah
autobahn, 45, 70, 74, 75
Axiotis, Ares D., 139

Badiou, Alain, 138
Bambach, Charles, 80, 91, 99, 175
Baudrillard, Jean, 1, 10, 56, 149
Bäumler, Alfred, 125
Beckenbauer, Franz, 69

Becker, Oskar, 96
beginning, the other, 42, 51
being
   and the paradox of the measure, 52
   as a verb, 53
   as questioning, 137
     and the problem of the prior
       claim, 137
   as such, 19, 27, 38, 71, 178
    as allegedly ontotheological, 28
    as community, 181
    as earth, 71
    as mystery, 74
    as nothing in the turning, 74
    as presencing, 14, 65, 158, *see also*
      presencing 20, 71, 164
    as the open, 163–164
     distinguished from the
      lighting, 164
    disclosed through the nothing,
      72
    distinguished from enowning,
      117
    distinguished from the being of
      entities, 19
    explained, 20
    as "the being of entities," 12–13
    understood as presence, 34, 38,
      40
    understood as the lighting, 164

being (*cont.*)
  history of, 9, 20, 25, 54
    and threat of relativism, 19–20,
      145–146
    "epochs" of, explained, 19, 20
    our late modern epoch,
      distinguished from the
      modern, 56, 59–61
    the five epochs of, 59
    response to poststructuralist
      critique of, 59
  understanding of, 9, 19–20
  finitude of, 54
  "technological" understanding of,
    see enframing
Benjamin, Walter, 125, 127
Bennington, Geoffrey, 137
Bildung (education), *see* education
Blanchot, Maurice, 1
Blattner, William D., 54
Blochmann, Elisabeth, 92
Bloom, Harold, 178
Boden, Margaret, 109
Bonnett, Michael, 169, 170
Borges, Jorge, 7
Borgmann, Albert, 48
Bostock, David, 33–34
Bourdieu, Pierre, 81
Bragg, Billy, 174
Brentano, Franz, 88
Brodsley, David, 70
Brooks, David, 149
Buber, Martin, 133, 134
Bultmann, Rudolph, 1
Byrne, David, 73

Caputo, John, 125
Carman, Taylor, 158
Carnap, Rudolf, 98
Catholicism, Heidegger's, 89–91
Cavell, Stanley, 91, 161
Celan, Paul, 82, 83
Cerbone, David, 107
claim, freeing, 20
Clark, Timothy, 152
clearing, 39, 40, 72
  as open and as lighting, 164
Cole, Bruce, 152

Collins, Jeff, 93
Collins, Randall, 81
communism, 65
community, *see* education
Confucian question, *see* National
    Socialism, lessons learned
Confucius, 85, 86
Connolly, William E., 108
conservativism, 46
constructivism, social, 45
Cooper, David, 139, 179
cosmopolitan, 45, *see also* Kant
crisis, historical, 93
critical theory, 57, *see also* Feenberg
Crowell, Stephen, 13, 79, 85, 87, 88,
  99, 100

Dallmayr, Fred, 80, 181
danger, the greatest, 20, 57, 64, 74,
  see also enframing
Dasein, 157, 165
  as world disclosing, 170
  finitude of, 54
  special nature of, 57
Dastur, Françoise, 137
death, 181
De Beistegui, Miguel, 52, 79, 87,
  88, 97, 100, 121, 132,
  136
deconstruction, 7, 10, 23, 38, 39, 40,
  41, 42
  explained, 7, 28, 141
  in Heidegger and Derrida, 7
De Fonteney, Elisabeth, 84
democratization, 49, 67–68, 75
Derrida, Jacques, 1, 2–4, 7, 10, 23, 27,
  34, 59, 60, 80, 85, 86, 100,
  121, 124, 125, 129, 131,
  134–135, 136–137, 138, 154,
  156, 178, 179
Descartes, René, 25
  category mistake of, 54
destiny, 50, 105
Dewey, John, 169
diachrony, 39
Dilthey, Wilhelm, 103, 113
divine, question of the, 15
double-forgetting, 16, 41

Dreyfus, Hubert L., 1, 8, 9, 36, 50, 52, 56, 59, 60, 62, 63–64, 68, 71, 72, 75, 79, 80, 81, 105, 108, 115, 120, 149, 165, 170, 179
dwelling, 159, 164

earth, 71, 74
Edler, Frank, 119
education
  contemporary crisis in, 4–5, 143
  ethical challenges in, 152
  etymology of, 161
  Heidegger's critique of, 61, 127–128, 142–143
    as enframing, 148–154, 157–158, 163
  Heidegger's deconstruction of, 141–143
  Heidegger's positive vision for future of, 119, 139, 142–143, 155–181
  Heidegger's views on
    and academic freedom, 123–128
    and community, 96–97, 101, 172–180, 181
      totalitarian distortions of, 126, 173–177, 180
    and distinctive challenges of modernity, 90
    and learning, 166–169
    and ontological freedom, 164
    and ontotheology, 172
    and pedagogy, 112, 162–169
    and teaching, 155, 162, 165–169
      distinguished from instructing, 168
  apologetic, 89–90
  as *Bildung*, 68, 90–91, 93, 101, 124, 153, 158–161, 162
  as *paideia*, 5, 68, 91, 142, 155–169
  as spiritual leadership, 92–93, 95, 99, 124, 133
  as vocationalism, 95
  authoritarian elements in, 116–118, 122–129
  historical development of, 85–86
  hoax concerning, 133, *see also* Allen; Axiotis 139
  individualistic elements in, 91–2, 97
  introduction to, 4–5
  Nietzsche's influence on, 99, 101–102, 103, 113, 124–128, 169
  in the service of ontological revolution, 158–159, 165, 172, 177, *see also* education, Heidegger's positive vision for future of; education, as *paideia*
  understood ontohistorically, 142–144, 146–147, 150
Ellul, Jacques, 48
Emad, Parvis, 139
enframing, 53–57
  and education, *see* education
  and greatest danger, 74, *see also* danger
  and the problem of the happy enframer, 57–58, 179
  as a critique of technologization of intelligibility, 45, 75
  distinguished from a critique of technical devices, 45, 75, 76
  as an ongoing transformation of intelligibility, 75
  as eclipse of *poiesis* by *technê*, 48
  as machination, 68
  as rooted in Nietzsche's ontotheology, 20–23, 43, 44, 45, 55–57, 68–69, 148–149, 172
  as the "technological" understanding of being, 21–23, 41–42, 44, 60
criticisms of Heidegger's understanding of,
  as ahistoricism, 48–49, 51, 58–61, 76–77
  as essentialism, 47–51, 76
  as Luddite, 45, 72, 73
  as one-dimensionalism (or totalizing), 47, 48, 51, 68–76
  as reactionary anti-modernism, 46, 74

enframing (*cont.*)
    as substantivism or fatalism, 47,
        48, 49–50, 51, 61, 62, 67, 76
    as fetishism, 50
    as heteronomism, 50
    as technophobic, 45, 47, 69
    Marxian, 46
    Heidegger's reading of the Shoah
        in terms of, 83
    relation between ontic and
        ontological in, 63–66, 75
enowning, 117
epochs, *see* being, history of
Ereignis (enowning), *see* enowning
essence, 52, 58, 144–145, *see also* being,
    history of; ontotheology;
    technology; truth
etymology, Heidegger's use of, 53
existentials, 54

fatalism, *see* enframing, criticisms of
    Heidegger's understanding
    of, as substantivism or
    fatalism
fate, distinguished from destiny, 50
Feenberg, Andrew, 3, 23, 45–47, 50,
    51, 52, 58–68, 70, 73, 76
Fichte, Johann Gottlieb, 100, 123,
    135, 153, 172, 177
finitude, 54
Flores, Fernando, 60, 68, 170
Ford, Henry, 83
Foucault, Michel, 1, 36, 59, 73, 94,
    175
fourfold, 157
Freedman, Jim, 64
freeway, *see* autobahn
Freud, Sigmund, 156
Friedman, Michael, 98
Fritsche, Johannes, 104, 105
fundamental ontology, *see* ontology,
    fundamental
Fynsk, Christopher, 105, 133

Gadamer, Hans-Georg, 1, 78, 81, 95,
    96, 97, 120, 156, 176
genealogy, 23, 29, 38
Geuss, Raymond, 58, 91, 161

Glazebrook, Trish, 60, 107
God
    belief in, 15
    death of, 20, 21
    question of, 15
Goethe, Johann Wolfgang von, 153
Graff, Gerald, 153
Guignon, Charles, 91, 103, 104, 113,
    116, 165

Habermas, Jürgen, 1, 10, 46, 48–49,
    62, 66
hands-on (*zuhanden*), 96
Hannay, Alastair, 91
Haskins, Charles, 100, 174
hearing (*hören*), 161
Hegel, G. W. F., 10, 15, 73
Heidegger
    alleged Occicentrism of, 8
    on *Being and Time*, 9
    on metaphysics, *see* ontotheology
    philosophical influence of, 1
    so-called turn in thinking of, 4, 10,
        117
Heideggerian hope, 20, 27, 51, *see also*
    beginning, the other
Heideggerianism, orthodox, 17
Heim, Michael, 67
Heraclitus, 39, 40–42, 85
hero, 21, *see also* Nietzsche
heterogeneity thesis, 66
Hill, R. Kevin, 21
Hiroshima, 83
historicality, 104–105, 107, 113
    distinguished from historicity, 114
historicity, 8–10, 20
history of being, *see* being, history of
Hitler, Adolf, 65, 79, 93, 133, 177
Hölderlin, Friedrich, 157
holism, ontological, 55, 147
Homer, 159
Horkheimer, Max, 96
Hsiao, Paul, 85
humanism, 160
Humboldt, Wilhelm von, 99–101, 123,
    151, 153, 173, 177
Hume, David, 25
hurry, 161

Husserl, Edmund, 83, 101–104, 106, 108, 116, 117
hydroelectric dam, 74, 75

idealism, temporal, 54
Ihde, Don, 48, 73
inception, 29
Internet, the, 45, 56, 70, 75, 149
Irigaray, Luce, 1, 10, 137
Isaiah, 85

Jaeger, Werner, 155, 156
Jaspers, Karl, 82, 86–87, 103, 167
Joyce, James, 159
Judaism, 64
Jünger, Ernst, 61, 175

Kadowaki, Shunsuke, 179
Kant, Immanuel, 7, 15, 20–21, 25, 46, 100, 106, 129, 132, 145
    and destiny of the enlightenment, 46
    and discursivity thesis, 54
    historicized, 54
    as murderer of God, 20, 21
    categories
        completeness of, 54
        substance, 54
    cosmopolitan vision of, 126
    extends Descartes' category mistake, 54
    on harshest of evils, 58
Kerr, Clark, 151
Kierkegaard, Søren, 25, 91
Kisiel, Theodore, 87, 88, 102, 174
Klee, Paul, 69
Kripke, Saul, 144–145
Kuhn, Thomas, 56, 71, 109, 115

Lacan, Jacques, 1
Laclau, Ernesto, 108
Lacoue-Labarthe, Philippe, 80, 83, 84, 108, 137
Lampert, Laurence, 148, 175
Lang, Berel, 79
late modernity, *see* enframing; being, history of

Lao Tzu, 85
Latour, Bruno, 48
leader (*Führer*), 94, 99
League of Nations, 126
Lefort, Claude, 108
left Heideggerians, 10, 136
Leibniz, Gottfried Wilhelm von, 15
Levinas, Emmanuel, 1, 60, 178
Lewis, David, 144
Locke, John, 106
Losurdo, Domenico, 79, 80, 175
Löwith, Karl, 79, 80, 104
Luther, Martin, 91, 124
Lyotard, Jean-François, 80, 81, 83, 137, 159

Marcuse, Herbert, 1, 23, 46, 47, 50, 51, 62, 64, 67, 81, 83, 84, 128
Marx, Karl, 49, 50, 57, 83
May 1968, 64, 66, 67, 136
MeetUp.org, 73
Mendieta, Eduardo, 73
Merleau-Ponty, Maurice, 1
metaphysics, *see* ontotheology
metontology, 13
Milchman, Alan, 79, 86, 87, 88
Mill, John Stuart, 129
modernity, 60, *see also* being, history of; education
morality, 21
Moran, Dermot, 7, 102
Mouffe, Chantal, 108
MoveOn.com, 73
myth, 38

Nancy, Jean-Luc, 108, 175, 180, 181
National Socialism
    Heidegger's critique of, 64, 85
    Heidegger's relation to, 4, 9, 65–66, 77, 78–86, 88, 125–126, 174–177
    and anti-Semitism, 82–84
    explained by his views on the university, 84–140
    lessons learned from, 84–85, 120–125, 129–140, 171–172, 177

National Socialism (*cont.*)
  politicization of the university by,
    86, 131–134
  supposed "inner truth and
    greatness" of, 128, 133
needlessness, need of, 57, *see also*
  danger, the greatest
Nietzsche, Friedrich, 2–4, 16, 25,
    26, 39, 65, 98, 124, 125,
    127, 159, 163, 174, *see also*
    education, ontotheology,
    enframing
  as Heidegger's hero, 105
  critique of Kant, 21
  on eternal recurrence, 148, *see also*
    enframing; ontotheology;
    will-to-will
  on "pre-Platonics," 32
  on superman, 61
  on will-to-power, 148, *see also*
    enframing; ontotheology;
    will-to-will
  revaluation of values in, 21
  will-to-will, 57
nihilism, 20, 21, 56–57, *see also*
  enframing
normativity, 45
Norris, Christopher, 81
nostalgia, 41, 45

Oakeshott, Michael, 168
Okrent, Mark, 18
Olafson, Frederick A., 62, 80, 81, 104,
    105
on-hand (*vorhanden*), 96
ontological
  as background of the ontic, *see*
    being, understanding of;
    enframing
  difference, 108
ontology, *see also* ontotheology
  fundamental, 13, 39, 114, 116–118,
    122–123, 171, 173
  regional, 115–118, 122
ontotheology, 2, 3–4, 5, 7–9, 10–43,
    53–57, 146–147
  and education, *see* education

and metaphysics of substance, 41
and other contemporary
  understandings of
  "metaphysics," 42
and technology, *see* enframing
as core content of metaphysics,
  12–16, 30
as crucial philosophical background
  for understanding
  Heidegger, 2, 10–11, 76–77
as double foundation of
  intelligibility, 17–20, 23, 38,
  39–41, 59
as ground of the sciences, 118–119
as historicization of Kant's
  categories, 54
confusions in Heidegger's
  development of, 13
different version of, shown in
  Table 1, 16
essence and existence in, 16, 29, 35
explained, 18–19
historical genealogy of, 28–41, *see
  also* genealogy
immanent critique of, 28
Nietzsche's, *see* enframing
ontological dimension of, 14, 17
origin of, 30–32, 38
role of metaphysician in, 25–26
theological dimension of, 14–16,
  17–18
Ott, Hugo, 83, 89, 91

Parmenides, 27, 34, 40–42
people (*Volk*), 64, 105, 135
perfectionism, Heidegger's, 101, 159,
  170–171, 177
Petzet, Heinrich W., 70, 74, 85
phenomenology, 18, 35, 36, 37–41, 69,
  70–71, 75, 112
  first law of, 56
  realism in Heidegger's, 36, 63, 64,
    96, 164
phusis (emerging), 40–42, 117, 118
Pindar, 159
Pinkard, Terry, 91
Pippin, Robert, 10, 46

Plato, 5, 21, 25, 26, 32–34, 36, 50, 53, 68, 132, 141–142, 143, 155, 157, 158–160, 161, 162, 168
Poe, Edgar Allen, 56
Pöggeler, Otto, 4, 80, 81, 85, 86, 87, 88, 94, 129–134
poiesis, 48
political, the, 108
polysemy, 156, 157
polytheism, Heidegger's, 15
postmodernism, 10
poststructuralism, 10, 28, 29
practices, marginal, 71
pragmatism, 25
presence, *see* being, as "the being of entities," understood as presence
presencing, 37–38, 40, 53, 117–118, 164, 167, *see also* being, as such
distinguished from presence, 37, *see also* being, as such, distinguished from the being of entities
Protestantism, Heidegger's, 91
proximity, law of, *see* phenomenology, first law of

quietism, Heidegger's alleged, 62, 66, *see also* enframing, criticisms of Heidegger's understanding of, as substantivism or fatalism

Rabinow, Paul, 36, 59, 81
Readings, Bill, 4, 152–153
realism, *see* phenomenology
redneck, 45, *see also* Rorty
releasement (*Gelassenheit*), 15, 38, 72, 156, 157, 161
resolve (*Entschlossenheit*), 156–157, 161
revolution, ontological, 64–65, 66, 75
compared with ontological progressivism, 64–67
Richardson, John, 55, 148, 165
Rickey, Christopher, 80
Ringer, Fritz, 99

Röhm purge, 79, 126
romantic asceticism, Heidegger's, 98
Rorty, Richard, 1, 45–46, 48, 80, 81–82
Rosenberg, Alan, 79, 86, 88

sacred, 71
Safranski, Rüdiger, 79, 82, 83, 86, 93, 94, 125, 167, 176
Sallis, John, 137
same, 23–24, 26–28, 29
Sartre, Jean-Paul, 1
saving power, 74
Scheler, Maria, 65
Scheler, Max, 65, 103
Schelling, F. W. J., 100, 173
Schiller, Friedrich, 153
Schlegel brothers, 153
Schleiermacher, Friedrich, 100, 153
Schopenhauer, Arthur, 174
Schürmann, Reiner, 9, 27, 39, 59, 62, 80, 81
science
crisis in, 110, *see also* Kuhn
"does not think," 110–13
guided by philosophy, 106–107, 114–123
positive, defined, 106–108
Scott, Charles, 132
September 11, 46
Sheehan, Thomas, 83, 175
Shenk, David, 56
Shirer, William, 83
Shoah, 78, 79, 82, *see also* Auschwitz
Heidegger's alleged silence concerning, 83–84
Sluga, Hans, 78, 79, 105, 133
socioanalysis, 81
Socrates, 12
sojourn (*Aufenthalte*), 159
Sokal, Alan, 23
Spengler, Oswald, 94–95, 97–98, 99, 105
Spielberg, Steven, 174
Spinosa, Charles, 60, 68, 75, 170
stab in the back, 93
Standish, Paul, 177, 178

Stenstad, Gail, 17
step back, 29–31, 32
Sternhall, Zeev, 102
Strawson, P. F., 7
Stump, David, 48
subjectivism, 54, 160
synchrony, 39

Taber, John, 159
Taylor, Charles, 1
teaching, *see also* education
    etymology of, 165–166
technê, 48, *see also* enframing
technicity, *see* enframing
technocracy, 64, 67
technology
    addiction to, 75
    and thankfulness, 71–72
    as "a beast off its leash," 69
    as ground of science, 111
    critical theory of, *see* Feenberg
    essence of, 52–53, 58, 68–69, 76, *see
        also* enframing
    Heidegger's call for a sublation of,
        61, 64, 73–74
    Heidegger's critique of, *see*
        enframing
    introduction to Heidegger's views
        on, 3, 44–47
    radical constructivism in
        philosophy of, 45, 48, 58, 73
television, 69
temporality, 54
Thales, 29–31, 32, 37, 40, 42, 166
theiology, 13
theology, 112, *see also* ontotheology
thing, 71
thinking, distinguished from
    philosophy, 110
Tillich, Paul, 1
totalitarianism, 43, *see also* National
    Socialism
transcendental, 54
truth, 144–145, 160

turn, the, *see* Heidegger, so-called turn
    in thinking of
turning, 74

understanding of being, *see* being,
    understanding of
university, *see also* education; National
    Socialism
    history of, 99–101
unthought, the, 29

Van Buren, John, 87, 88, 89, 91, 94
Van Gogh, Vincent, 71
Vigliotti, Robert, 89
Von Meysenbug, Malvida, 125

Wagner, Richard, 65
Ward, James, 167
Weber, Max, 49, 94–95, 96, 99,
    101–102, 103
Weimar Republic, 93
Wessel, Horst, 65–66
Wiggershaus, Rolf, 96
will-to-will, 51
Wissenschaft (knowledge), 94, 101, 102,
    132, 135, 150–151, *see also*
    science
    and objectivity, 96–98
Wittgenstein, Ludwig, 9, 52, 146–147,
    150, 167
Wolin, Richard, 62, 79, 81, 82, 83, 84,
    98, 104–105, 131, 178
Wood, David, 178
Woodstock, 64
world, 71
world disclosure, 68, 170
Wrathall, Mark A., 15, 54, 157
Wyschogrod, Edith, 83

Young, Julian, 62, 72, 79, 83, 84, 89,
    93, 132, 175, 177, 180

Zimmerman, Michael, 66, 79, 80, 175
Ziolkowski, Theodore, 100